I0792887

IMAGES
of America

Los Angeles's Historic Filipinotown

KONSULADO PANLAHAT NG PILIPINAS — LOS ANGELES — CONSULATE GENERAL OF THE PHILIPPINES

MESSAGE

I wish to congratulate Carina Monica Montoya for her book on *Historic Filipinotown*, a monumental undertaking in gathering history that dates back to the early part of the twentieth century when young Filipinos, who were mostly single males, lived in a section of downtown Los Angeles that came to be known as Little Manila.

The book preserves the memories of the place where Filipinos first settled in Los Angeles. Today, the Town's Filipino population is a minority overshadowed by an expanding Hispanic population; but the book remains nevertheless as relevant as ever, as the Town continues to throb as the cultural heart of Filipinos in Los Angeles and still harbors one of the highest concentrations of Filipino Americans in Southern California.

The Town still hosts some Filipino establishments that include restaurants, churches, medical clinics, Filipino service organizations and institutions, such as the Aristocrat, Bahay Kubo, Remy's on Temple Art Gallery, the Filipino American Library, the Pilipino Workers Center (PWC), Filipino American Community of Los Angeles (FACLA), Filipino American Service Group, Inc. (FASGI), Search to Involve Pilipino Americans (SIPA), to name a few.

It is encouraging that the Historic Filipinotown Neighborhood Council and the Rotary Club of Historic Filipinotown are among those leading the efforts to develop the area. In November 2006, I joined the few remaining Filipino veterans in witnessing the unveiling by L.A. City Council's President Eric Garcetti of the first monument in Lake Street Park dedicated to and honoring the Filipino soldiers who fought for the United States in World War II.

But for us, the history of Historic Filipinotown is far from over. We look forward to a future when Filipinos would come back in droves, re-establish their domiciles, businesses and landmarks, and eventually reclaim the area, so that Historic Filipinotown would cease to be "Historic" and simply be known as "Filipinotown."

May this book further re-awaken the Filipino in us and enable us to cherish the sacrifices and headways of those who came before us.

Mabuhay!

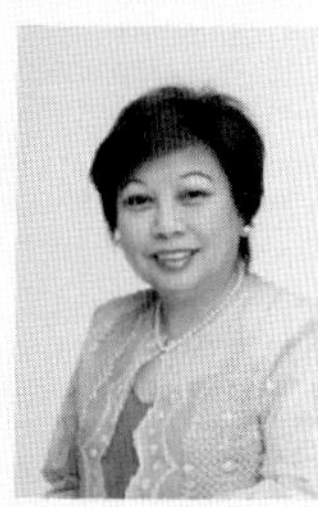

Mary Jo B. Aragon

MARY JO BERNARDO ARAGON
Consul General

3600 Wilshire Blvd., Suite 500, Los Angeles, CA 90010
Tel. (213) 639-0980; Fax (213) 639-0990; E-mail: losangelespc@aol.com; Website: www.pcgenla.org

Born in Manila, Consul General Mary Jo Bernardo Aragon is the first female the Philippine government has appointed as consul general for the Los Angeles post. A career diplomat who has achieved the rank of chief of Mission II, she has been instrumental in the promotion of cultural affairs in Historic Filipinotown by her active participation and assistance in community activities and events. (Courtesy of the Los Angeles Consul General of the Philippines.)

ON THE COVER: Hundreds of Filipino Federation of America, Inc., members gathered at the federation's headquarters in Los Angeles for its first annual national convention, held on December 23, 1927. For more information about the federation, see pages 16 and 17. (Courtesy of the Filipino Federation of America, Inc.)

IMAGES
of America

LOS ANGELES'S HISTORIC FILIPINOTOWN

Carina Monica Montoya
Foreword by Eric Garcetti

ARCADIA
PUBLISHING

ISBN 978-0-7385-6954-3

Published by Arcadia Publishing
Charleston SC, Chicago IL, Portsmouth NH, San Francisco CA

Printed in the United States of America

Library of Congress Catalog Card Number: 2008935197

For all general information contact Arcadia Publishing at:
Telephone 843-853-2070
Fax 843-853-0044
E-mail sales@arcadiapublishing.com
For customer service and orders:
Toll-Free 1-888-313-2665

Visit us on the Internet at www.arcadiapublishing.com

To the Filipino community of Los Angeles, then and now

Contents

ACKNOWLEDGMENTS

This book would not have been possible without the generous support of the Filipino community, associations, and historical organizations in Los Angeles.

I want to especially thank my editors at Arcadia Publishing, Jerry Roberts, for his professional guidance; and Lori Gildersleeve, for her patience and professionalism. Thanks also to my publisher, Devon E. Weston, for her support in making my second book in this series possible.

I also want to thank Carolyn Kozo Cole, senior librarian, Photograph Collection/History and Genealogy Department of the Los Angeles Public Library, for her generosity, assistance, and support of this book and for the use of the many images from the Shades of L.A. Archives.

I am indebted to Sthanlee B. Mirador and Peter Gonzaga for their generosity in providing their photographs taken in and around Historic Filipinotown.

My deepest appreciation goes to all who shared my vision of this book and generously contributed to it: Faustino "Peping" Baclig, Filipino-American Service Group, Inc.; Joe Bernardo; Mary Jo Bernardo Aragon, Philippine consul general of Los Angeles; Carlene Sobrino Bonnivier, novelist; Ryan Carpio, field deputy for Eric Garcetti; Enrique de la Cruz, professor of Asian American studies at California State University–Northridge; Scott Davis, Arcadia Publishing; Prosy Abarquez-Delacruz, J.D., writer; Steven De La Vega; Kenny and Shirley Dionzon; Filipino American Library; Filipino Federation of America, Inc.; First Christian Church; Eric Garcetti, president, Los Angeles City Council, District 13; Cheri Gaulke, artist; Joselyn Geaga-Rosenthal, owner of Remy's on Temple art gallery; Gerald Gubatan; Reme A. Grefalda, librarian in charge at the Library of Congress, Washington, D.C., Asian American Collection; Florante Peter Ibanez; John Hermann; Joel F. Jacinto, executive director of Search to Involve Pilipino Americans (SIPA); Carol O. Kimbrough, lecturer on Asian American studies; Juliet Lagmay-Akiaten; Jonathan Lorenzo, administrator of the Filipino American Library; Linda Nietes, owner of Philippine Book Expressions; John Mina, president of the Filipino American Library; Ann Morales; Elvisa Ordonio; Angelina and Vitorio Orlanes; Victor Orlanes Jr.; Christine Oshima; Cecile Ramos, president of Historic Filipinotown Neighborhood Council; David Rockello, vice president and chief information officer of Historic Filipinotown Neighborhood Council; Imelda Rodriguez; Carmen Salindong; Alexander Sanchez; Eliseo Art Silva, artist/muralist; Celina Taganas-Duffy; Elson Trinidad; Phil Ventura; Valerie Villarta; George Villanueva; Jonathan Yap, director of Remy's on Temple; and all the other helpful individuals who contributed in many ways to make this book a reality.

FOREWORD

Filipino Americans have made important contributions to Los Angeles's culture, economy, and community since our city was founded. After generations of families and businesses that had settled in Little Manila and Bunker Hill were moved in the 1960s, Filipino Americans began to establish a community in the Temple-Beverly corridor. For many years, the community worked to create a strong neighborhood that reflected the rich Filipino culture. The area just west of downtown Los Angeles became known to Filipino Americans throughout the region as an area where the community could receive services, patronize Filipino American–owned businesses, and celebrate their cultural heritage.

Underlying decades of collaboration between residents, business owners, and community organizations was a longing for a neighborhood where Filipino Americans could share the community's history and culture with each other and the rest of Los Angeles. In August 2002, the Los Angeles City Council unanimously approved my legislation that officially designated an area in the Temple-Beverly corridor as Historic Filipinotown. The community celebrated this milestone, but it was only the beginning of a new chapter for the neighborhood.

Today thousands of Filipino Americans live alongside neighbors from around the world in Los Angeles's Historic Filipinotown. Vibrant Filipino American businesses line the neighborhood's streets and are part of a new Historic Filipinotown Chamber of Commerce. Numerous community-based organizations such as Search to Involve Pilipino Americans, Filipino American Service Group, Pilipino Workers Center, Filipino American Community of Los Angeles, and the Filipino American Library offer educational opportunities, job training, health care, and many other services to local residents.

Lake Street Park provides a beautiful backdrop to the Filipino World War II Veterans Memorial by Cheri Gaulke that we unveiled in 2006. In 2007, we opened Unidad Park, home to one of the nation's largest Filipino American murals, *Gintong Kasaysayan, Gintong Pamana* by Eliseo Art Silva. Even the neighborhood's streets themselves recall its Filipino heritage. Stamped into the concrete crosswalks at major intersections are beautiful, intricate patterns inspired by traditional Filipino weave patterns. Purple orchid trees common to the Philippines are planted up and down Temple Street, and decorative medallions denoting Historic Filipinotown hang on streetlights.

Looking at a map of Los Angeles neighborhoods, Historic Filipinotown lies between the 101 Freeway, Glendale Boulevard, Hoover Street, and Beverly Boulevard. But the perseverance and diligence of Filipino Americans who worked to create this neighborhood know no bounds. I am deeply honored to be part of Historic Filipinotown's new history. Mabuhay!

—Eric Garcetti, president, Los Angeles City Council
Los Angeles, California

INTRODUCTION

The history of the Filipinos in Los Angeles dates back to the 1920s when a wave of Filipino immigrants, who were mostly young unmarried males, arrived in Los Angeles largely in response to America's agricultural industries' need for workers, particularly in California. For many, it seemed like a wonderful opportunity to earn money, and for others, it would be an opportunity to further their educations. However, the reality of living in America at the turn of the 20th century for many immigrants, particularly Filipinos, was met with jobs restricted to stoop labor in the agricultural fields and menial service-related positions in the city. White America's general attitude toward people of color created many restrictions for the new settlers—where they could live, where they could work, and who they could marry. All these factors had a significant impact on the Filipinos in California, resulting in an unstable life that prevented any permanent attachment to a place, but more significantly, a lost generation as a result of more than two decades of restrictive immigration and more than a century of enforced anti-miscegenation laws.

For more than two decades, the Filipino community, which was still mostly males, was located in an impoverished section of downtown Los Angeles called Little Manila. Filipino-owned restaurants, barbershops, pool halls, and an employment agency were established, and Little Manila became the nucleus where Filipinos lived, socialized, congregated, and networked among compatriots to find work. Hollywood studios in need of ethnic-type extras for films, among others in need of cheap labor, would merely drive to First and Main Streets to solicit Filipinos.

The first movement of the Los Angeles Filipino community out of the Little Manila area came in the 1940s as a result of a combination of racial tensions between Filipinos and African Americans and the city's redevelopment of the Little Manila area, which included the demolition of its buildings, hotels, and apartments. Although population growth and redevelopments began to change and reshape the city, restrictive laws and obstacles of discrimination that affected Filipinos still remained intact.

Many relocated a few blocks west to the Bunker Hill area while others dispersed throughout the city in search of inexpensive housing accommodations. Although Filipinos were able to reestablish some businesses and find affordable housing in Bunker Hill, within a decade, a second movement was necessitated because of a city development project that would once again demolish buildings and residences. Relocation a few more blocks west brought them into the Temple-Beaudry area. By the late 1940s, the anti-miscegenation laws were lifted, and new immigration laws allowed Filipino wives and fiancées of Filipino servicemen, among others, to immigrate to America. This marked the beginning of a growing Filipino family community with a need to find stability by attachment to a place. The Temple-Beaudry area was one of the first areas where Filipino families attempted to settle, but the area was considered one of the oldest and most dilapidated sections of the city and was slated to be redeveloped in the post–World War II era by the demolition of buildings and residences. This marked the third forced movement of the Filipino community, to the Temple-Beverly corridor.

By the early 1950s, Filipinos were able to buy land in America, and many Filipino families in Los Angeles purchased their first homes in the Temple-Beverly corridor. Filipino-owned businesses, establishments, churches, and organizations flourished in the corridor throughout the years, resulting in the community's attachment to a place. The relatively recent designation of Historic Filipinotown is representative of this attachment. Today new Filipino-owned businesses, establishments, and organizations are sprouting up around the corridor, adding new life to an old community.

One

LITTLE MANILA

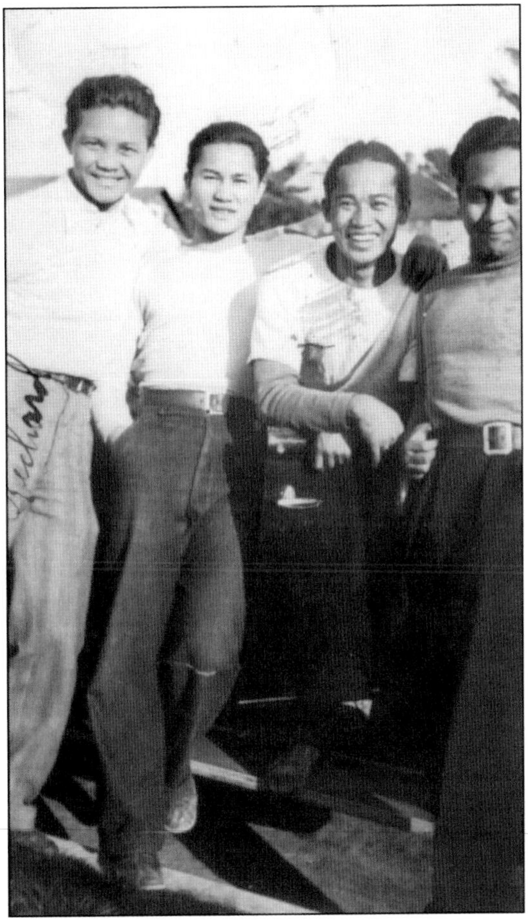

Richard Dionzon (far left) is pictured with friends in downtown Los Angeles in the 1920s. Early settlers were mostly young males with no parental control or supervision. Restrictions on where Filipinos could live and socialize limited them to an impoverished section of downtown Los Angeles, particularly First and Main Streets, where inexpensive hotels, pool halls, and taxi dance halls flourished. The area came to be known as Little Manila. (Courtesy of Kenny Dionzon.)

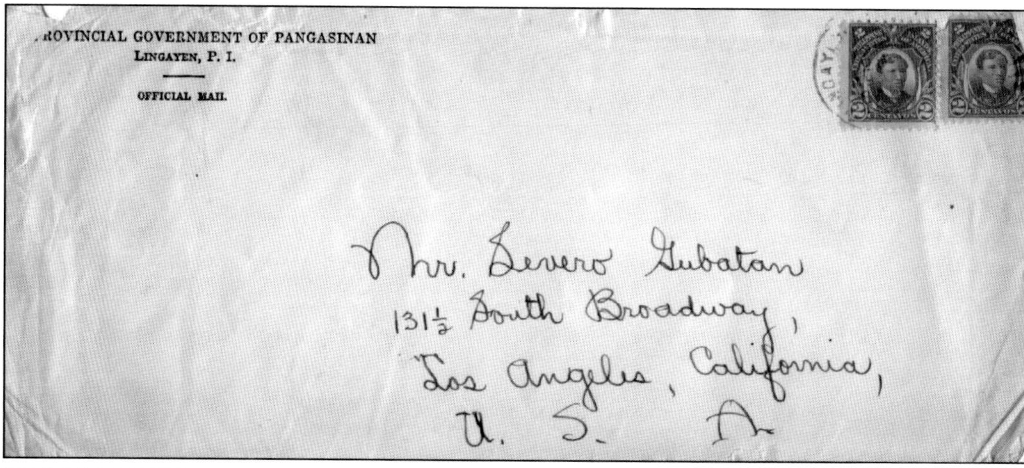

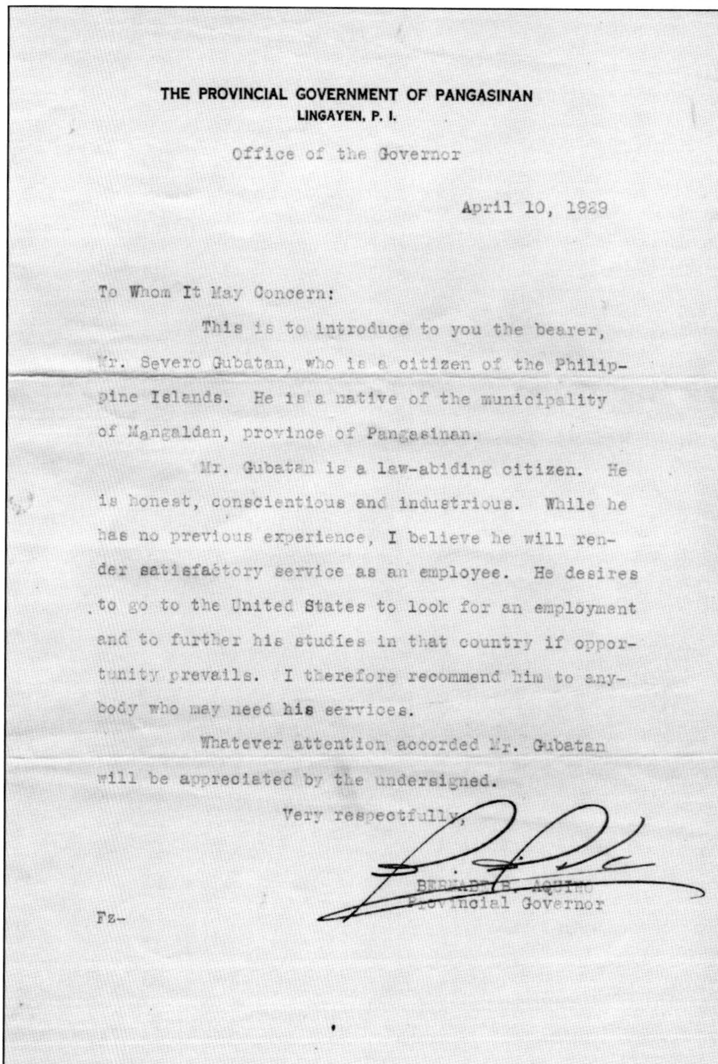
THE PROVINCIAL GOVERNMENT OF PANGASINAN
LINGAYEN, P. I.

Office of the Governor

April 10, 1929

To Whom It May Concern:

This is to introduce to you the bearer, Mr. Severo Gubatan, who is a citizen of the Philippine Islands. He is a native of the municipality of Mangaldan, province of Pangasinan.

Mr. Gubatan is a law-abiding citizen. He is honest, conscientious and industrious. While he has no previous experience, I believe he will render satisfactory service as an employee. He desires to go to the United States to look for an employment and to further his studies in that country if opportunity prevails. I therefore recommend him to anybody who may need his services.

Whatever attention accorded Mr. Gubatan will be appreciated by the undersigned.

Very respectfully,

Provincial Governor

Fz-

A character recommendation letter dated April 10, 1929, from the provincial governor of Pangasinan in the Philippines, was written on behalf of Severo Gubatan and addressed to any prospective employer in the United States. It is unknown if the letter assisted Severo in obtaining a job as a "pantryman," or restaurant worker, in the downtown area near Sixth and Spring Streets because most Filipinos in the city were already relegated to service-related positions. One day, Severo tossed a Caucasian man into a trash can in the restaurant after the man had taunted him and called him a dog. Above, the envelope shows that the letter was mailed to Severo Gubatan's residence on South Broadway in downtown Los Angeles. (Both, courtesy of Gerald Gubatan.)

Eugene Manantan (left) and a friend are aboard a U.S. ship in 1940. Some U.S. Navy sailors later attained U.S. citizenship and went on to complete their educations. In 1934, there was reported to be one known Filipino lawyer, an ex-serviceman, who practiced law in Los Angeles. (Courtesy of Shades of L.A. Archives/Los Angeles Public Library.)

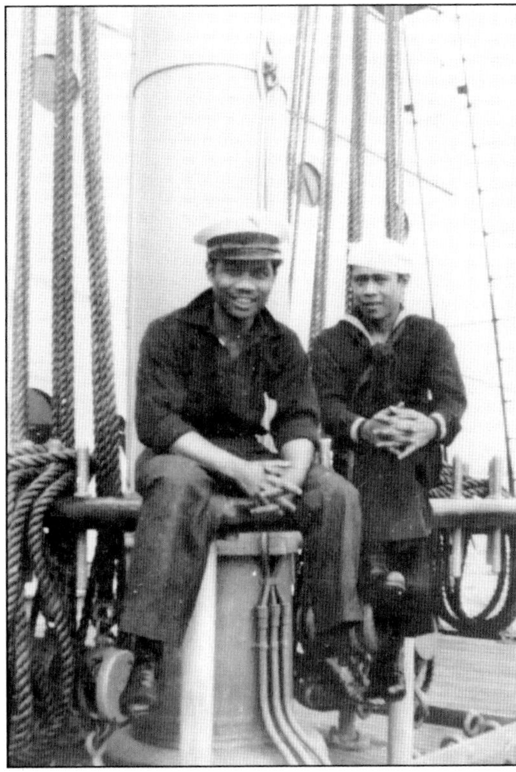

Below, Richard Dionzon (seated, second from left) is seen here with fellow ship stewards and cooks in the U.S. Navy in the 1920s. Many Filipinos served in the armed forces as an avenue to attain U.S. citizenship. After Dionzon's enlistment was completed, he was granted citizenship in 1937 and settled in Los Angeles. (Courtesy of Kenny Dionzon.)

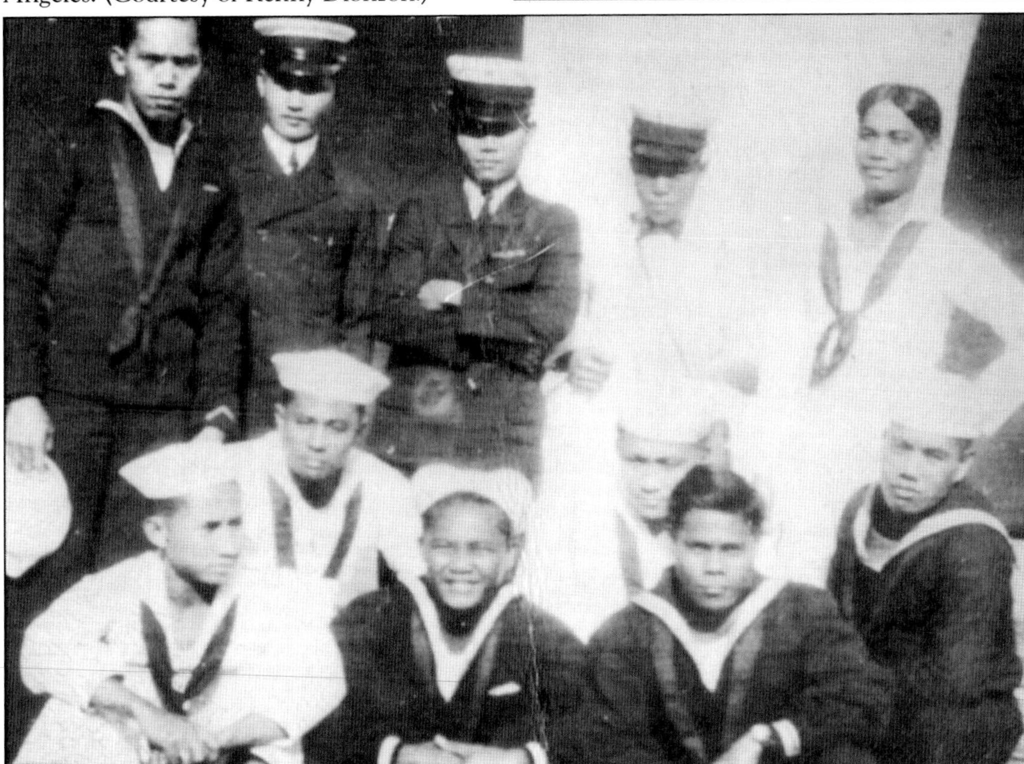

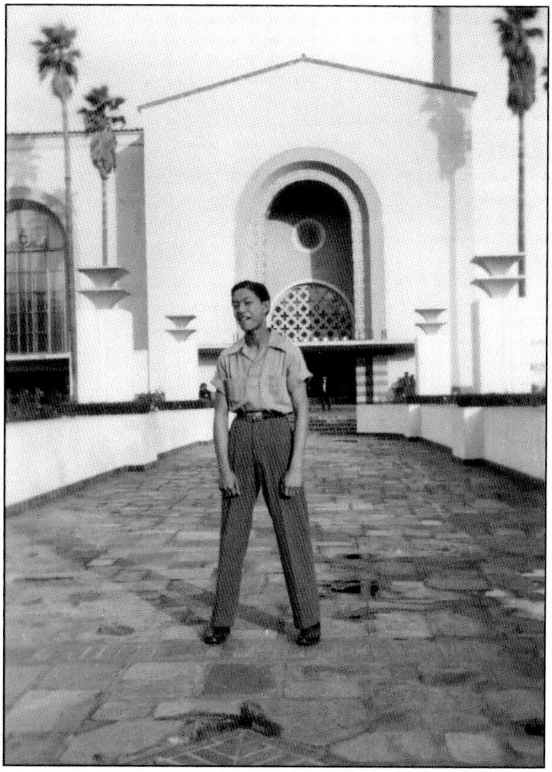

This 1945 photograph of a young Filipino man was taken in front of Union Station. Completed in 1939, Union Station consolidated all intercity rail lines. Because many Filipinos were not permanent residents of the city, trains provided extensive mobility to travel outside of Los Angeles County and California to agricultural areas, where field work could be found during certain months of the year. (Courtesy of Security Pacific National Bank.)

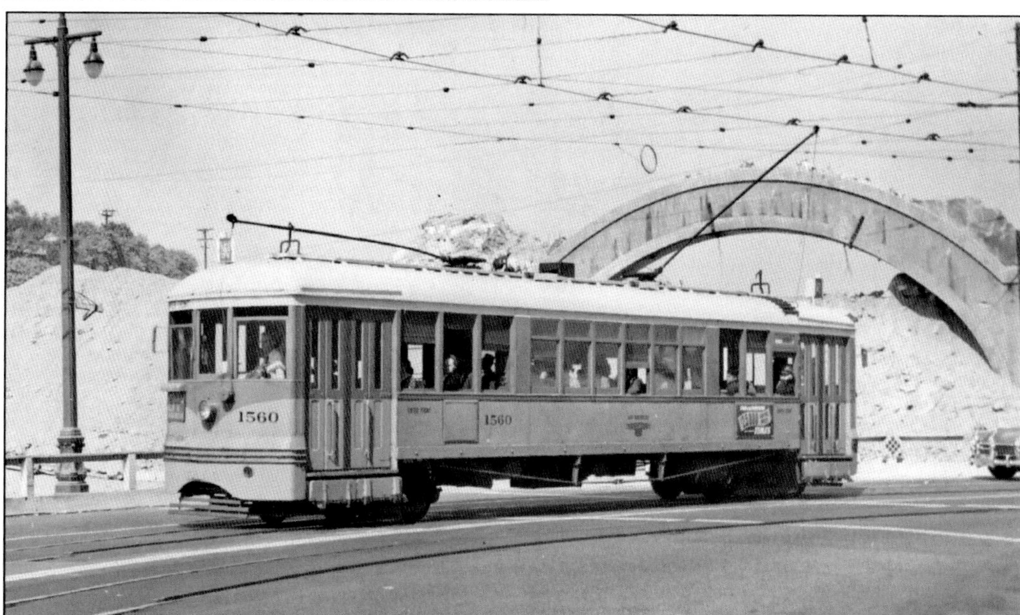

A full electric Los Angeles Railway Yellow Car travels past the mostly demolished Broadway tunnel in preparation for the building of the new Hollywood freeway in 1949. The tunnel ran from a short block north of Temple Street to just south of Sunset Boulevard. Intercity public transportation and cars made it possible and convenient to work across town. (Courtesy of Security National Bank.)

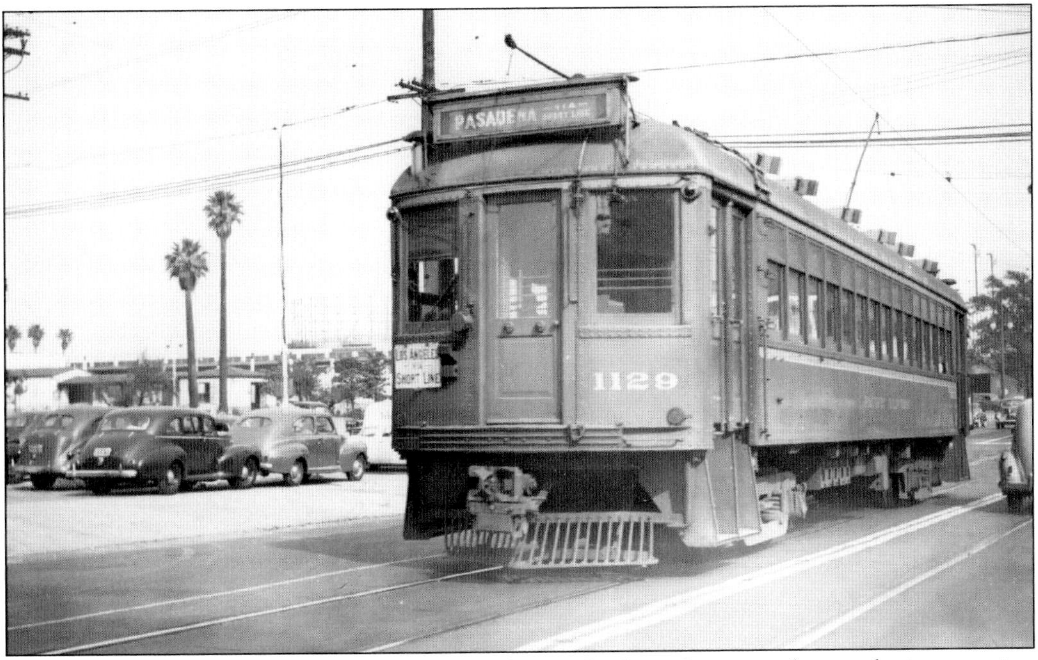

A 1940s photograph of this Pasadena Pacific Electric Railway Car was taken at the intersection of Aliso and Alameda Streets. The electric car ran between Los Angeles and Pasadena via the short line and traveled far north of the city and back to downtown Los Angeles on the same line. (Courtesy of Security Pacific National Bank.)

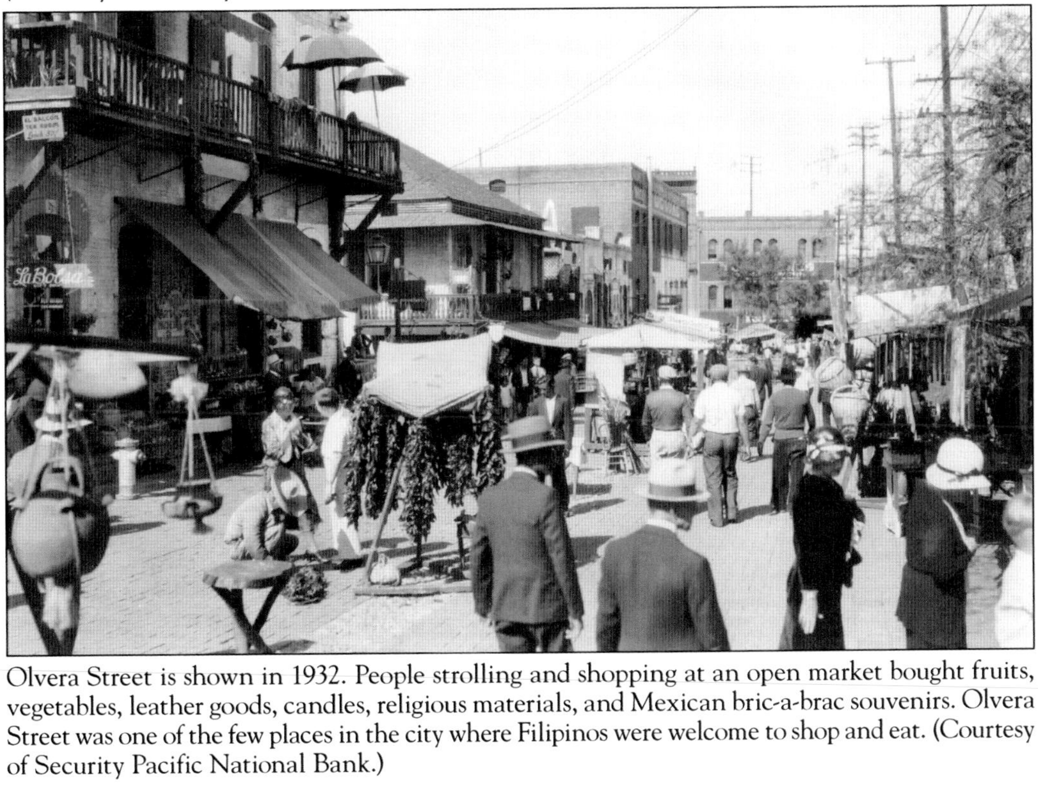

Olvera Street is shown in 1932. People strolling and shopping at an open market bought fruits, vegetables, leather goods, candles, religious materials, and Mexican bric-a-brac souvenirs. Olvera Street was one of the few places in the city where Filipinos were welcome to shop and eat. (Courtesy of Security Pacific National Bank.)

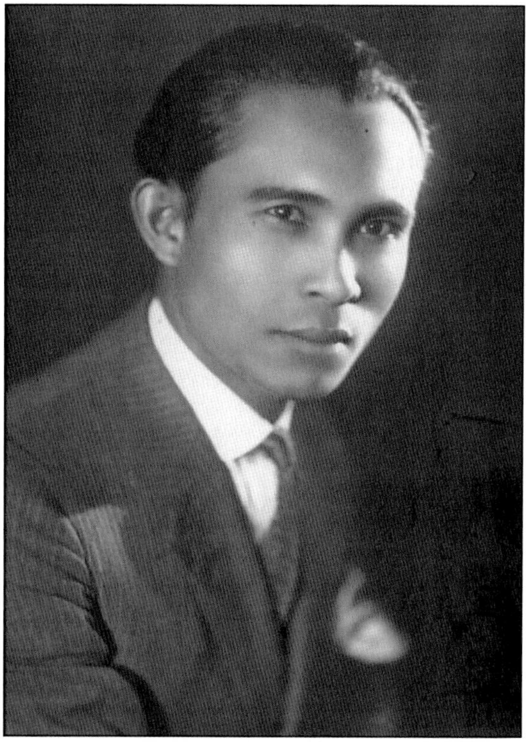

This 1920s portrait is of Hilario C. Moncado (1898–1956). Born in Balamban, Cebu, one of the many islands in the Philippines, Moncado devoted his life to the betterment of native Filipinos, many from the provinces of Cebu, Ilocos, and Mindanao. In 1924, he was the editor and publisher of a monthly publication called *News Service*, which in 1926 became the *Filipino Nation*. Both publications focused on establishing permanent relations between Americans and Filipinos. In 1925, Moncado founded the Filipino Federation of America, Inc., one of the country's first and largest Filipino organizations. Its headquarters was located at 428 Stack Building at Fourth Street and Broadway. (Courtesy of the Filipino Federation of America, Inc.)

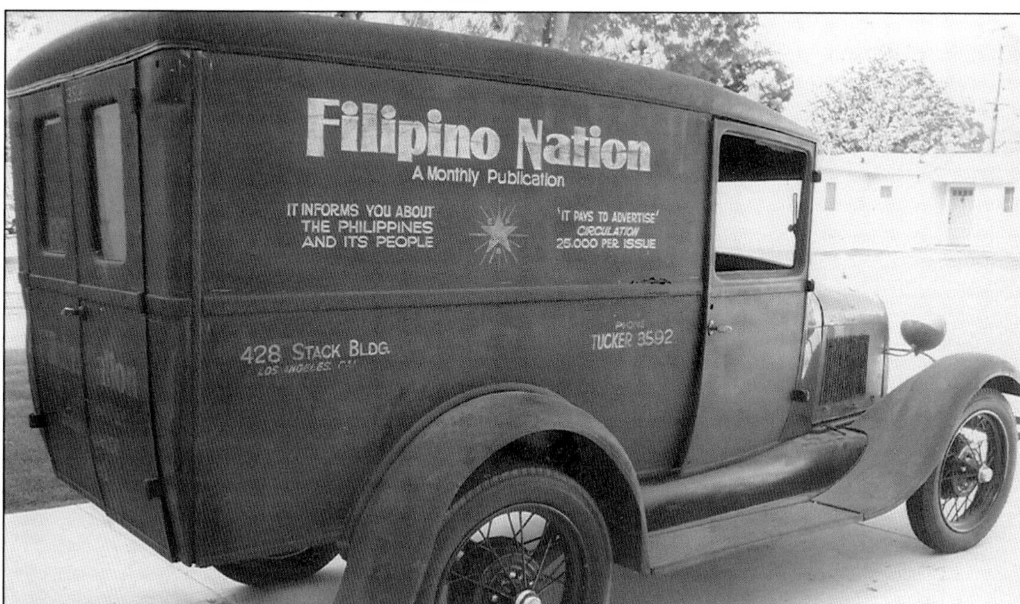

Pictured is a 1926 *Filipino Nation* delivery truck. *Filipino Nation* was a 52-page magazine with a monthly circulation of 25,000 copies. By the 1930s, there were approximately 11 Filipino newspapers in circulation—*Associated Filipino Press*, *New Deal*, *Philippine Star Press*, *Filipino Youth*, *Filipino Voice*, *Philippine Tribune*, *Modern Philippines*, *East*, *Philippine American Business*, and *Ang Bantay*, printed in the native language. Most publications consisted of two to six pages, with some in magazine and pamphlet form. (Courtesy of the Filipino American Library.)

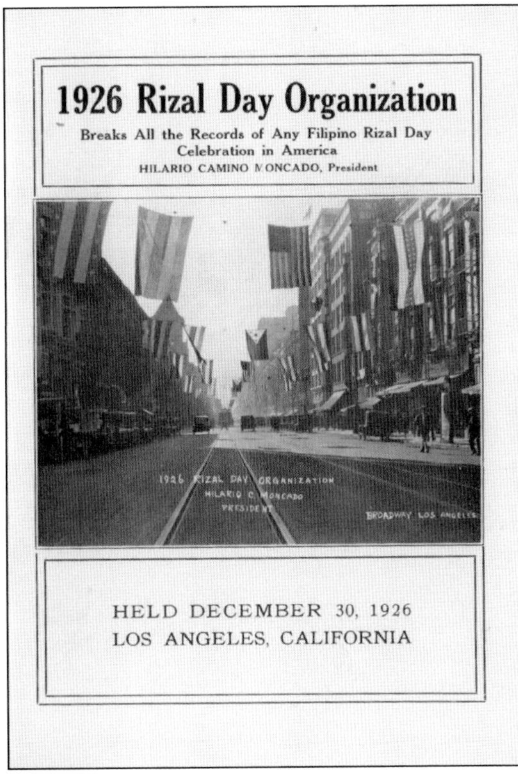

1926 Rizal Day Organization

Breaks All the Records of Any Filipino Rizal Day Celebration in America

HILARIO CAMINO MONCADO, President

HELD DECEMBER 30, 1926
LOS ANGELES, CALIFORNIA

The front and back covers seen here are from a Rizal Day celebration pamphlet authored by Hilario C. Moncado, president of the joint Rizal Day celebration held on December 30, 1926, at the Bovard Auditorium of the University of Southern California. The celebration was in honor of the anniversary of the death of Jose Rizal (1861–1896), a Filipino revolutionary leader and national hero who, through his writings, exposed the Spanish tyrannical rule in the Philippines. Rizal Day is one of the most celebrated events among Filipinos. (Courtesy of the Filipino Federation of America, Inc.)

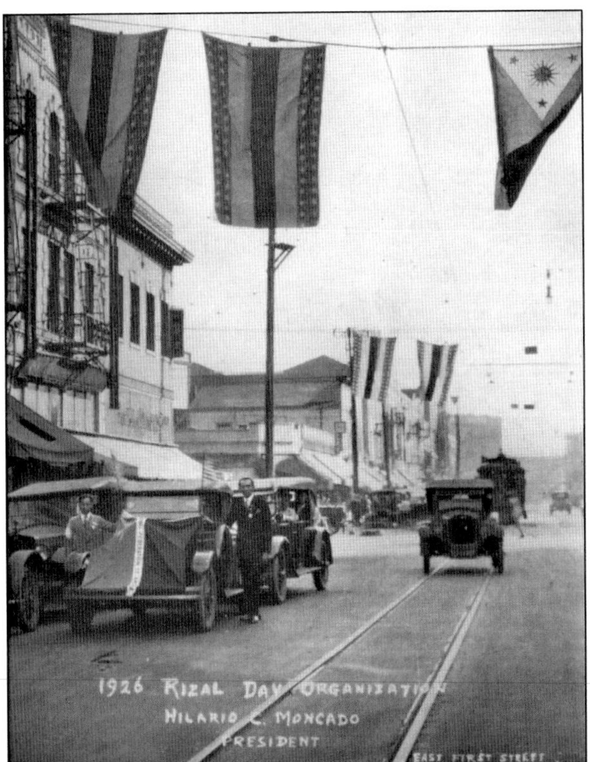

Despite discrimination against Filipinos, Moncado was the first Filipino to display the Philippine flags—for the Rizal Day celebration. In Los Angeles, the flags were displayed on two major downtown streets: Broadway (above) and East First Street (left). (Courtesy of the Filipino Federation of America, Inc.)

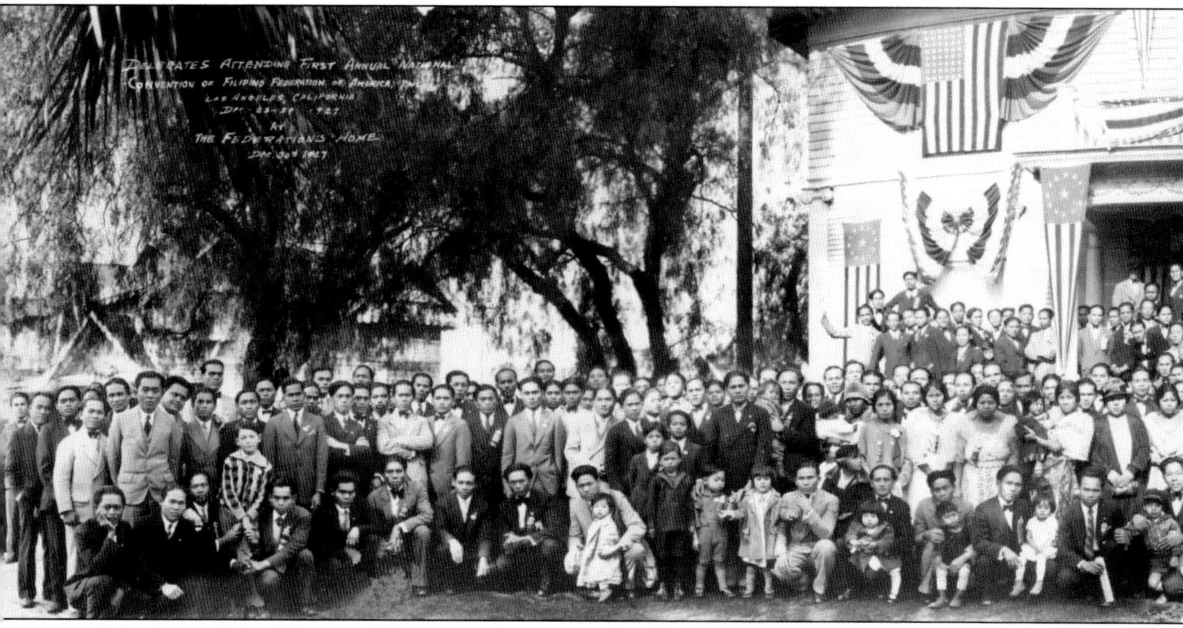

Members of the Filipino Federation of America, Inc., pose for this 1927 photograph, taken during their first convention in front of a home in Los Angeles, which was purchased by the federation to house its president and officers, located at 2289 West Twenty-fifth Street. The federation was founded by Hilario C. Moncado on December 27, 1925, and was incorporated on April 2, 1927, as a fraternal, semireligious organization and nonprofit corporation. Its sole purpose was to create a better relationship between Americans and Filipinos and to serve its fellow man. Its motto is

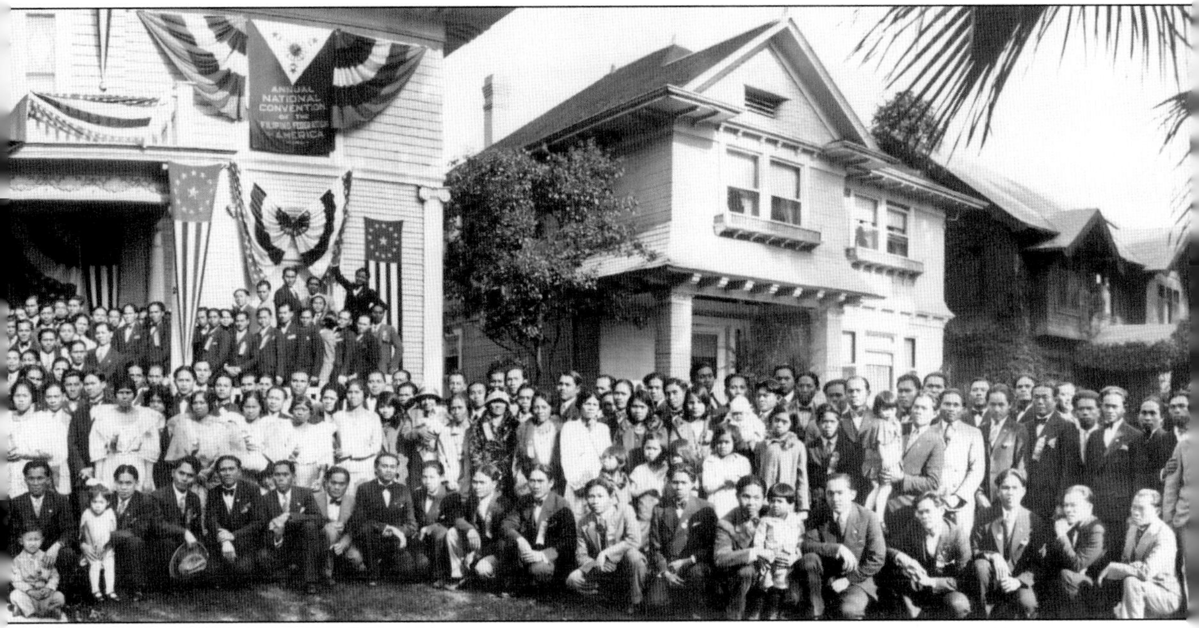

"Humanity be Served." Other early organizations also founded for the betterment of Filipinos include the Filipino Barristers Association, Filipino Catholic Club, Pangasinan Association, Filipino Christian Fellowship, Filipino Patriotic Association, La Union Association, Sons of Cebu, Filipino Christian Association of Southern California, Cagayan Valley Association, Filipino Alumni Association, and the Caballeros de Dimas-Alang. (Courtesy of the Filipino Federation of America, Inc.)

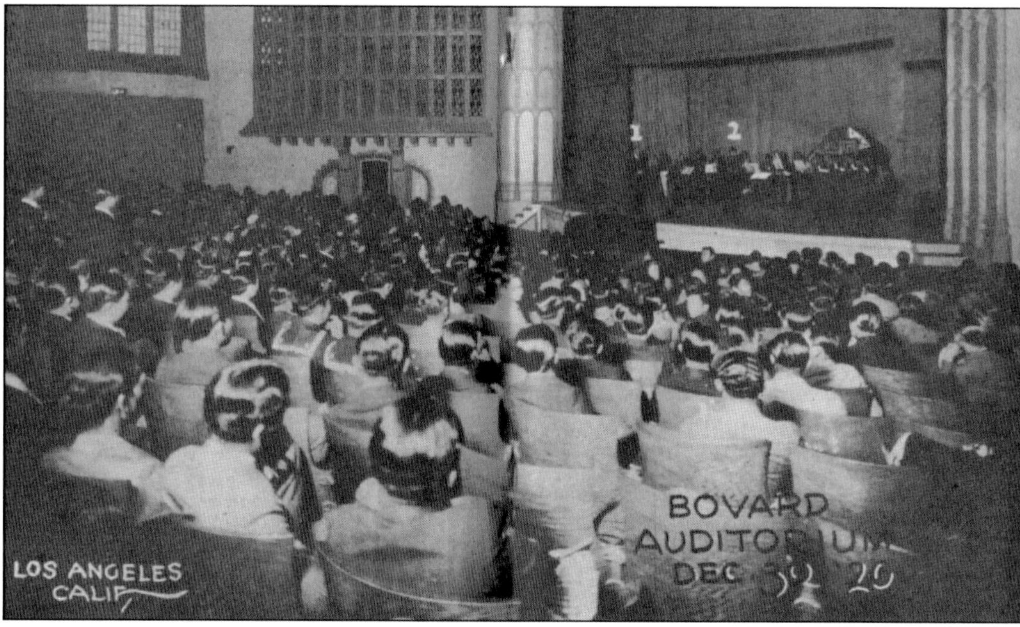

Rizal Day was celebrated at Bovard Auditorium at the University of Southern California in 1926. Oratorical and declamation contests sponsored by Filipino associations were held with the subject centered on the life of Jose Rizal and his philosophy, and how he influenced the Filipino national life. The Philippine Junior House of Representatives and the Filipino Varsity Debating Club specifically trained for these events. (Courtesy of the Filipino Federation of America, Inc.)

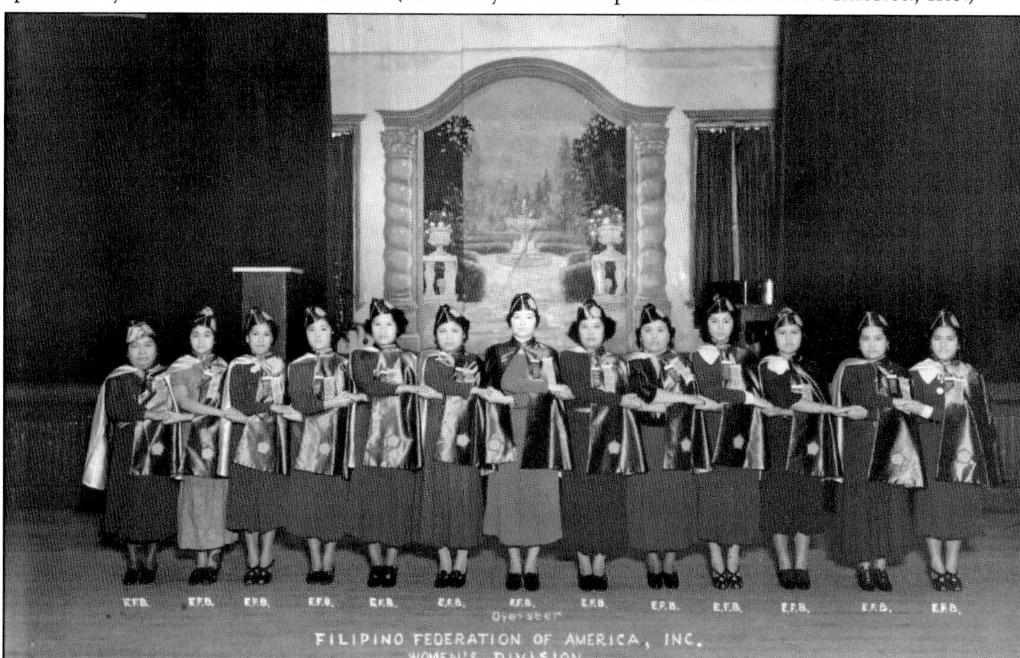

The Filipino Federation of America, Inc., was divided into 12 divisions and 12 lodges, with each lodge having a women's division. Pictured above is the women's division of Lodge 5, Division 1 on December 28, 1937. (Courtesy of the Filipino Federation of America, Inc.)

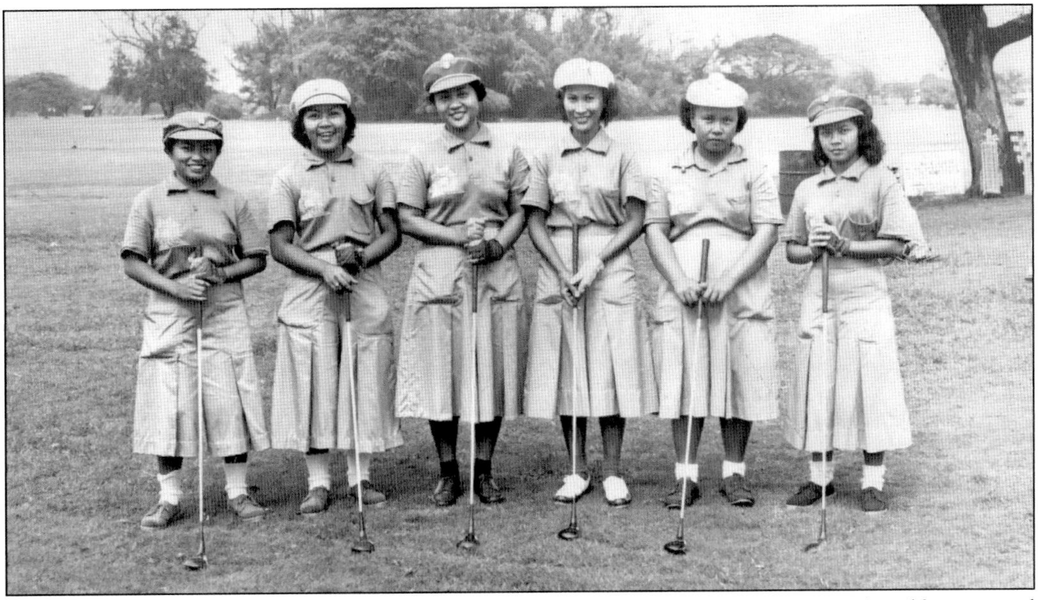

Above is a 1920s photograph of the Filipino Federation of America, Inc., women's golf team, and the photograph below shows four individuals on the federation's men's golf team. The federation espoused the common goal of healthy living and promoted a relatively meat-free diet and exercise lifestyle, particularly by participating in the game of golf and martial arts. However, since Filipinos were restricted from patronizing many establishments, federation members often played golf on less than exclusive courses and without club affiliations. (Both, courtesy of the Filipino Federation of America, Inc.)

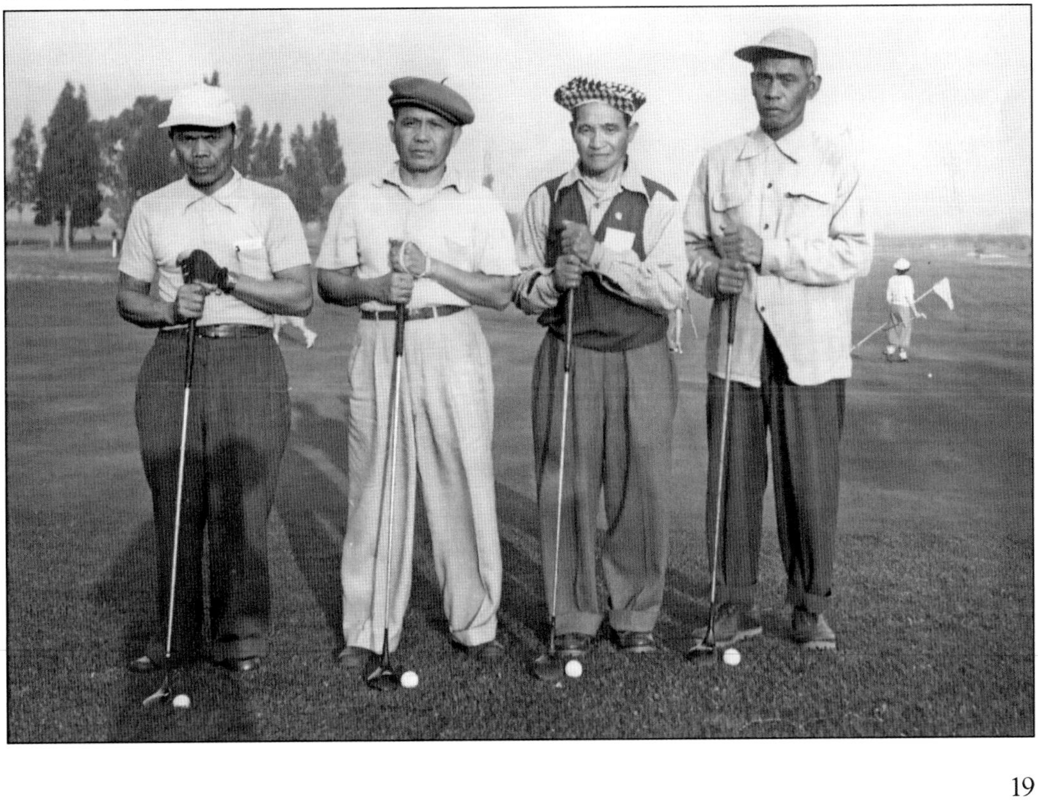

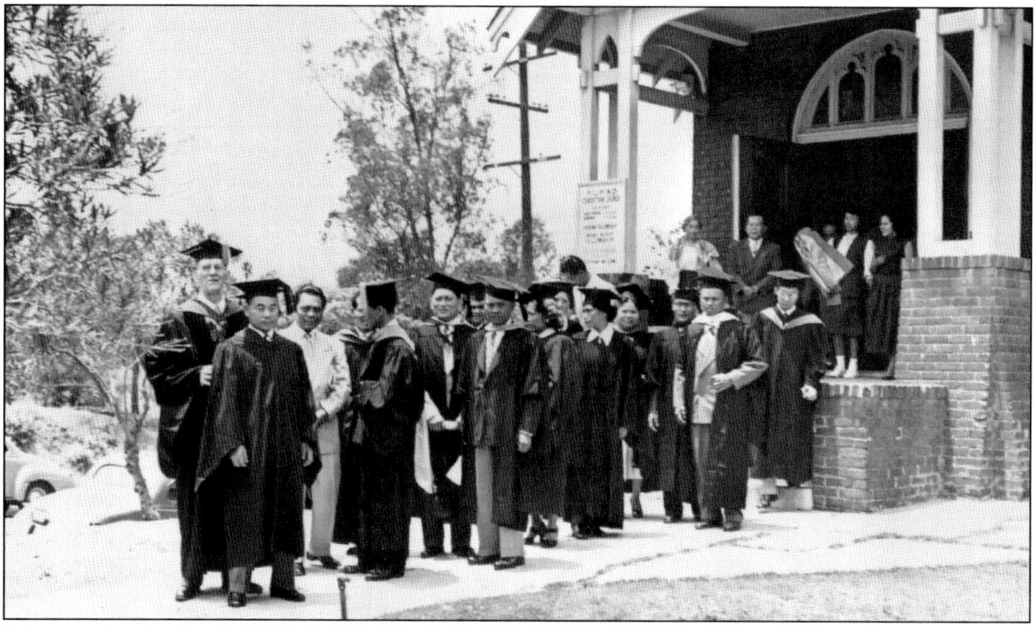

Filipino alumni homecoming is celebrated in 1951 at the Filipino Christian Church. Founded in 1933, it is the oldest Filipino church in America. Located at 301 North Union Street, it was designated as a Historical Cultural Monument by the Cultural Heritage Commission of the City of Los Angeles in 1998. (Courtesy of Shades of L.A. Archives/Los Angeles Public Library.)

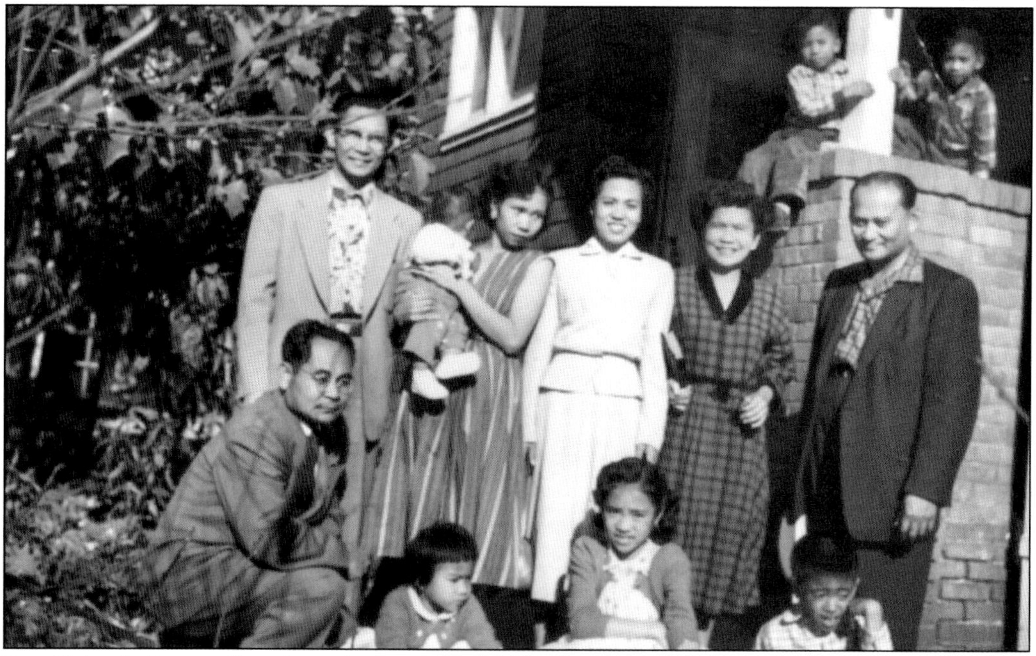

Rev. Felix A. Pascua (kneeling, first row, far left) and members of the Filipino Christian Church pose for this photograph in front of the church in 1956. With the help of Roy Morales and Helen Summers Brown, the church later provided space for the Pilipino American Reading Room and Library (PARRAL) to operate from 1985 to 1994. Ming Menez and Tania Azores were founding members of PARRAL. (Courtesy of First Christian Church.)

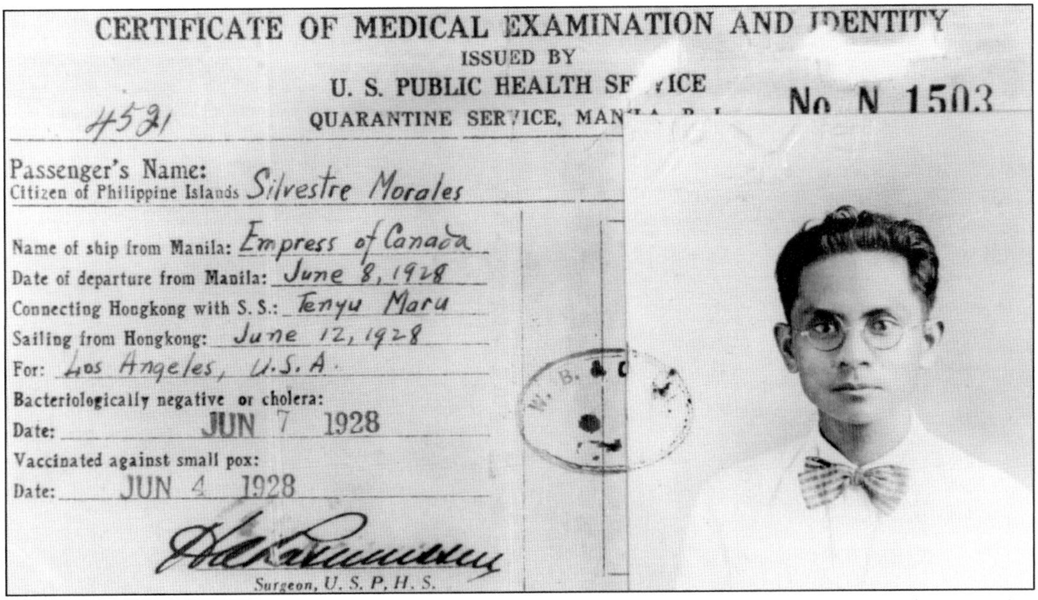

CERTIFICATE OF MEDICAL EXAMINATION AND IDENTITY
ISSUED BY
U. S. PUBLIC HEALTH SERVICE
QUARANTINE SERVICE, MANILA, P. I.

4531 No N 1503

Passenger's Name:
Citizen of Philippine Islands Silvestre Morales

Name of ship from Manila: Empress of Canada
Date of departure from Manila: June 8, 1928
Connecting Hongkong with S. S.: Tenyu Maru
Sailing from Hongkong: June 12, 1928
For: Los Angeles, U.S.A.
Bacteriologically negative or cholera:
Date: JUN 7 1928
Vaccinated against small pox:
Date: JUN 4 1928

Surgeon, U. S. P. H. S.

This Certificate of Medical Examination and Identity was issued to Silvestre Morales in 1930. In 1928, thirteen Filipino students from the California Christian College founded the Filipino Christian Fellowship, which provided assistance to Filipinos, who were mostly males, in Los Angeles. In 1933, the fellowship founded the Filipino Christian Church with the help of Rev. Silvestre Morales, Rev. Felix A. Pascua, students, and others. In 1932, the fellowship was located at First and San Pedro Streets. It later relocated to Bunker Hill. (Courtesy of Shades of L.A. Archives/ Los Angeles Public Library.)

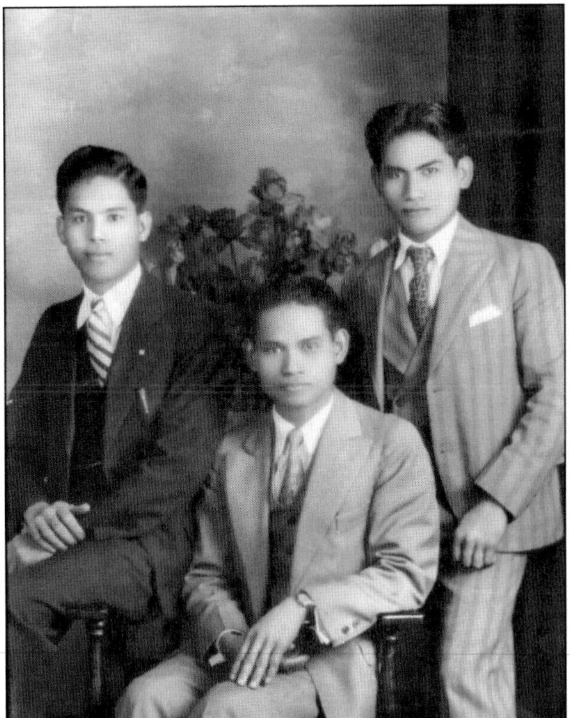

Pioneers of the Filipino Christian Fellowship in the 1930s are, from left to right, Rev. Casiano Coloma, Ponciano Balderama, and Ed G. Balderama. (Courtesy of First Christian Church.)

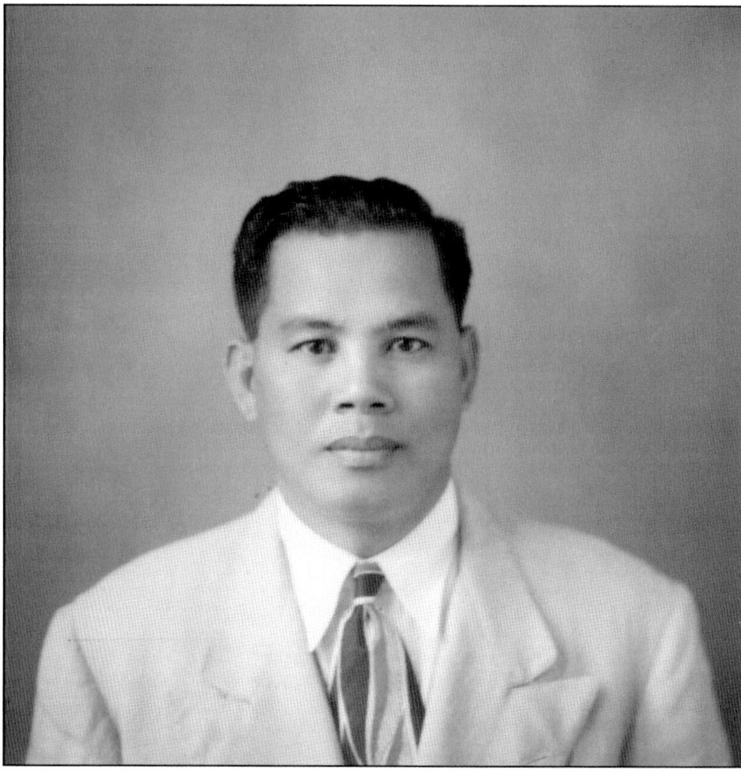

These portraits of Rev. Casiano Coloma (left) and his wife, Esperaza Coloma (below), of the First Christian Church, were taken in the 1940s. Reverend Casiano served the church in an unofficial capacity as assistant pastor for three years during World War II when Reverend Pascua voluntarily relinquished the pastorate to serve in the U.S. Army. When Pascua returned, he resumed his ministerial duties at the church. (Courtesy of First Christian Church.)

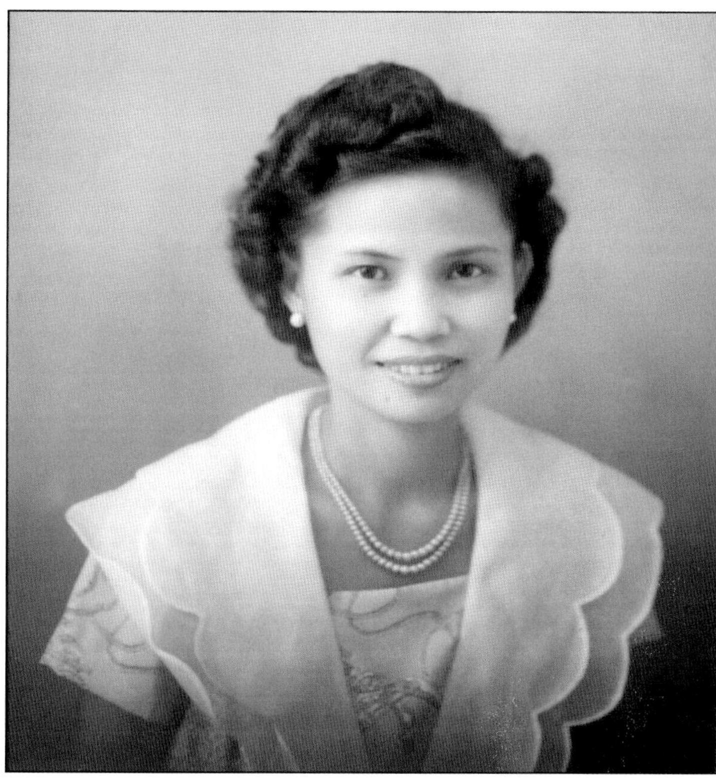

Esperaza Coloma was active in the church during her husband's ministry. In addition to providing spiritual guidance to its members, the church fostered social and individual attention by encouraging group recreational activities such as attending camp events, sports activities, and singing in the church choir. (Courtesy of First Christian Church.)

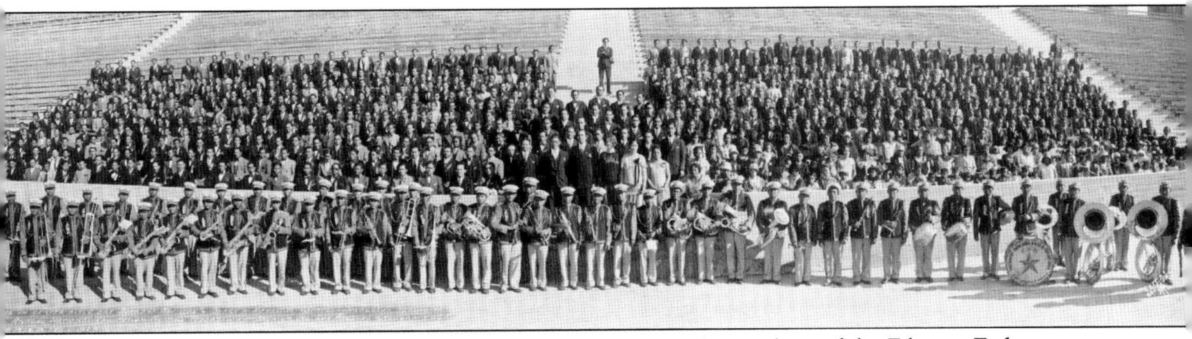

Hilario C. Moncado (standing in back, center aisle) is seen with members of the Filipino Federation of America, Inc., at the Los Angeles Coliseum during its second annual national convention, held from December 23, 1928, to January 1, 1929. Standing in the center aisle are the board of advisors and the board of managers. Seated are delegates of the federation. The federation promoted music appreciation and had its own musical band, called the Gamut Orchestra, that performed at annual federation-sponsored concerts. (Courtesy of the Filipino Federation of America, Inc.)

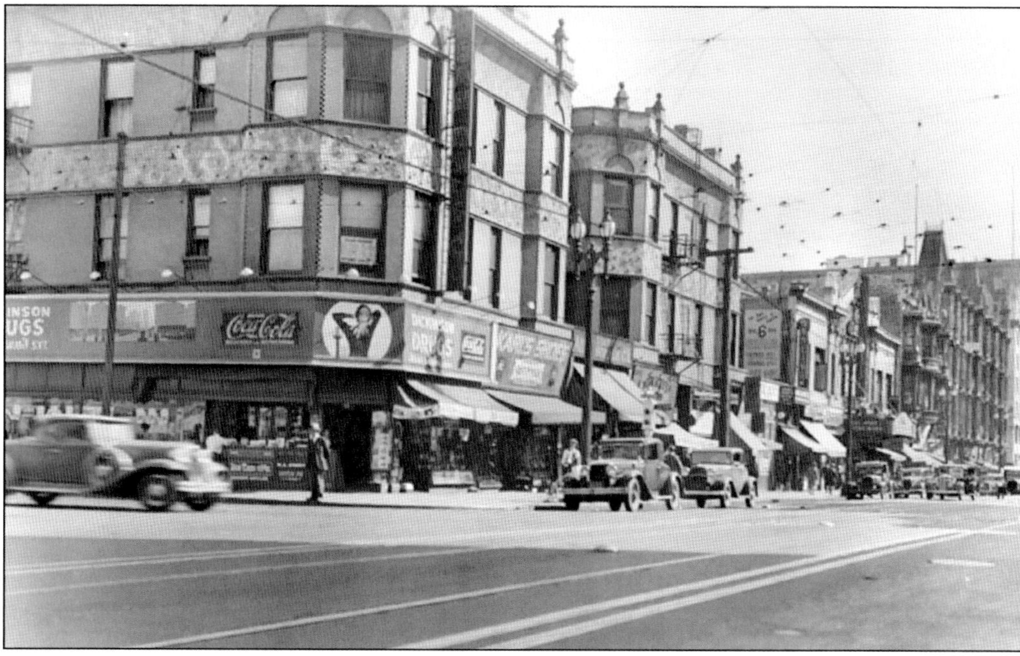

Main Street in Los Angeles is pictured in the 1930s. Filipino-owned pool halls, such as the Eagle, Luzon, and Manila pool halls, were located in the area near First and Second Streets and Main and Los Angeles Streets. Pool halls were a popular recreational pastime and provided congregation places for Filipinos to socialize. (Courtesy of Los Angeles Public Library.)

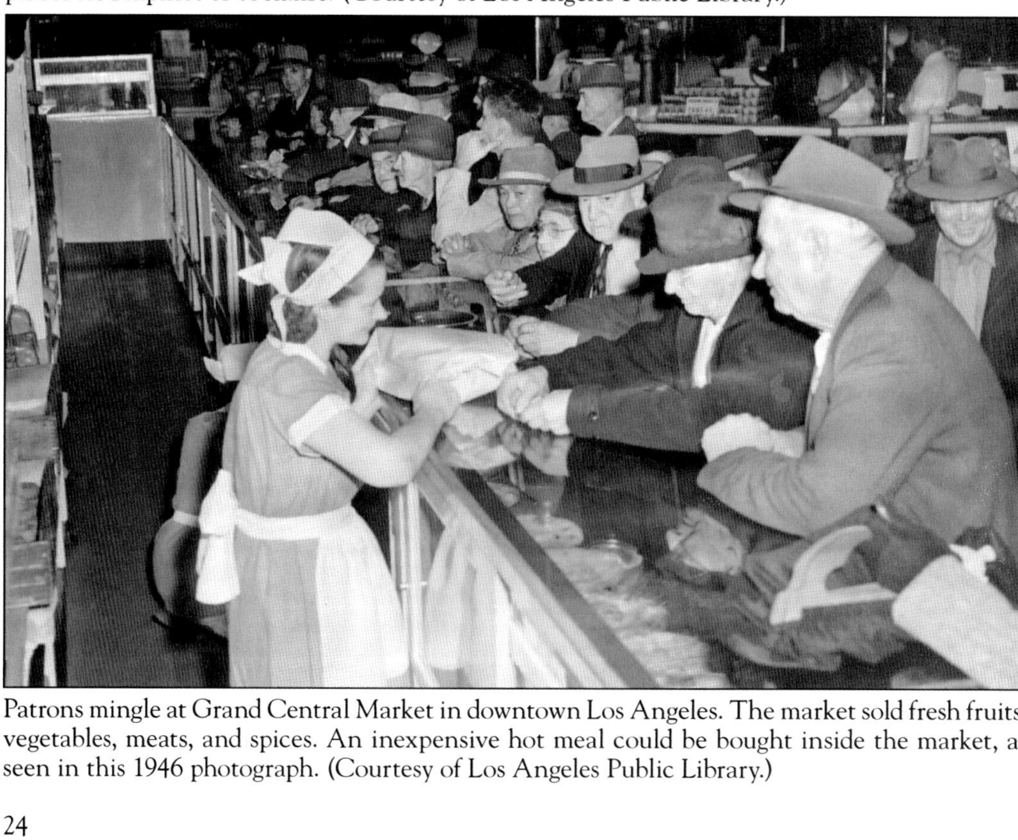

Patrons mingle at Grand Central Market in downtown Los Angeles. The market sold fresh fruits, vegetables, meats, and spices. An inexpensive hot meal could be bought inside the market, as seen in this 1946 photograph. (Courtesy of Los Angeles Public Library.)

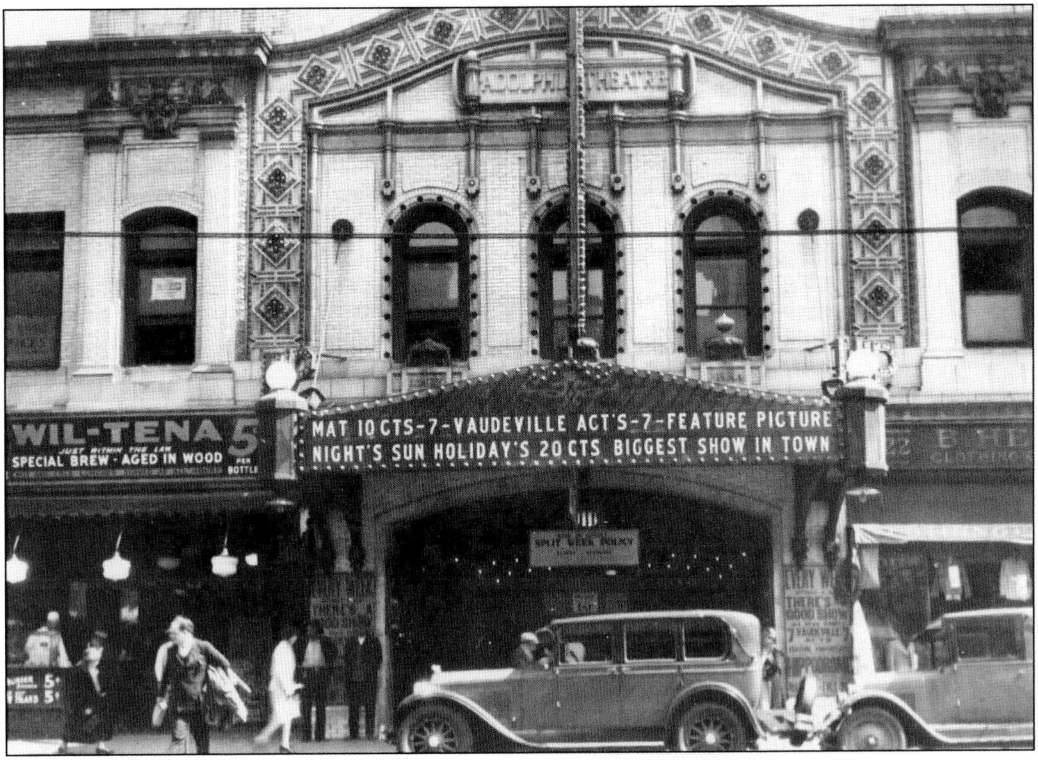

A 1928 photograph shows the Adolphus Theater, located at 320 South Main Street. The theater later became a taxi dance hall called the Hippodrome. By the 1930s, there were nine dance halls on Main Street—the Olympic, Royal, Palais, Liberty, One Eleven, Red Mills, Hidalgo, and Danceland. Other dance halls frequented by Filipinos included the Four Hundred One Ballroom, Roseland, Rizal Cabaret, Montezuma, and the Tiffany Dance Hall. (Courtesy of Security Pacific National Bank.)

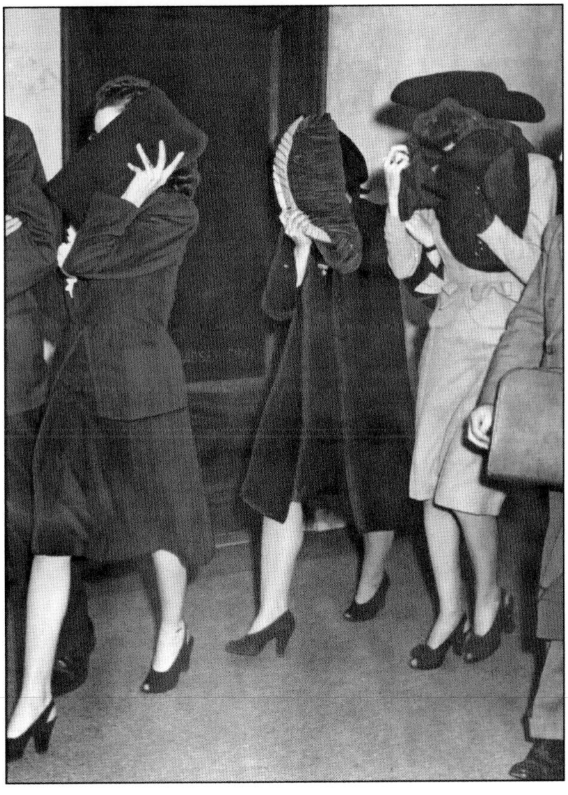

In 1943, dancers at the Roseland taxi dance hall were called to testify in a grand jury probe of the slaying of William Lederer, the Roseland dance hall proprietor. The women hiding their faces from the camera as they appeared for questioning are, from left to right, Eunice Cullen, Dorothy Cox, and Mary Derry. Public disturbances and arrests involving Filipinos were often associated with dance halls. (Courtesy of the *Herald-Examiner* Collection.)

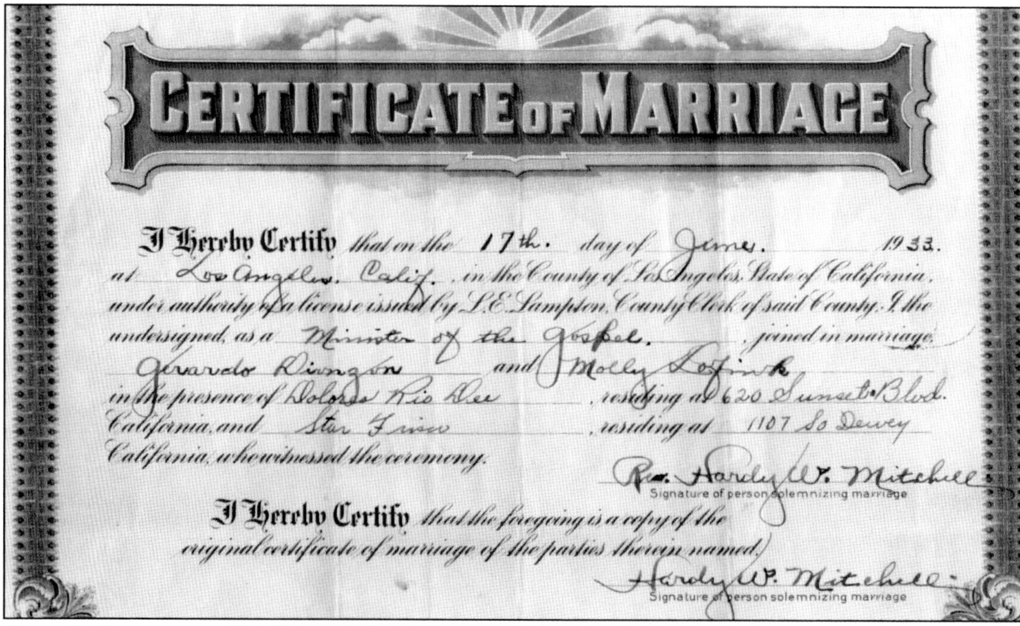

CERTIFICATE OF MARRIAGE

I Hereby Certify that on the 17th. day of June. 1933. at Los Angeles, Calif. in the County of Los Angeles State of California, under authority of a license issued by L.E. Lampson, County Clerk of said County, I the undersigned, as a Minister of the Gospel, joined in marriage Gerardo Dionzon and Molly Lofink in the presence of Dolores Rio Dee, residing at 620 Sunset Blvd. California, and Star Frisco, residing at 1107 So Dewey California, who witnessed the ceremony.

Rev. Hardy W. Mitchell
Signature of person solemnizing marriage

I Hereby Certify that the foregoing is a copy of the original certificate of marriage of the parties therein named.

Hardy W. Mitchell
Signature of person solemnizing marriage

Gerardo Dionzon and Molly Lofink, a Caucasian woman, married in 1933 after Salvador Roldan challenged a California anti-miscegenation law that prohibited interracial marriages between whites and "Mongolians, Negroes, Mulattos, and persons of mixed blood," arguing that Filipinos were Malayan. He won the case and was allowed to marry, but two months later, the statute was amended to include Malay. (Courtesy of Kenny Dionzon.)

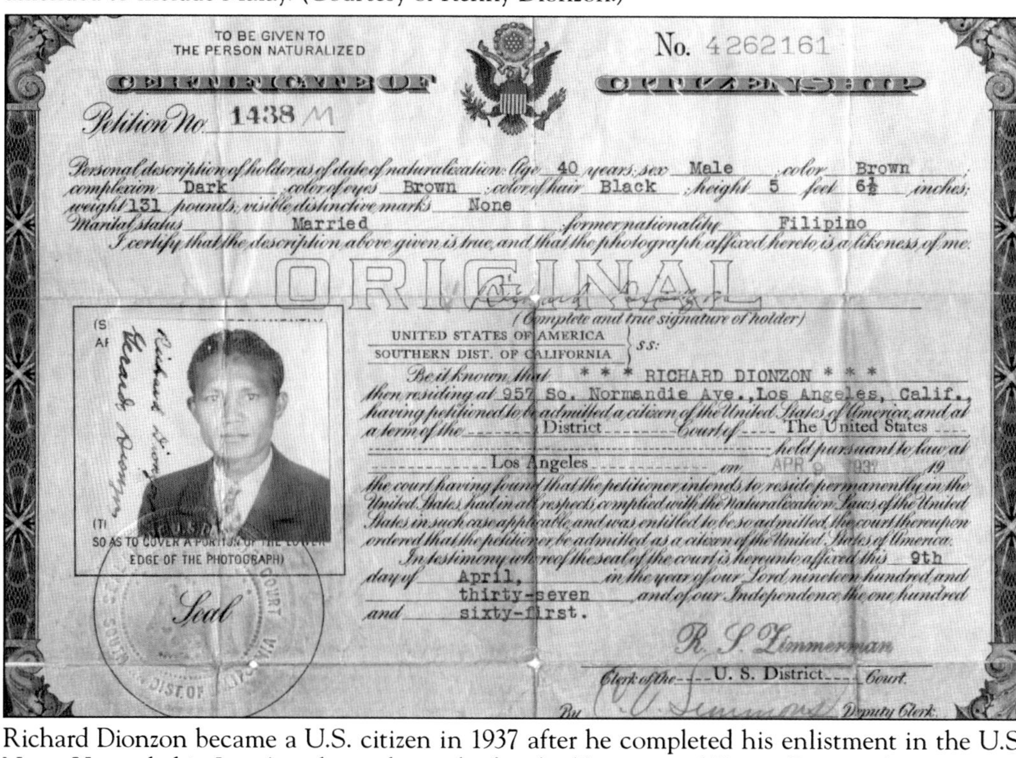

TO BE GIVEN TO THE PERSON NATURALIZED

No. 4262161

CERTIFICATE OF CITIZENSHIP

Petition No. 1438 M

Personal description of holder as of date of naturalization: Age 40 years; sex Male color Brown complexion Dark color of eyes Brown color of hair Black height 5 feet 6½ inches; weight 131 pounds; visible distinctive marks None
Marital status Married former nationality Filipino

I certify that the description above given is true, and that the photograph affixed hereto is a likeness of me.

ORIGINAL

(Complete and true signature of holder)

UNITED STATES OF AMERICA
SOUTHERN DIST. OF CALIFORNIA } ss:

Be it known that * * * RICHARD DIONZON * * * then residing at 957 So. Normandie Ave., Los Angeles, Calif., having petitioned to be admitted a citizen of the United States of America, and at a term of the District Court of The United States held pursuant to law at Los Angeles on APR 9 1937 19 the court having found that the petitioner intends to reside permanently in the United States, had in all respects complied with the Naturalization Laws of the United States in such case applicable, and was entitled to be so admitted, the court thereupon ordered that the petitioner be admitted as a citizen of the United States of America.

In testimony whereof the seal of the court is hereunto affixed this 9th day of April, in the year of our Lord nineteen hundred and thirty-seven and of our Independence the one hundred and sixty-first.

Seal

R. S. Zimmerman
Clerk of the U. S. District Court.
By Deputy Clerk.

Richard Dionzon became a U.S. citizen in 1937 after he completed his enlistment in the U.S. Navy. He settled in Los Angeles and raised a family. (Courtesy of Kenny Dionzon.)

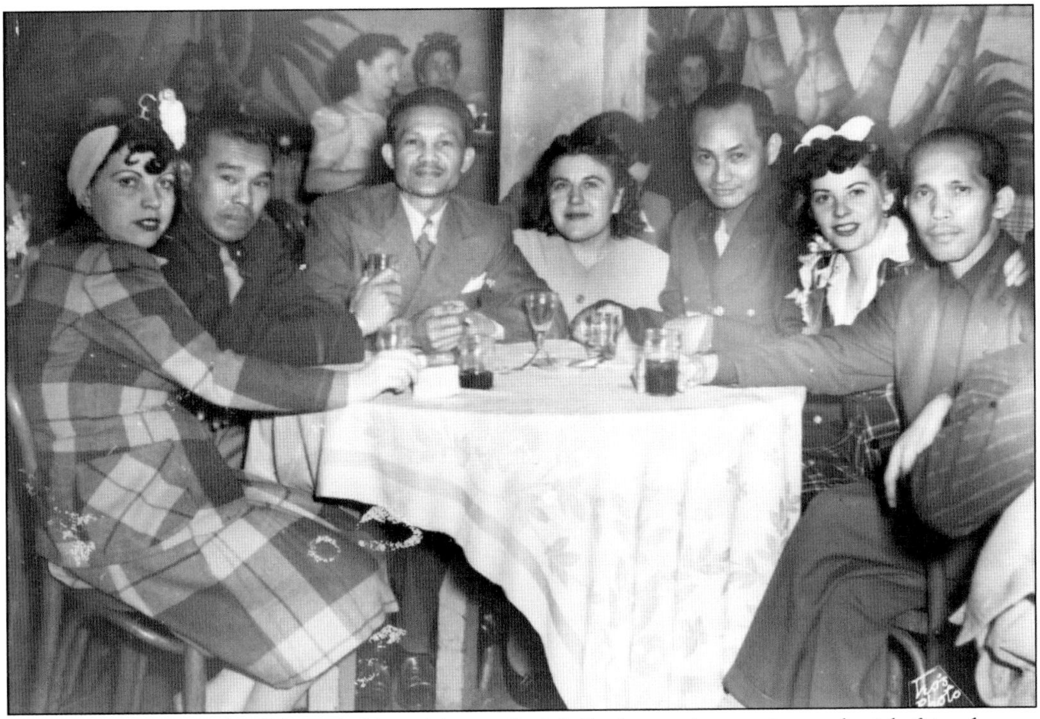

Richard Dionzon (third from left) and his wife, Molly (center), are pictured with friends at a nightclub in downtown Los Angeles in the 1930s. (Courtesy of Kenny Dionzon.)

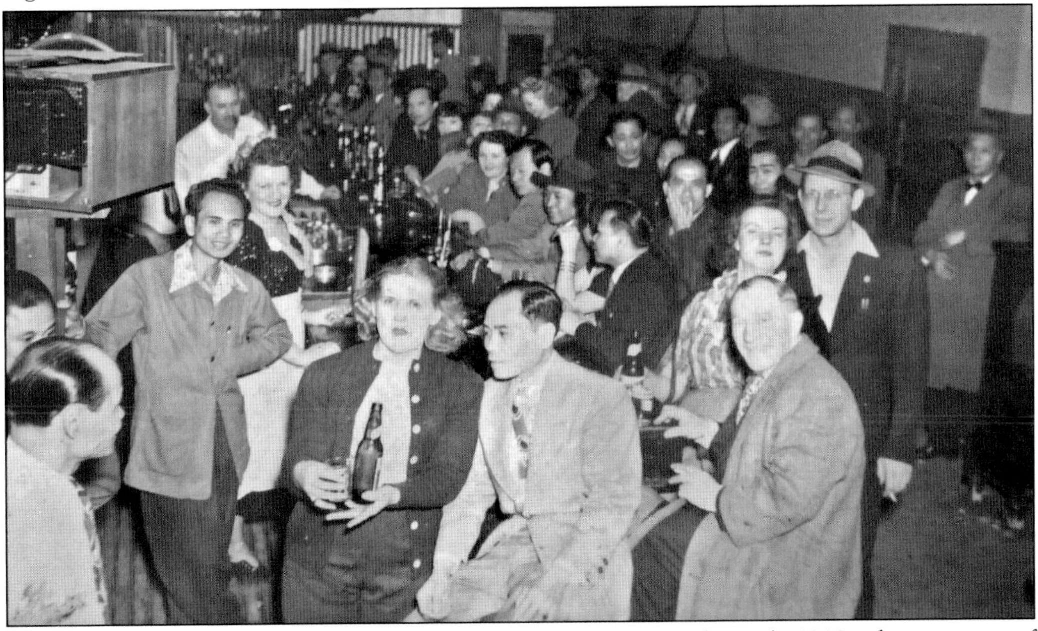

Pictured is one of several bars around First and Main Streets in the early 1940s, the core area of downtown where Filipinos lived and congregated. Filipinos were forced to live in this impoverished section of the city and were restricted from socializing and obtaining most services outside of the downtown area. The area around First and Main Streets was also known as the "Red Light District." (Courtesy of the author.)

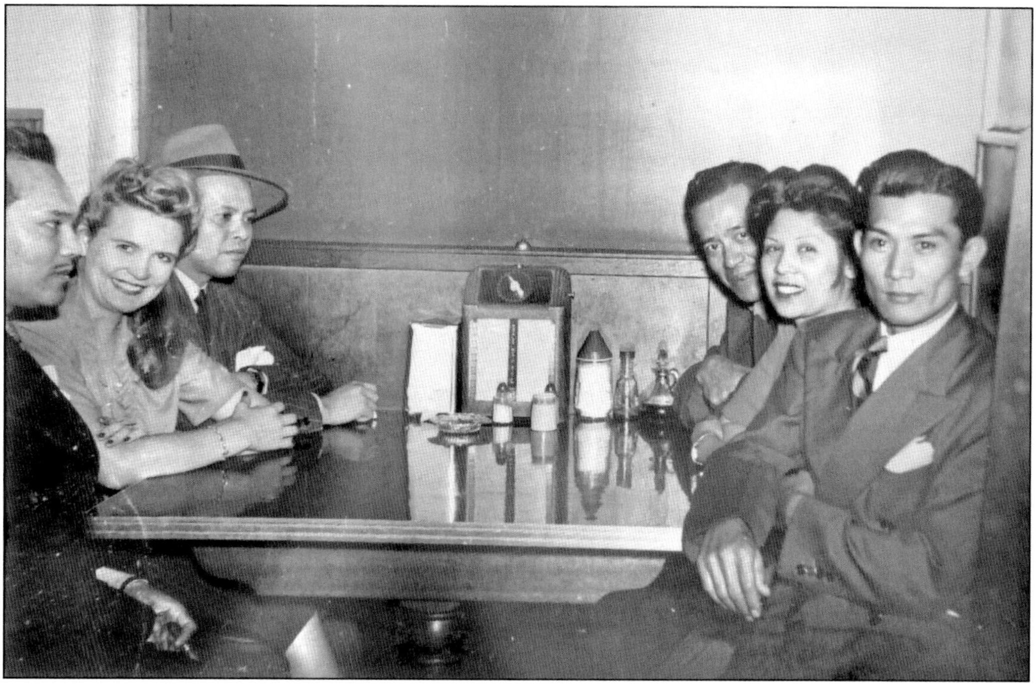

Tommy Montoya (far left) and his friends visit a diner in Little Manila in the 1930s. By 1940, there were 22 restaurants in and around Little Manila, including Ace Café, Busy Bee, Fagel Asuncion, Luzon, La Divisoria, L.V.M., La Union, Lucky Spot, Moonlight, Three Stars, York Lunch, and My-T-Good Café, to name a few. (Courtesy of the author.)

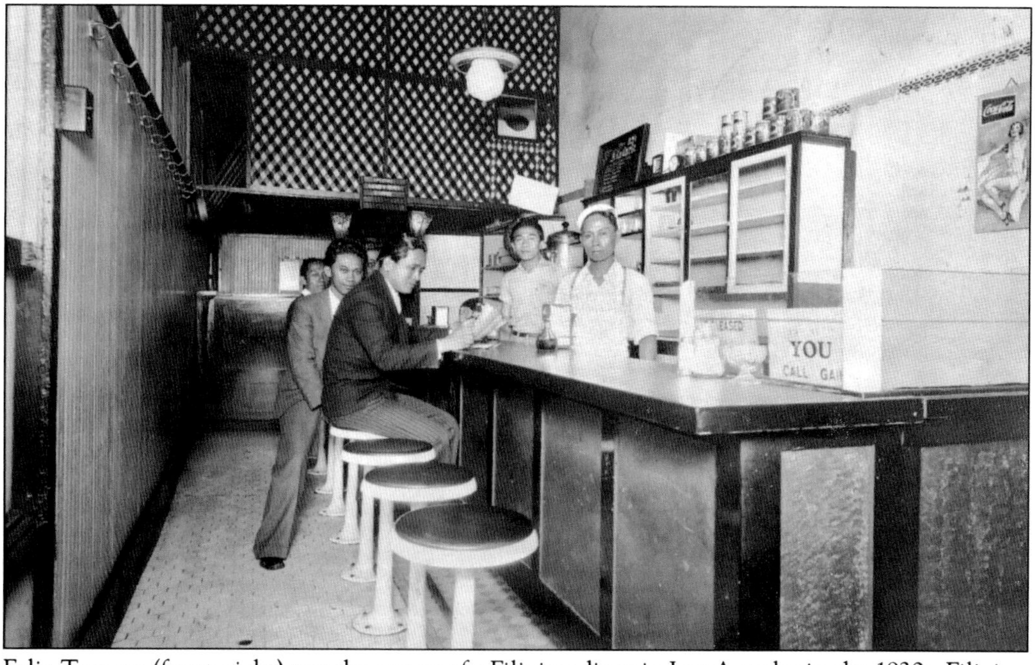

Felix Taganas (front, right) was the owner of a Filipino diner in Los Angeles in the 1930s. Filipino diners and cafés offered ethnic dishes and a place where Filipinos could dine without being confronted or refused service. (Courtesy of Jenny Ochale and Celina Taganas-Duffy.)

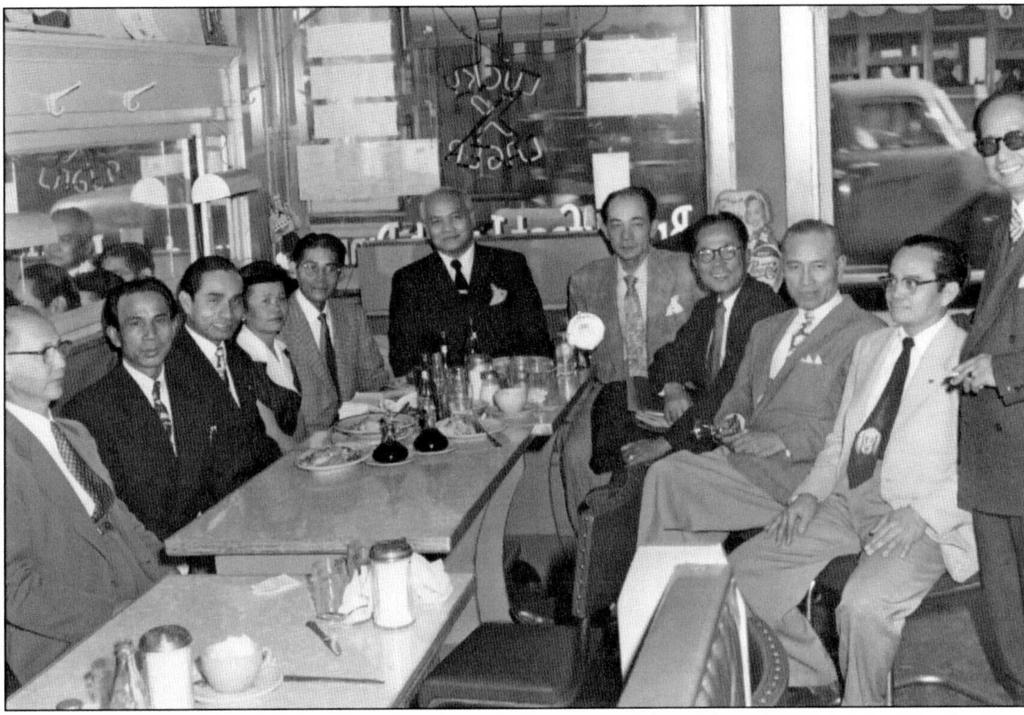

Numeriano D. Lagmay (third from left) is shown with friends at the Filipino-owned Lucky Spot Café in the 1950s. (Courtesy of Benita Q. Lagmay and Numeriano D. Lagmay.)

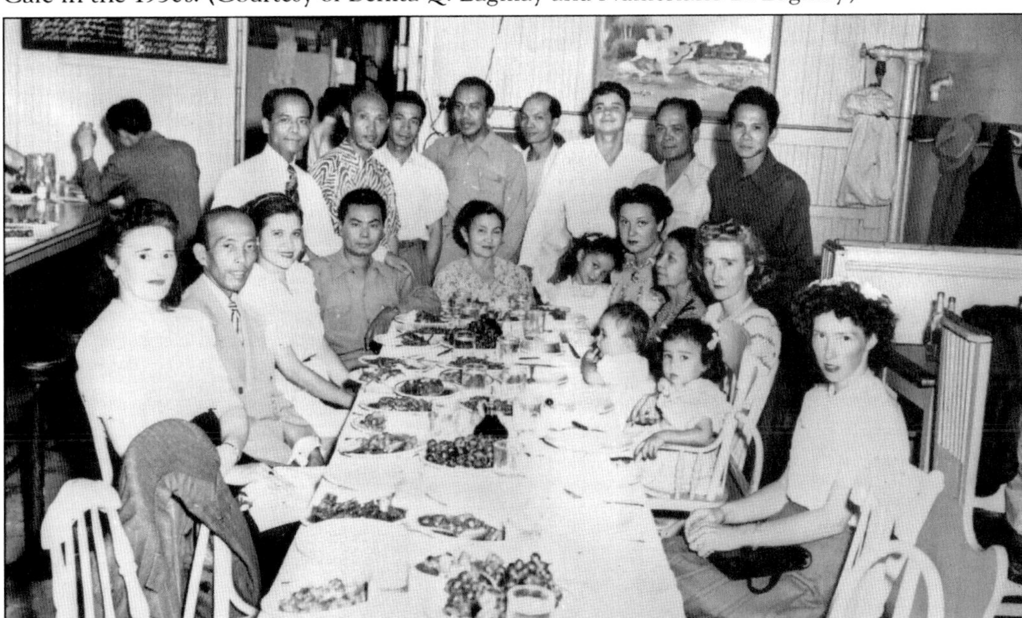

Here is a 1952 photograph of members of the Ferrer family and their friends at the L.V.M. Café. The acronym stood for Luzon, Visayas, and Mindanao, all islands in the Philippines. The restaurant was located on East First Street. Pictured are, from left to right, (seated) two unidentified, Anne Ferrer, and Eddie Ferrer; (standing behind Eddie) Joe Abrigo; (standing fourth from right) Gene Aquino. All others are unidentified. (Courtesy of Shades of L.A. Archives/Los Angeles Public Library.)

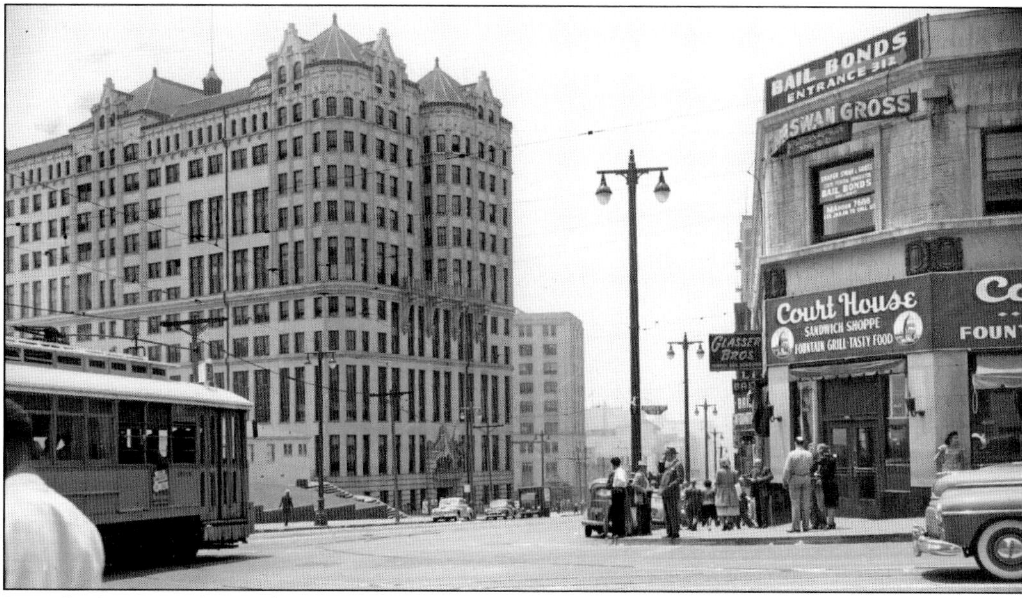

Temple Street and Broadway are seen here in this 1945 photograph. Although most Filipinos congregated in the area of First and Main Streets, they also resided on and around Temple Street, Broadway, and Hill Street near First Street; Fremont Street between Third and Fourth Streets; Grand Avenue and Hope Street; Figueroa Street at First and California Streets; California and Pavilion Streets; Centennial and Temple Streets; Boylston Street; Burlington Street; and Weller Street between San Pedro and Los Angeles Streets. (Courtesy of Security Pacific National Bank.)

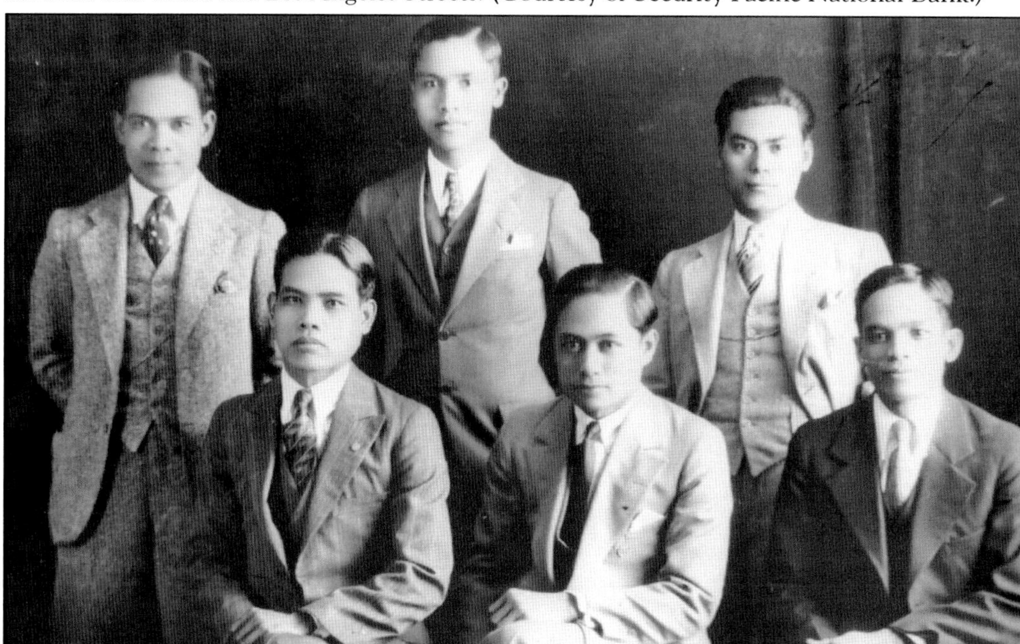

Here is a portrait of members of the Mapandan Association of Los Angeles in 1930. The organization was named after the town where the members were from. It provided mutual aid to its members, as well as promoting cultural and sports activities. One member has been identified as Eddie Ferrer (standing, right). (Courtesy of Shades of L.A. Archives/Los Angeles Public Library.)

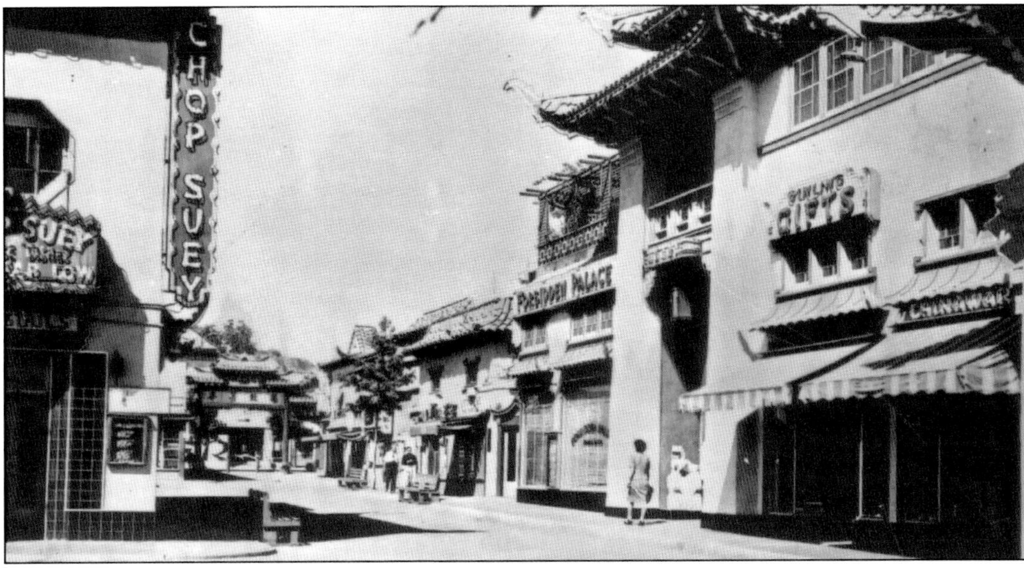

This view of new Chinatown in 1938 shows various restaurants and gift shops. A partial view of the Chop Suey restaurant can be seen on the left side of the image, while the Forbidden Palace restaurant is visible in the center. What is not visible are the gambling dens that were hidden deep within the buildings and were frequented by Filipinos. (Courtesy of Security Pacific National Bank.)

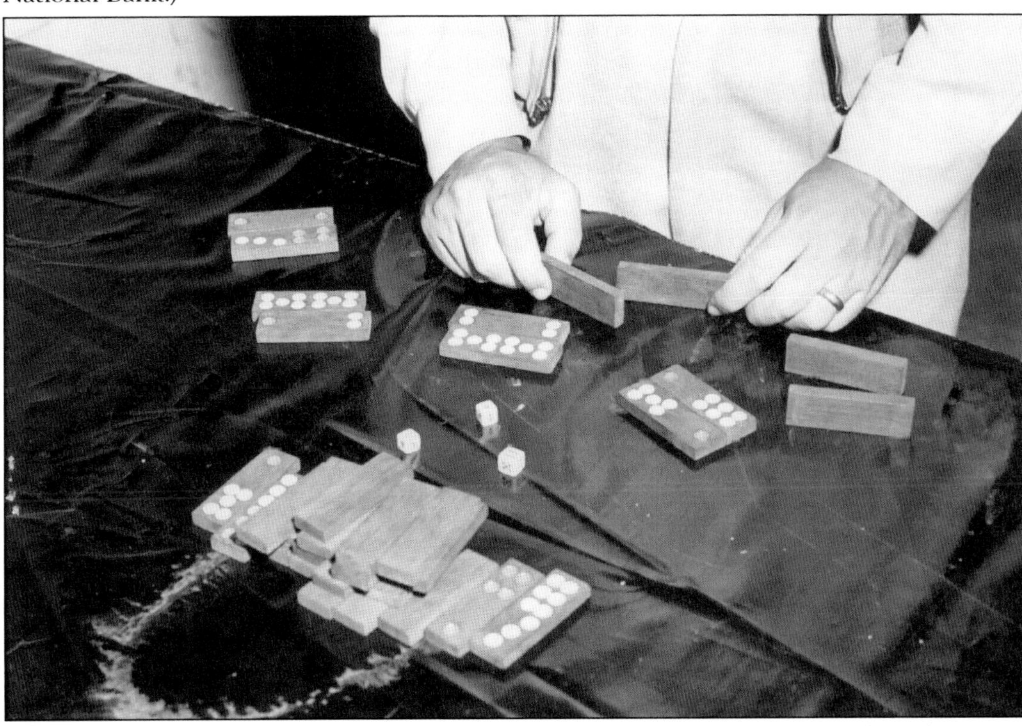

Pai Gow or *Pi Que* (Chinese dominoes) was a popular illegal gambling game played in Chinatown. Secret gambling dens were usually located in innocent-appearing restaurants. A labyrinth of passages leading to a secret room often hid the dens. This 1954 photograph was taken in a gambling den on North Spring Street. (Courtesy of Los Angeles Public Library.)

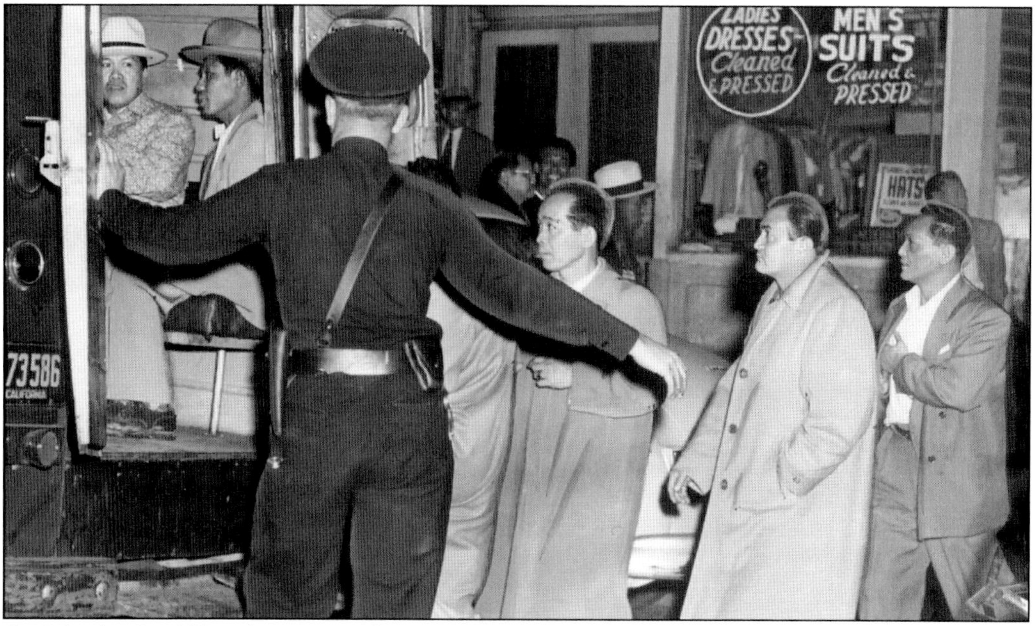

On March 12, 1953, police arrested 26 suspects in a raid on a basement gambling den located at 816 West Temple Street. Suspects are seen boarding a paddy wagon after an elaborate fan-tan parlor was discovered. Fan-tan was typically a game consisting of a square marked in the center of a table with its sides marked with numbers that players placed bets on. (Courtesy of Los Angeles Public Library.)

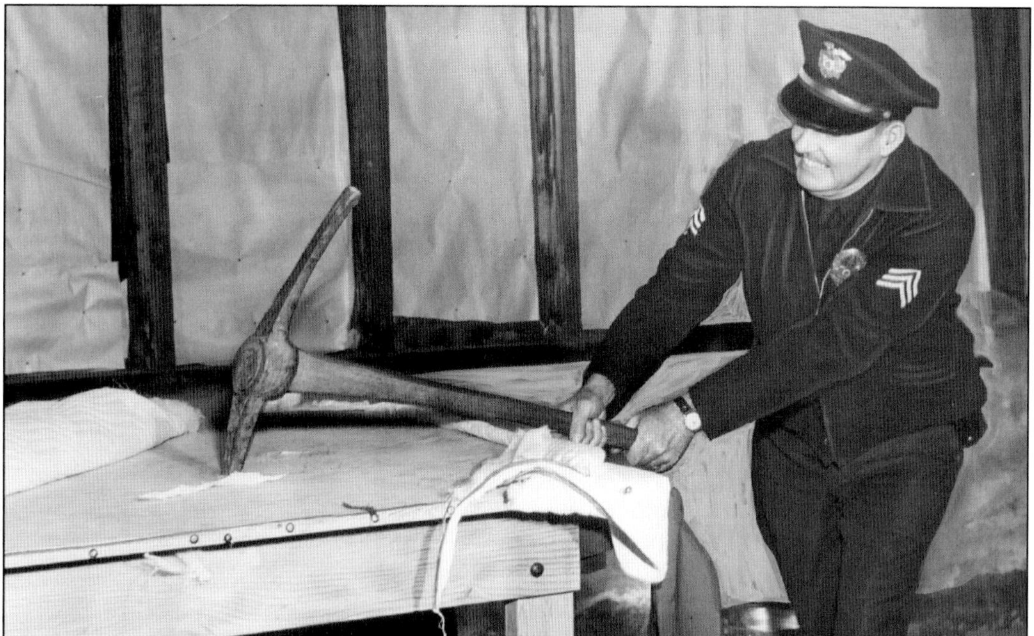

Sgt. Don Houghton axes a gaming table while a vice squad destroys equipment seized in the raid on a Chinese gambling den at 816 West Temple Street in 1953. (Courtesy of Los Angeles Public Library.)

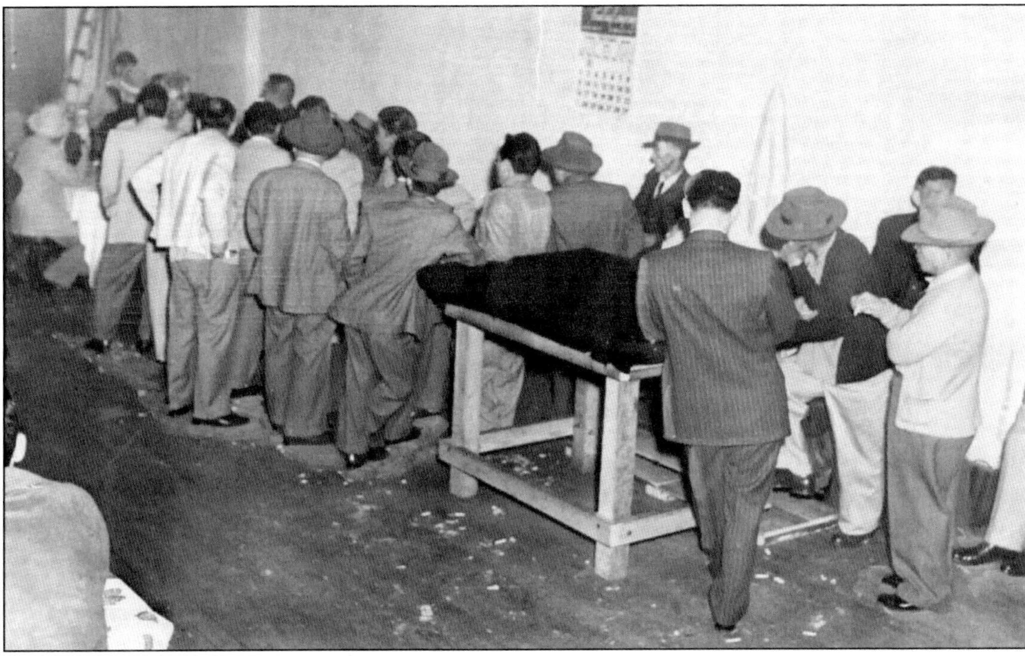

Another gambling den is seen raided by the Los Angeles Police Department (LAPD) vice squad in downtown Los Angeles in 1950. Pictured are some of the 70 customers who were booked on gambling charges. Chinese checkers, fan-tan, and other games were illegally played for money. (Courtesy of Los Angeles Public Library.)

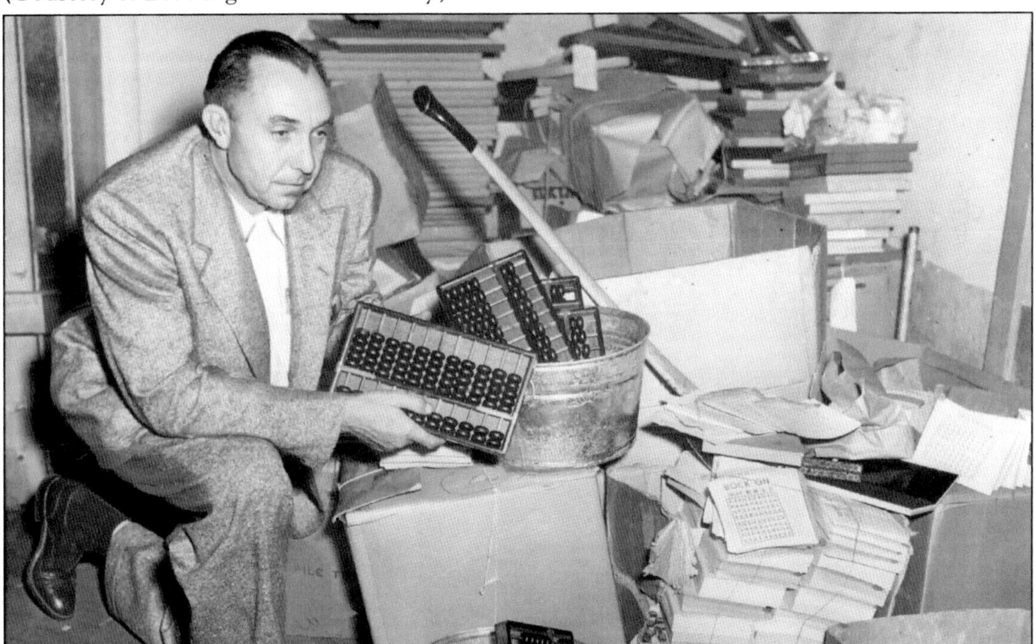

A 1951 photograph of detective Lt. Bob Hall shows him examining abacuses, lottery tickets, and other items seized in a raid at 4133½ Third Street. Eight men were arrested on gambling charges. Police said the gambling den took in several hundred dollars a day. (Courtesy of the *Herald-Examiner* Collection.)

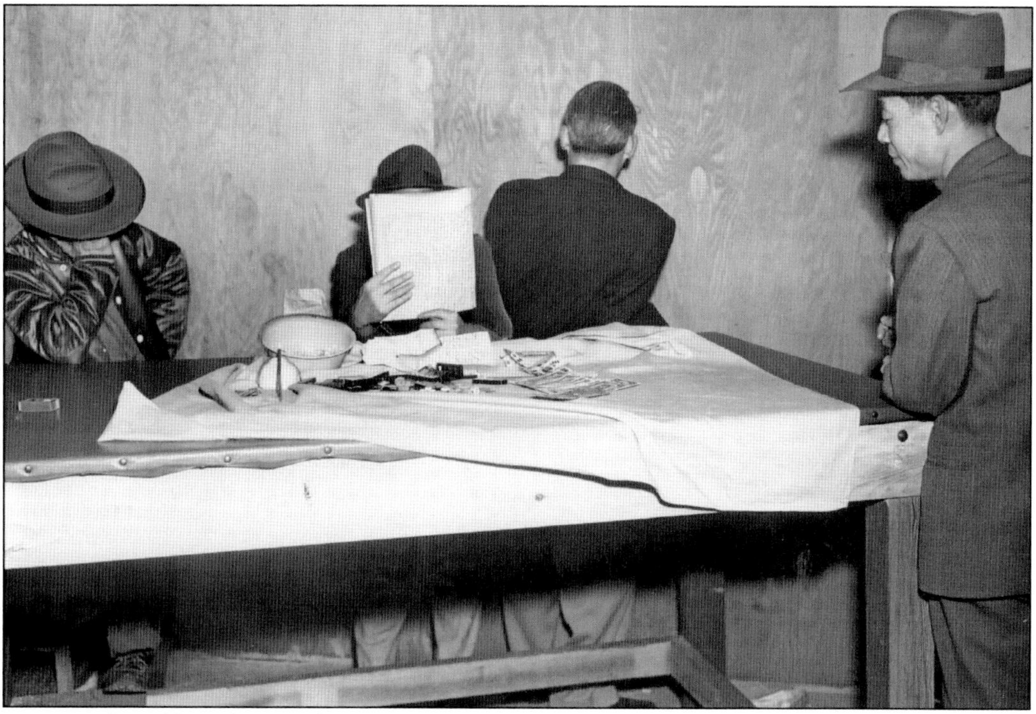

Money and gambling chips can be seen on the gaming table as more suspects are arrested in Chinatown in a gambling den in this 1954 photograph. (Courtesy of Los Angeles Public Library.)

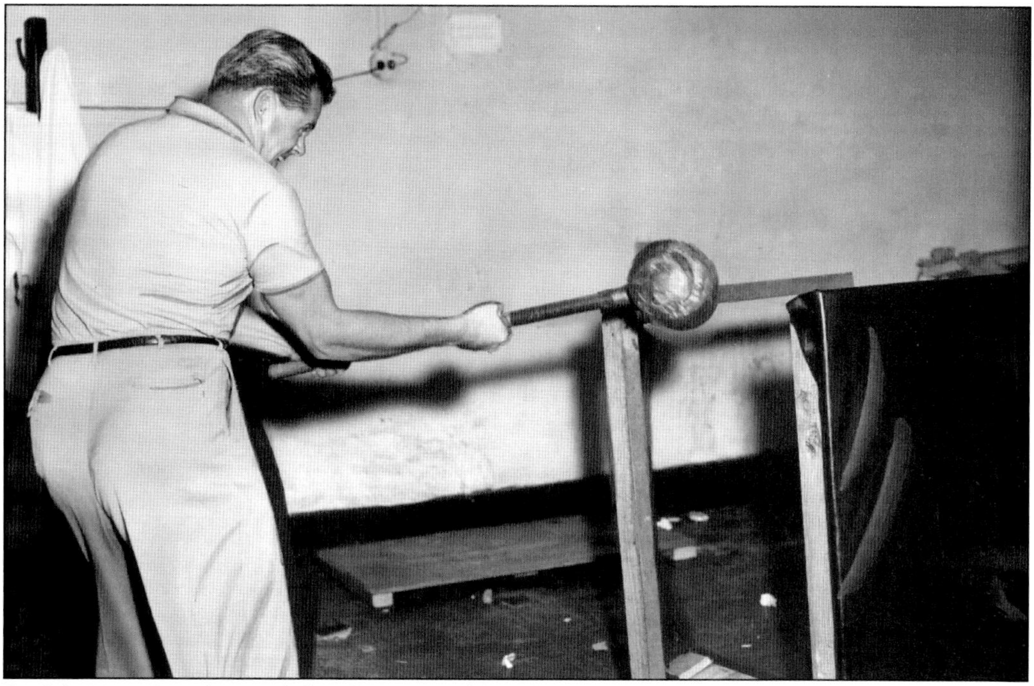

On July 28, 1954, police raided a Chinese gambling den at 505½ East First Street. City administrative vice squads entered the den by sledge-hammering three successive doors and then destroyed the gaming tables with a sledge hammer. (Courtesy of Los Angeles Public Library.)

Pictured is a 1940s map of Little Tokyo. First, Main, and Los Angeles Streets intersected in Little Tokyo. Both the Japanese and Chinese had established their own communities, Little Tokyo and Chinatown respectively. From the 1920s to the mid-1940s, Filipinos resided and established businesses in a small section of Little Tokyo, calling it Little Manila. (Courtesy of the *Herald-Examiner* Collection.)

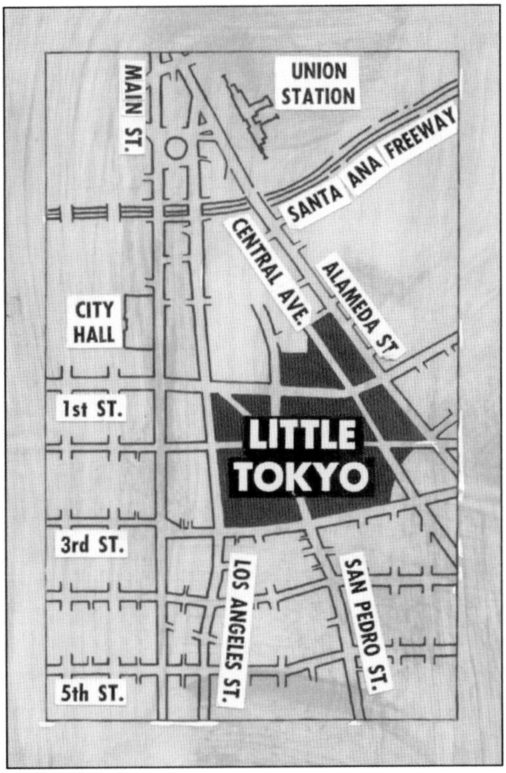

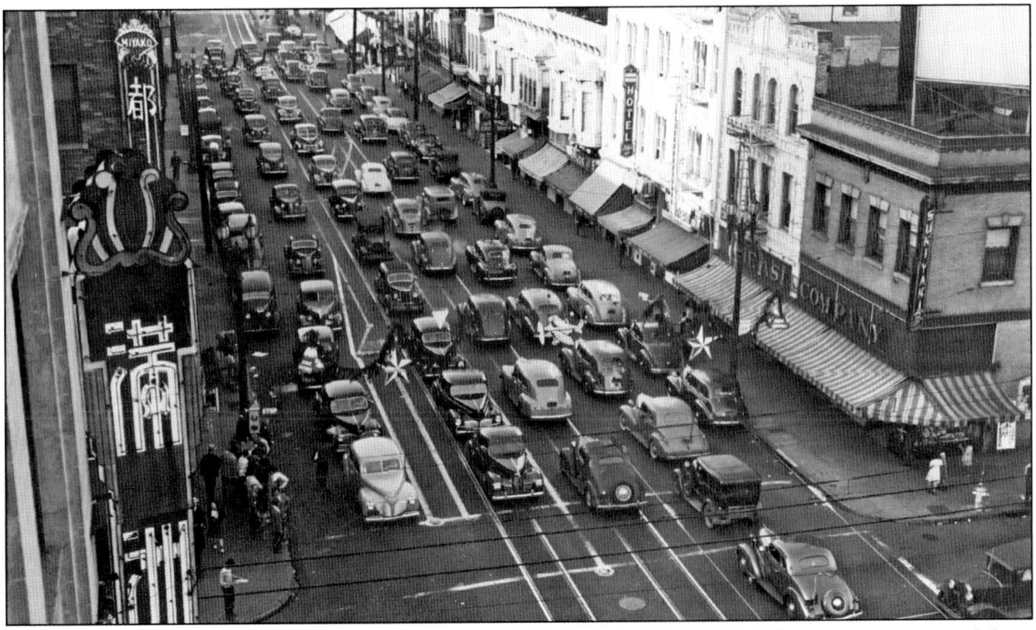

This aerial view of Little Tokyo looks down on First Street in 1941. The intersection at Main and First Streets was the core area of downtown where Filipinos congregated since the 1920s. By the 1930s, there were seven barbershops, 12 restaurants, the Philippine Chamber of Commerce of Southern California, and five Filipino business corporations, as well as several pool halls and taxi dance halls. (Courtesy of the *Herald-Examiner* Collection.)

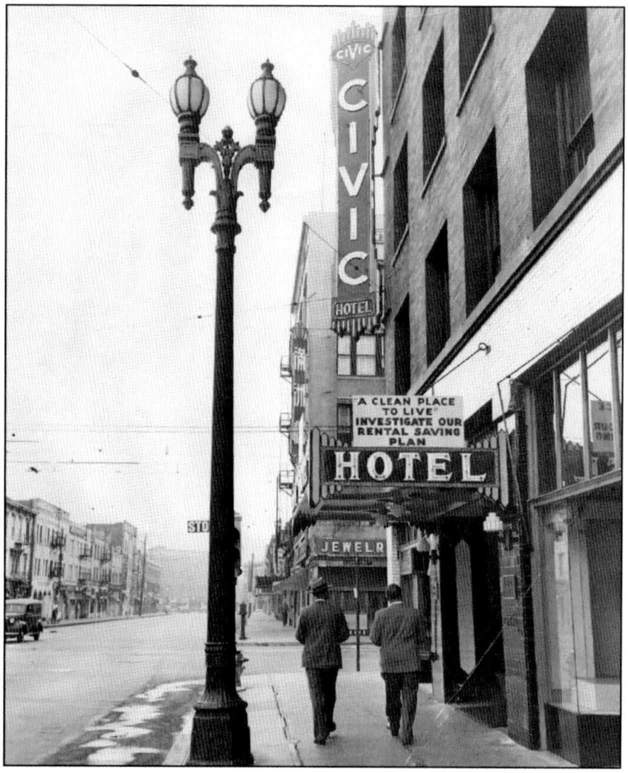

This is a 1942 photograph of First and San Pedro Streets in Little Tokyo. In and around First and Main Streets were seven Filipino-owned businesses and organizations, including the Philippine Mercantile Company, Guideons Trading Corporation, Filipino Utopia Medical Service, Philippine Importing Company, Orlanes Philippine Products Company, and the Legionarios Club. (Courtesy of the *Herald-Examiner* Collection.)

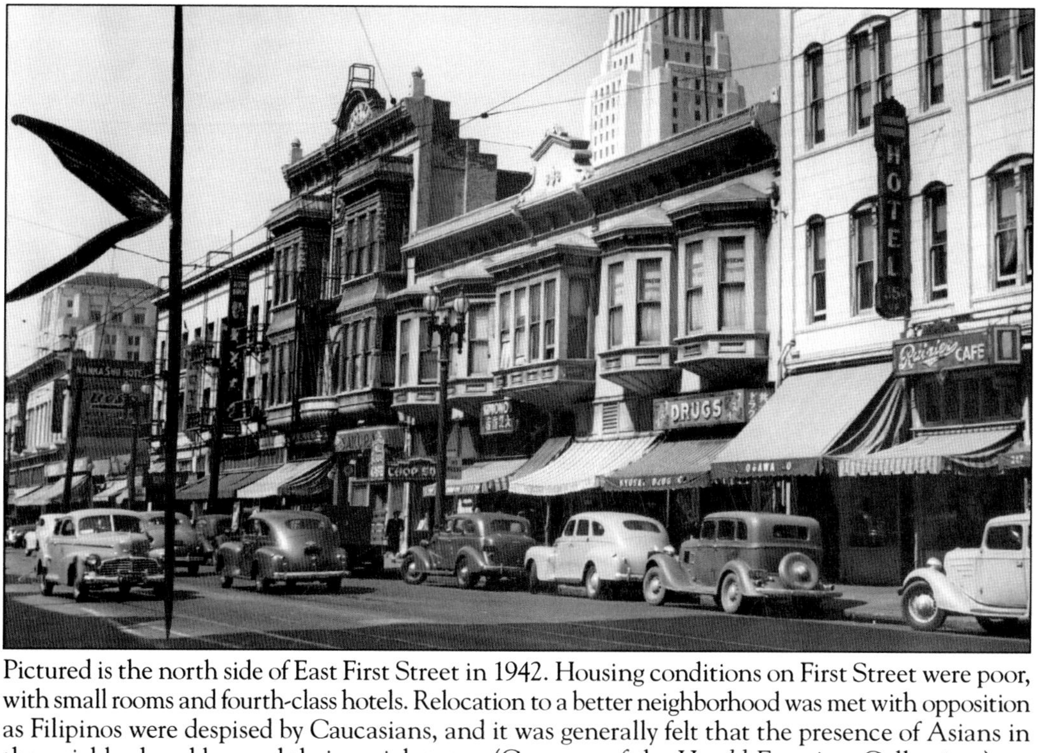

Pictured is the north side of East First Street in 1942. Housing conditions on First Street were poor, with small rooms and fourth-class hotels. Relocation to a better neighborhood was met with opposition as Filipinos were despised by Caucasians, and it was generally felt that the presence of Asians in the neighborhood lowered their social status. (Courtesy of the *Herald-Examiner* Collection.)

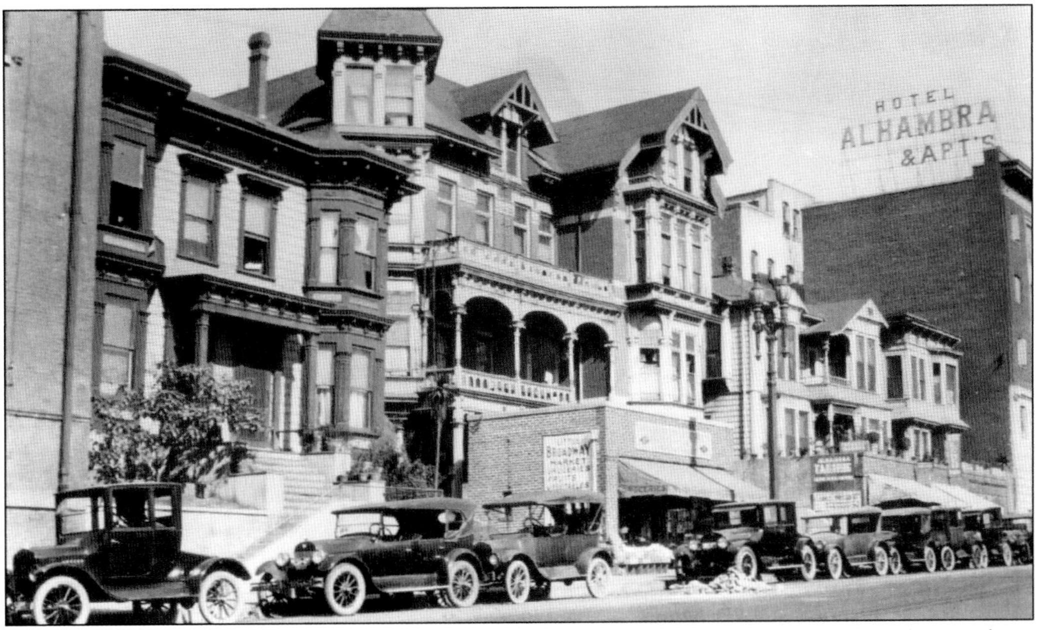

A 1920 photograph shows a row of houses on Broadway near Temple Street. The Little Broadway Market and the Hotel Alhambra and Apartments can be seen. Although the nucleus of the Filipinos' social life was around First and Main Streets, affordable boarding rooms and single apartments were to be found on California Street, Broadway, and Temple Street. (Courtesy of Security Pacific National Bank.)

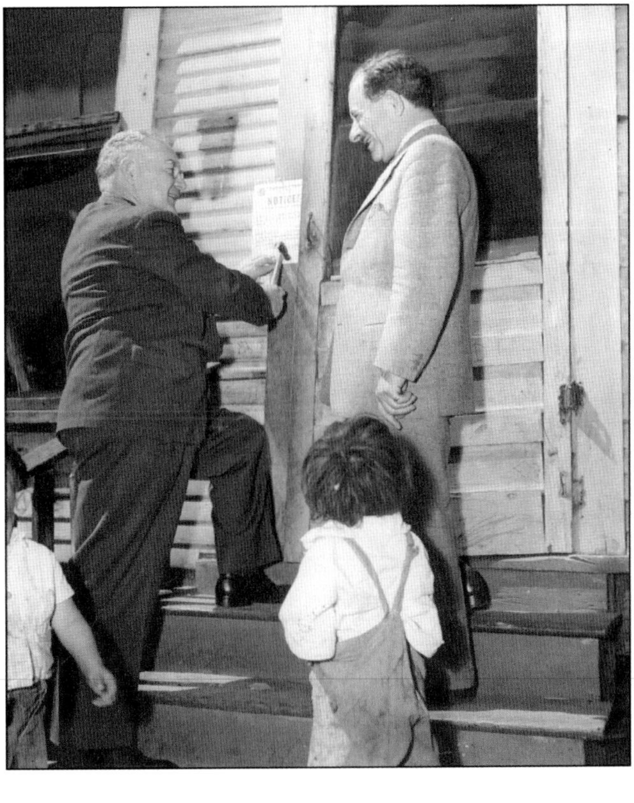

A notice to abate overcrowded and unhealthy conditions was posted by Mayor Fletcher Bowron in 1944 at the start of a campaign to clean up conditions in Little Tokyo, which by the early 1940s was becoming home for thousands of war workers who were mostly African Americans. Tensions developed between African Americans and Filipinos that led to some reported incidents of physical violence. (Courtesy of the *Herald-Examiner* Collection.)

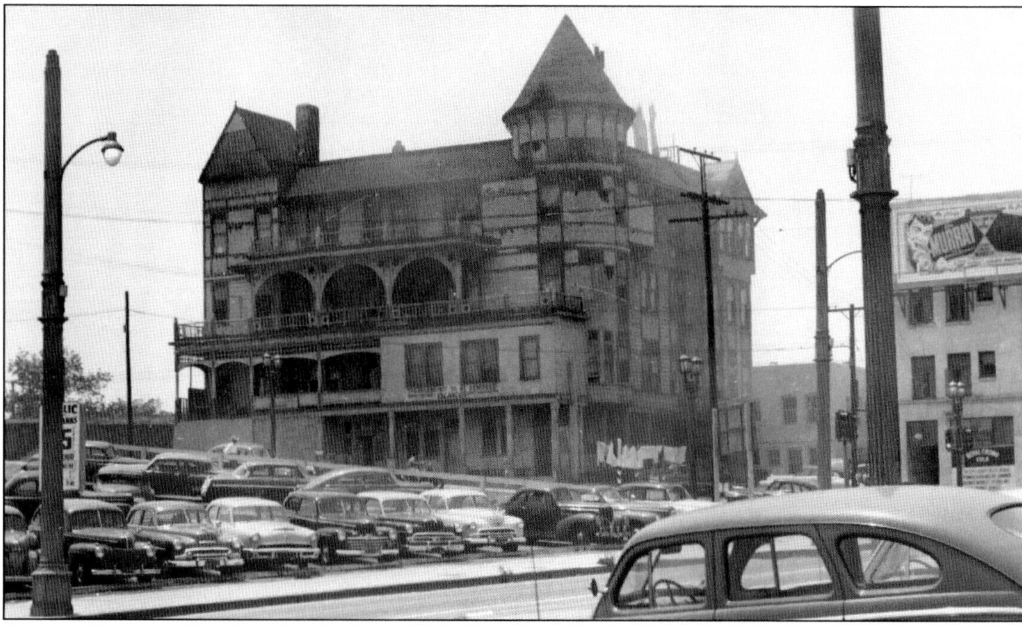

A large four-story, multi-unit residence on Grand Avenue, south of Temple Street, is seen in 1953. Because many Filipinos resided in temporary spaces at hotels, boardinghouses, and apartments, the transitional lifestyle prevented them from securing an attachment to one place. Those who held seasonal and migratory jobs found the lifestyle practical, but it made for an unsettled life for others. (Courtesy of Security Pacific National Bank.)

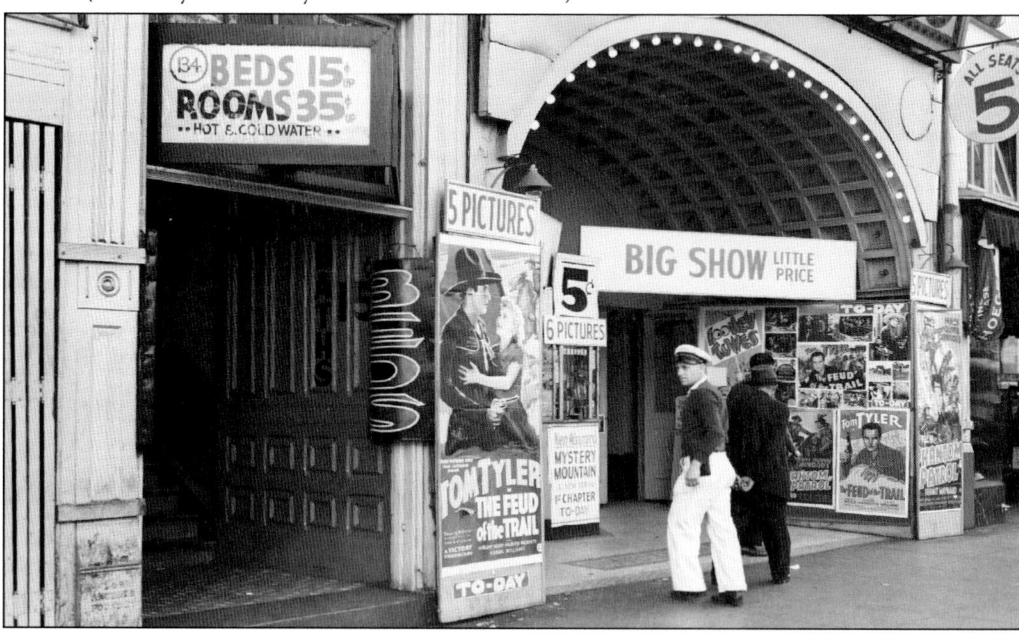

A flophouse is seen at 134 South Main Street in 1920. Flophouses offered cheap lodging, and occupants generally shared bathroom facilities. People who lived in flophouses were a step above homelessness. Next door to this flophouse is a movie theater with signs that read: "All seats .5 cents." Some Filipinos found it more economical to sleep in a movie theater rather than rent a room, particularly during the Depression years. (Courtesy of Los Angeles Public Library.)

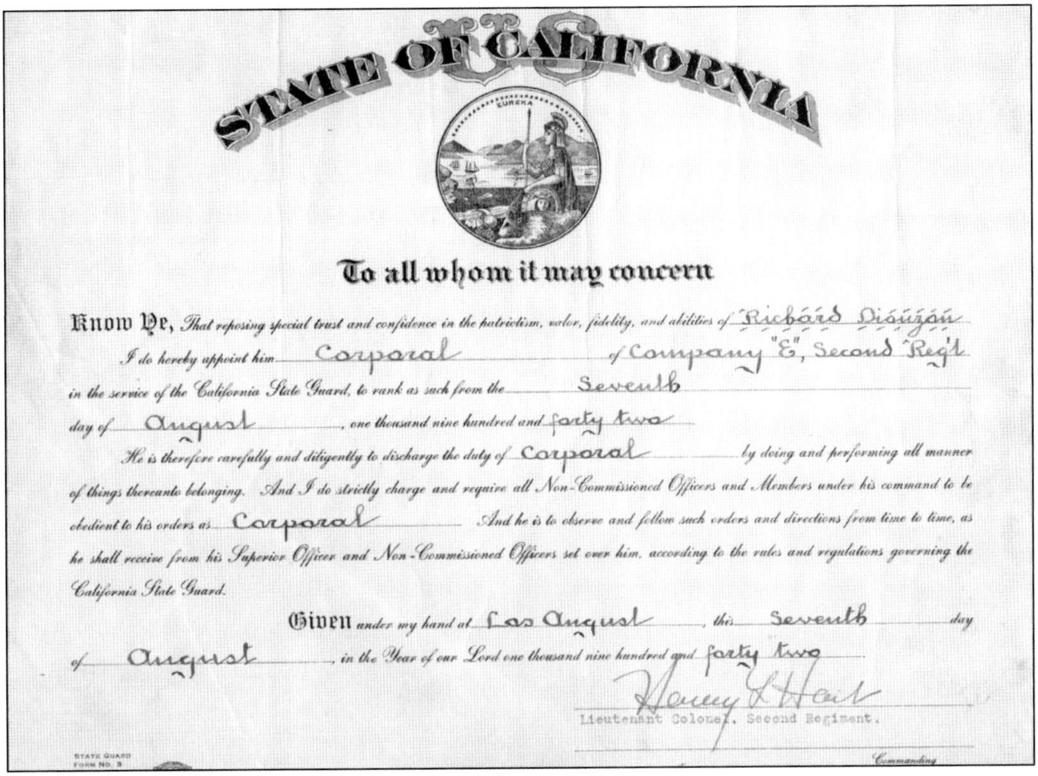

STATE OF CALIFORNIA

EUREKA

To all whom it may concern

Know Ye, That reposing special trust and confidence in the patriotism, valor, fidelity, and abilities of Richard Dionzon

I do hereby appoint him Corporal of Company "E", Second Reg't in the service of the California State Guard, to rank as such from the Seventh day of August, one thousand nine hundred and forty two

He is therefore carefully and diligently to discharge the duty of Corporal by doing and performing all manner of things thereunto belonging. And I do strictly charge and require all Non-Commissioned Officers and Members under his command to be obedient to his orders as Corporal And he is to observe and follow such orders and directions from time to time, as he shall receive from his Superior Officer and Non-Commissioned Officers set over him, according to the rules and regulations governing the California State Guard.

Given under my hand at Los Angeles, this Seventh day of August, in the Year of our Lord one thousand nine hundred and forty two

Henry L. Hart

Lieutenant Colonel, Second Regiment.

Commanding

STATE GUARD FORM NO. 3

After completing his enlistment in the U.S. Navy and being granted U.S. citizenship, Richard Dionzon enlisted in the California State Guard in 1942 and was appointed to the rank of corporal of Company E, 2nd Regiment. (Courtesy of Kenny Dionzon.)

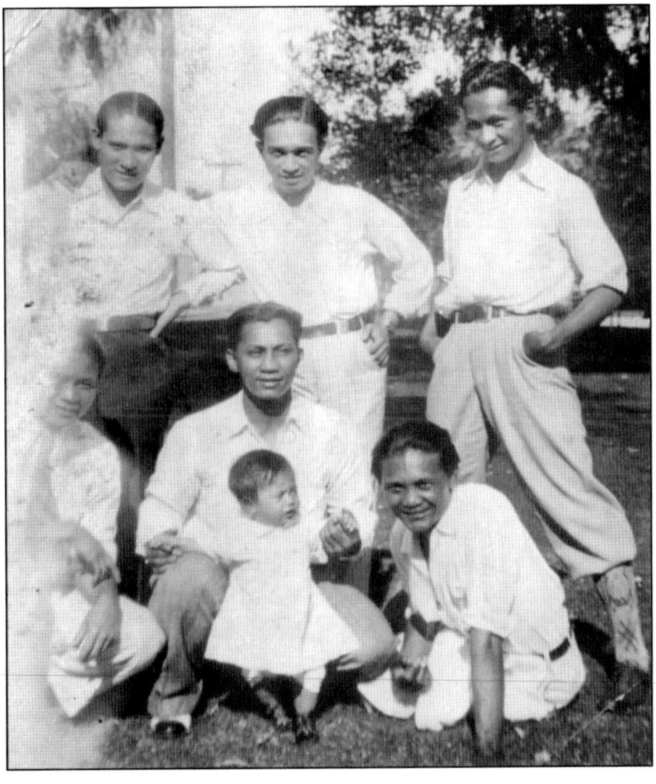

Pictured is Richard Dionzon in the 1930s with his young son Kenny (child) and friends in downtown Los Angeles. Filipinos were thought to be involved in gangs because they usually travelled in groups, but their need to exist in groups was the result of economic necessity and a sense of security in a city that discriminated against people of color. (Courtesy of Kenny Dionzon.)

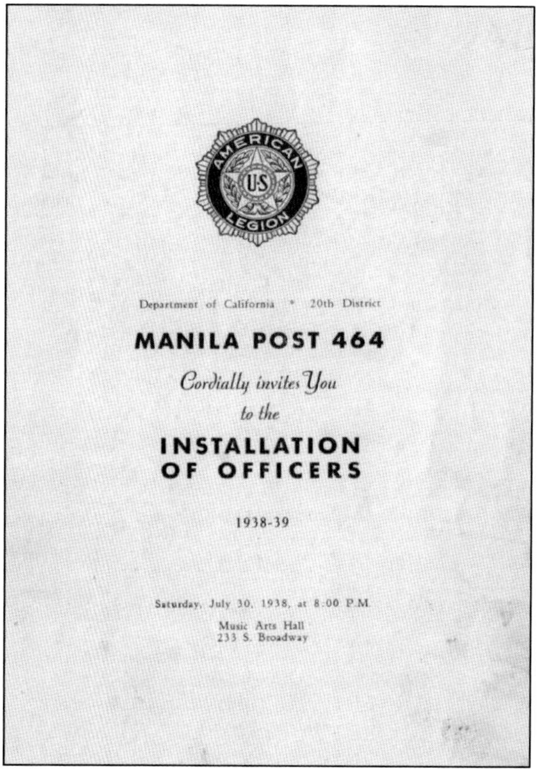

Department of California * 20th District

MANILA POST 464

Cordially invites You

to the

INSTALLATION
OF OFFICERS

1938-39

Saturday, July 30, 1938, at 8:00 P.M.

Music Arts Hall
233 S. Broadway

Pictured is a program for the American Legion Manila Post 464 installation of officers on Saturday, July 30, 1938, at 8:00 p.m. at the Music Arts Hall, located at 233 South Broadway. Manila Post 464 sponsored fund-raising and charitable events that assisted members and their families. (Courtesy of Kenny Dionzon.)

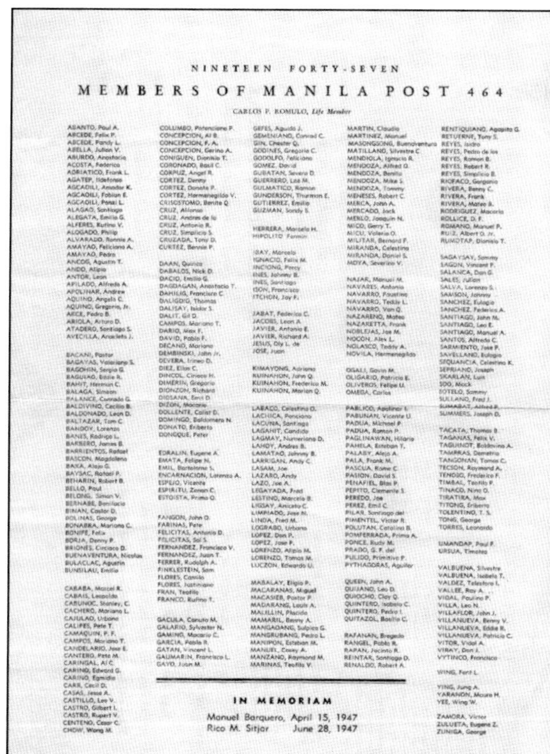

NINETEEN FORTY-SEVEN

MEMBERS OF MANILA POST 464

CARLOS P. ROMULO, *Life Member*

ABANTO, Paul A.
ABCEDE, Felix P.
ABCEDE, Pandy L.
ABELLA, Julian V.
ABURDO, Anastacio
ACOSTA, Federico
ADRIATICO, Frank L.
AGATEP, Ildefonso
AGCAOILI, Amador K.
AGCAOILI, Fabian E.
AGCAOILI, Ponsi L.
ALAGAO, Santiago
ALEGATA, Emilio G.
ALFERES, Rufino V.
ALOGADO, Philip
ALVARADO, Ronnie A.
AMAYAO, Feliciano A.
AMAYAO, Pedro
ANCOG, Agustin T.
ANDO, Alipio
ANTOR, Leon
APILADO, Alfredo A.
APOLINAR, Andrew
AQUINO, Angelo C.
AQUINO, Gregorio, Jr.
ARCE, Pedro B.
ARIOLA, Arturo D.
ATADERO, Santiago S.
AVECILLA, Anacleto J.

BACANI, Pastor
BAGAYAS, Valeriano S.
BAGOHIN, Sergio G.
BAGULAO, Eddie R.
BAHIT, Herman C.
BALAGA, Simeon
BALANCE, Conrado G.
BALDIVINO, Cecilio B.
BALDONADO, Leon D.
BALTAZAR, Tom C.
BANDOY, Lorenzo
BANES, Rodrigo L.
BARBERO, James B.
BARRIENTOS, Rafael
BASCON, Magdaleno
BAXA, Alejo G.
BAYSAC, Rafael P.
BEHARIN, Robert B.
BELLO, Paul
BELONG, Simon V.
BERNABE, Bonifacio
BINAN, Castor D.
BOLINAS, George
BONABRA, Mariano C.
BONIFE, Felix
BORJA, Denny P.
BRIONES, Circiaco D.
BUENAVENTURA, Nicolas
BULACLAC, Agustin
BUNSILAU, Emilio

CABABA, Marcel R.
CABAIS, Leopoldo
CABUNOC, Stanley, C.
CACHERO, Mariano L.
CAJULAO, Urbano
CALIPES, Pete T.
CAMAQUIN, P. F.
CAMPOS, Mariano T.
CANDELARIO, Jose E.
CANTERO, Pete M.
CARINGAL, Al C.
CARINO, Edward G.
CARINO, Egmidio
CARR, Cecil D.
CASAS, Jesse A.
CASTILLO, Leo V.
CASTRO, Gilbert L.
CASTRO, Rupert V.
CENTENO, Cesar C.
CHOW, Wong M.

COLLUMBO, Potenciano P.
CONCEPCION, Al B.
CONCEPCION, F. A.
CONCEPCION, Gerino A.
CONIGUEN, Dionisio T.
CORONADO, Basil C.
CORPUZ, Angel R.
CORTEZ, Denny
CORTEZ, Donato P.
CORTEZ, Hermenegildo V.
CRISOSTOMO, Benito Q.
CRUZ, Alfonso
CRUZ, Andres de la
CRUZ, Antonio R.
CRUZ, Simplicio S.
CRUZADA, Tony D.
CURTEZ, Bennie P.

DAAN, Quirico
DABALOS, Nick D.
DACIO, Emilio G.
DAGDAGAN, Anastacio T.
DAHILIG, Franciscο C.
DALIGDIG, Thomas
DALISAY, Isidor S.
DALIT, Gil D.
CAMPOS, Mariano T.
DARIO, Max F.
DAVID, Pablo F.
DECANO, Mariano
DEMBINSKI, John Jr.
DEVERA, Irineo D.
DIEZ, Elias C.
DINCOL, Ciriaco H.
DIMERIN, Gregorio
DIONZON, Richard
DIOSANA, Emil D.
DIZON, Macario
DOLLENTE, Calist D.
DOMINGO, Baldomero N.
DONATO, Eriberto
DONGQUE, Peter

EDRALIN, Eugene A.
EMATA, Felipe N.
EMIL, Bartolome S.
ENCARNACION, Lorenzo A.
ESPEJO, Vicente
ESPIRITU, Zenon C.
ESTOISTA, Primo O.

FANGON, John O.
FARINAS, Pete
FELICITAS, Antonio D.
FELICITAS, Sal S.
FERNANDEZ, Francisco V.
FERNANDEZ, Juan T.
FERRER, Rudolph A.
FINKLESTEIN, Sam
FLORES, Camilo
FLORES, Justiniano
FRAN, Teofilo
FRANCO, Rufino T.

GACULA, Canuto M.
GALARIO, Sylvester N.
GAMINO, Macario C.
GARCIA, Pablo R.
GATAN, Vincent L.
GAUMARIN, Francisco L.
GAYO, Juan M.

GEFES, Agudo J.
GEMENIANO, Conrad C.
GIN, Chester Q.
GODINES, Gregorio C.
GODOLFO, Feliciano
GOMEZ, David
GUBATAN, Severo D.
GUERRERO, Lee M.
GULMATICO, Ramon
GUNDERSON, Thurmon E.
GUTIERREZ, Emilio
GUZMAN, Sandy S.

HERRERA, Marcelo H.
HIPOLITO, Fermin

IBAY, Marcelo
IGNACIO, Felix M.
INCIONG, Percy
INES, Johnny B.
INES, Santiago
ISON, Francisco
ITCHON, Jay F.

JABAT, Federico C.
JACOBS, Leon A.
JAVIER, Antonio E.
JAVIER, Richard A.
JESUS, Oly L. de
JOSE, Juan

KIMAYONG, Adriano
KUINAHON, John Q.
KUINAHON, Frederico M.
KUINAHON, Marion Q.

LABACO, Celestino O.
LACHICA, Ponciano
LACUNA, Santiago
LAGAHIT, Candido
LAGMAY, Numeriano D.
LAHOY, Andres B.
LAMATAO, Johnny B.
LARRIGAN, Andy C.
LASAM, Joe
LAZARO, Andy
LAZO, Joe A.
LEGAYADA, Fred
LESTINO, Marcelo B.
LIGSAY, Aniceto C.
LIMPIADO, Jose M.
LINDA, Fred M.
LOGRABO, Urbano
LOPEZ, Don P.
LOPEZ, Jose P.
LORENZO, Alipio M.
LORENZO, Tomas M.
LUCZON, Edwardo U.

MABALAY, Eligio P.
MACARANAS, Miguel
MACASIEB, Pastor P.
MADARANG, Louis A.
MALILLIN, Placido
MAMARIL, Benny A.
MANGAOANG, Sulpicio G.
MANGRUBANG, Pedro L.
MANIPON, Esteban M.
MANUEL, Casey A.
MANZANO, Raymond M.
MARINAS, Teofilo V.

MARTIN, Claudio
MARTINEZ, Manuel
MASONGSONG, Buenaventura
MATILLANO, Silvestre C.
MENDIOLA, Ignacio R.
MENDOZA, Alfred O.
MENDOZA, Benito
MENDOZA, Mike S.
MENDOZA, Tommy
MENESES, Robert C.
MERCA, John A.
MERCADO, Jack
MERLO, Joaquin N.
MICO, Gerry T.
MICU, Valerio O.
MILITAR, Bernard F.
MIRANDA, Celestino
MIRANDA, Daniel S.
MOYA, Severino V.

NAJAR, Manuel M.
NAVARES, Antonio
NAVARRO, Faustino
NAVARRO, Teddy L.
NAVARRO, Van Q.
NAZARENO, Mateo
NAZARETTA, Frank
NOBLEJAS, Joe M.
NOCON, Alex L.
NOLASCO, Teddy A.
NOVILA, Hermenegildo

OGALI, Gavin M.
OLIGARIO, Patricio E.
OLIVEROS, Felipe U.
OMEGA, Carlos

PABLICO, Apolinar L.
PABUNAN, Vicente U.
PADUA, Michael P.
PADUA, Ramon P.
PAGLINAWAN, Hilario
PAHELA, Esteban T.
PALABY, Alejo A.
PALA, Frank M.
PASCUA, Rome C.
PASION, David S.
PENAFIEL, Blas P.
PEPITO, Clemente S.
PEREDO, Joe
PEREZ, Emil C.
PILAR, Santiago del
PIMENTEL, Victor R.
POLUTAN, Catalino B.
POMFERRADA, Primo A.
PONCE, Rudy M.
PRADO, G. F. del
PULIDO, Primitivo P.
PYTHAGORAS, Aguiler

QUEEN, John A.
QUIJANO, Leo D.
QUIOCHO, Clay Q.
QUINTERO, Isabelo C.
QUINTERO, Pedro I.
QUITAZOL, Basilio C.

RAFANAN, Bregedo
RANGEL, Pablo R.
RAPAN, Jacinto R.
REINTAR, Santiago D.
RENALDO, Robert A.

RENTIQUIANO, Agapito G.
RETUERNE, Tony S.
REYES, Isidro
REYES, Pedro de los
REYES, Ramon B.
REYES, Robert R.
REYES, Simplicio B.
RIOFACO, Gorgonio
RIVERA, Benny C.
RIVERA, Frank
RIVERA, Mateo B.
RODRIGUEZ, Macario
ROLLICE, D. F.
ROMANO, Manuel P.
RUIZ, Albert O. Jr.
RUMOTAP, Dionisio T.

SAGAYSAY, Sammy
SAGON, Vincent P.
SALANCA, Dan G.
SALES, Julian
SALVA, Lorenzo S.
SAMSON, Johnny
SANCHEZ, Eulogio
SANCHEZ, Federico A.
SANTIAGO, John M.
SANTIAGO, Leo E.
SANTIAGO, Manuel A.
SANTOS, Alfredo C.
SARMIENTO, Jose P.
SAVELLANO, Eulogio
SEQUANCIA, Celestino K.
SEPRIANO, Joseph
SKARLAN, Luis
SOO, Mock
SOTELO, Sammy
SULLANO, Fred J.
SUMABAT, Alfred P.
SUMMERS, Joseph D.

TACATA, Thomas B.
TAGANAS, Felix V.
TAGUINOT, Baldovino A.
TAMPRAS, Demetrio
TANGONAN, Tomas C.
TECSON, Raymond A.
TENOSO, Frederico F.
TIMBAL, Teofilo P.
TINACO, Nino O.
TIRATIRA, Max
TITONG, Eriberto
TOLENTINO, T. S.
TONG, George
TORRES, Leonardo

UMANDAP, Paul P.
URSUA, Timoteo

VALBUENA, Silvestre
VALBUENA, Isabelo T.
VALDEZ, Telesforo I.
VALLEE, Roy A.
VIDAL, Paulino P.
VILLA, Leo N.
VILLAFLOR, John J.
VILLANUEVA, Benny V.
VILLANUEVA, Eddie R.
VILLANUEVA, Patricio C.
VITOR, Vidal A.
VIRAY, Don J.
VYTINCO, Francisco

WING, Fent L.

YING, Jung A.
YARANON, Mauro H.
YEE, Wing W.

ZAMORA, Victor
ZULUETA, Eugene Z.
ZUNIGA, George

IN MEMORIAM

Manuel Barquero, April 15, 1947
Rico M. Sitjar June 28, 1947

This is a list of members belonging to the American Legion of Manila Post 464 in 1947. Although most Filipino clubs and organizations were mainly fraternal and social, some organizations, such as Manila Post 464, were founded on the concept of personal development by keeping their members active in organization and community activities, and away from harmful pastimes, such as taxi dance halls, pool halls, and gambling dens. (Courtesy of Kenny Dionzon.)

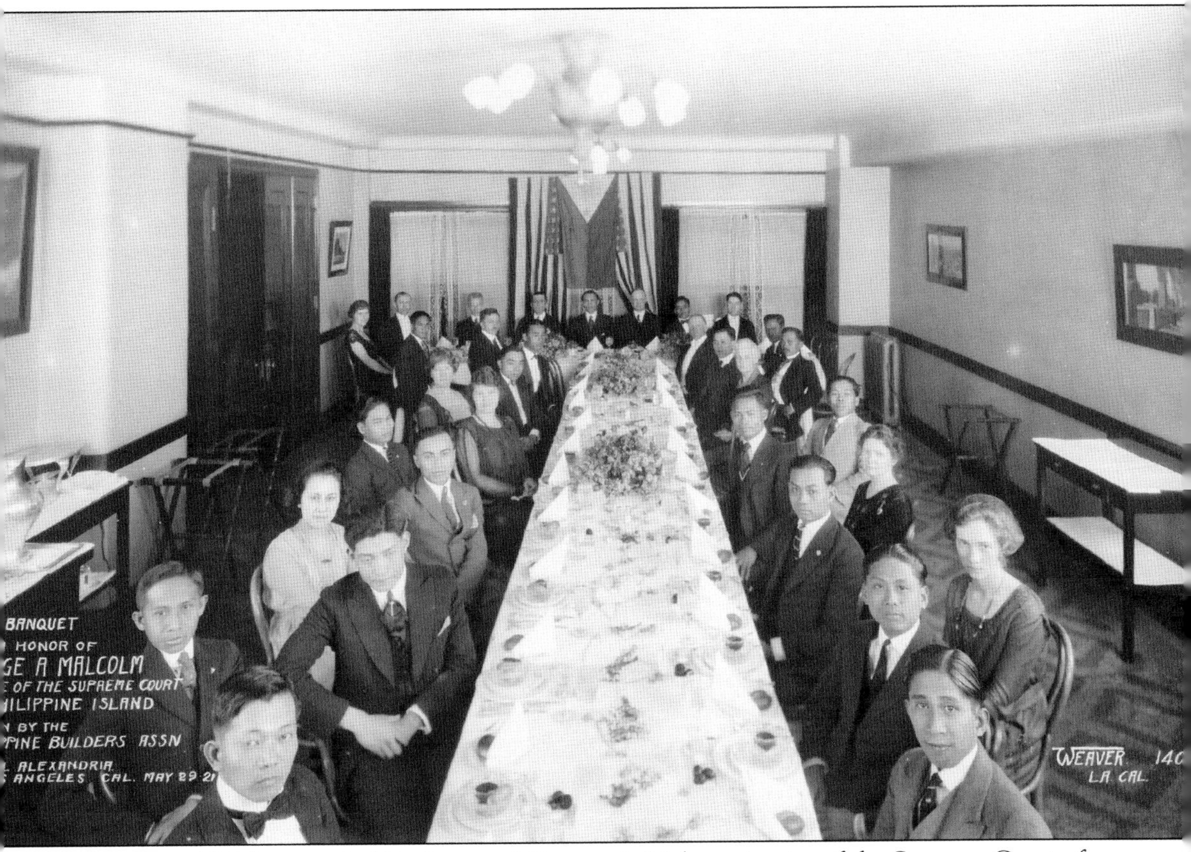

Pictured is a 1929 banquet held in honor of George A. Malcom, justice of the Supreme Court of the Philippine Islands, and hosted by the Philippine Builders Association at the Hotel Alexandria in Los Angeles. Among those attending were several members of the Filipino Federation of America, Inc., including Hilario C. Moncado, seated (center) at the head of the table. The Filipino Federation of America, Inc., attended and hosted many formal events, some of which were political in nature, all in the spirit of creating a better relationship between Americans and Filipinos, and for the betterment of Filipinos in America. By the 1930s, there were 64 Filipino clubs and organizations in Los Angeles. Other early organizations also founded in the 1930s and 1940s for the betterment of Filipinos included the Caballeros de Dimas-Alang, Inc.; Cabugao Club; Filipino American Citizens, Inc.; Filipino Community of Los Angeles, Inc.; Knights of the Cross; Legionarios del Trabajo; Pangasinan Association of Southern California; Santa Maria Association; Asinganian Club; Filipino Athletic Club; Filipino Patriotic Association of California; and USC Philippines Trojan Club. (Courtesy of the Filipino Federation of America, Inc.)

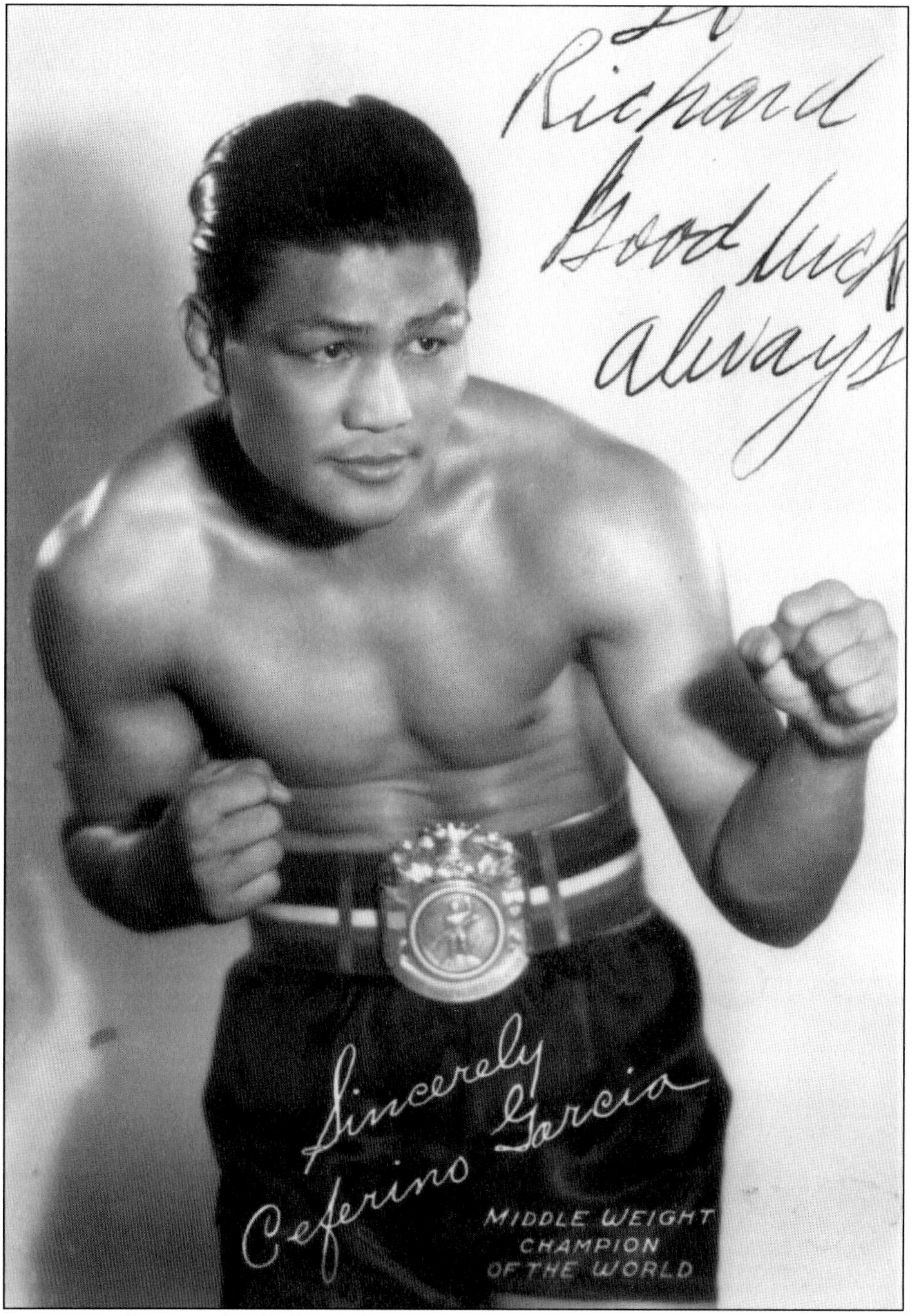

This is a 1920s photograph of Filipino boxer Ceferino Garcia. Born in Tondo, Manila, he held the most victories and became the world champion among Filipino middleweight boxers. Boxers fought every Tuesday and Friday evenings at two primary arenas in Los Angeles—the Olympic Stadium in downtown Los Angeles and the American Legion Stadium in Hollywood. Other popular Filipino boxers in the 1920s and1930s included Speedy Dado, Young Tommy, Francisco "Pancho Villa" Guilledo, Pablo Dano, and Pete Sarmiento, to name a few. High-stakes gambling was associated with boxing fights. (Courtesy of Kenny Dionzon.)

Many amateur boxers and prizefighters trained at the Main Street Gym, located at 318½ Main Street and seen in this 1930 photograph. Admission was 50¢. Boxers at the gym were often called to fight in "semi-wind up" events in prizefight rings where boxing matches were staged. (Courtesy of Los Angeles Public Library.)

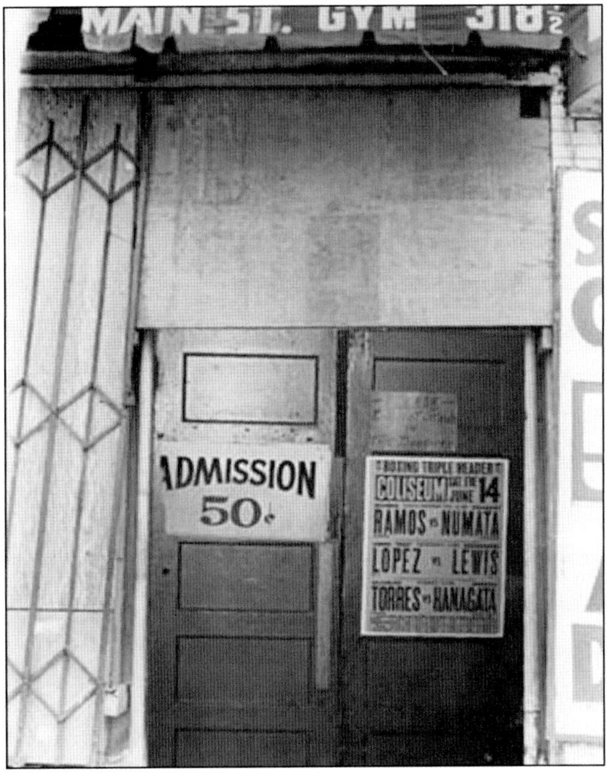

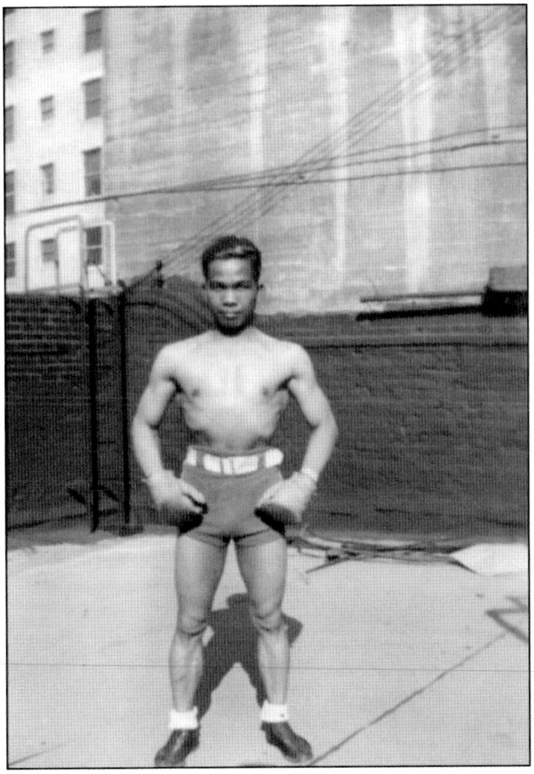

Pictured is Severo Gubatan atop a roof in downtown Los Angeles in the early 1930s. Because recreational activities open to Filipinos were limited, boxing was one of the most popular activities for both spectators and participants. (Courtesy of Gerald Gubatan.)

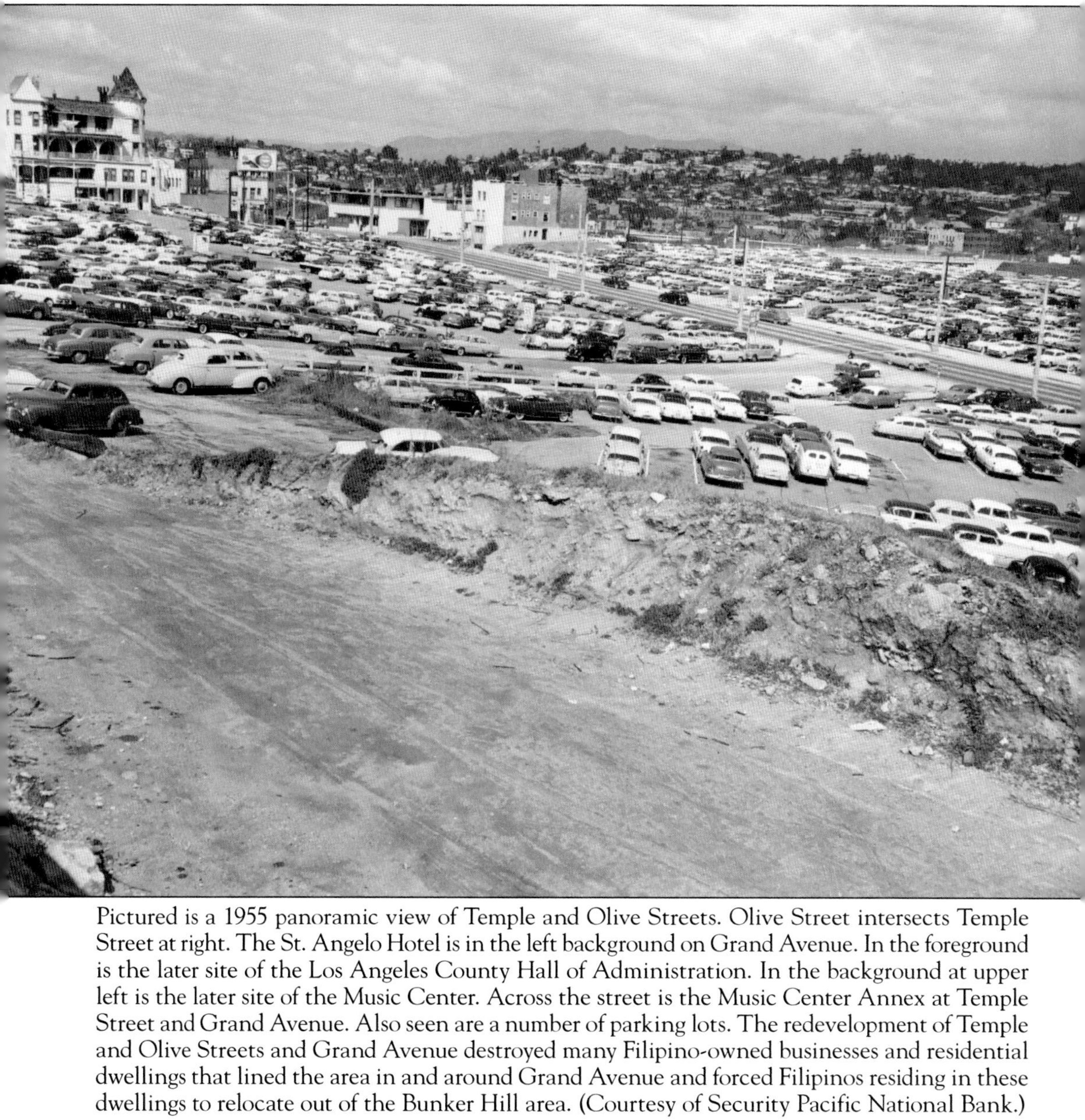

Pictured is a 1955 panoramic view of Temple and Olive Streets. Olive Street intersects Temple Street at right. The St. Angelo Hotel is in the left background on Grand Avenue. In the foreground is the later site of the Los Angeles County Hall of Administration. In the background at upper left is the later site of the Music Center. Across the street is the Music Center Annex at Temple Street and Grand Avenue. Also seen are a number of parking lots. The redevelopment of Temple and Olive Streets and Grand Avenue destroyed many Filipino-owned businesses and residential dwellings that lined the area in and around Grand Avenue and forced Filipinos residing in these dwellings to relocate out of the Bunker Hill area. (Courtesy of Security Pacific National Bank.)

Two

BUNKER HILL

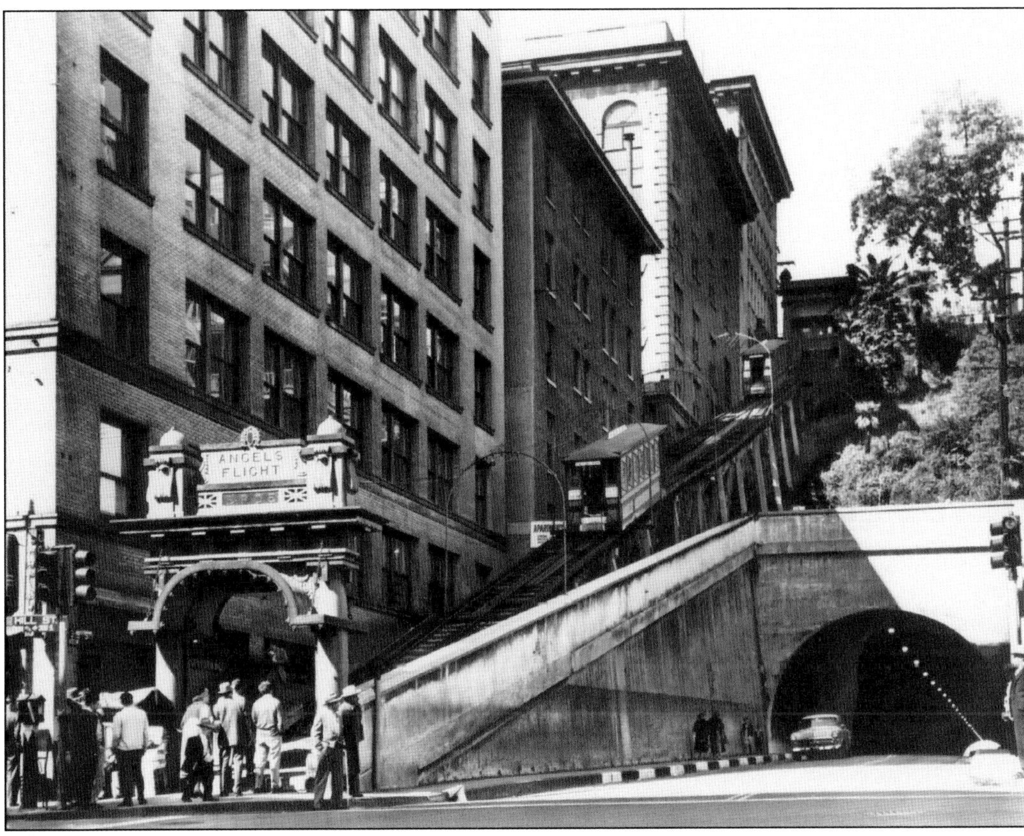

This view up Bunker Hill and Angels Flight was taken from Hill Street at the Third Street tunnel in 1940. Angels Flight was the shortest paying railway in the world. Two cable cars named *Olivet* and *Sinai* were a means of transportation from Hill Street up to the Victorian neighborhood called Bunker Hill. By the 1940s, many of the wealthy Bunker Hill residents had relocated to more desirable neighborhoods in the city to escape the intrusion of non-whites moving into the neighborhood. The beautiful Victorian homes in Bunker Hill were converted into boardinghouses and, shortly after their conversion, began to show signs of dilapidation and neglect. (Courtesy of Security Pacific National Bank.)

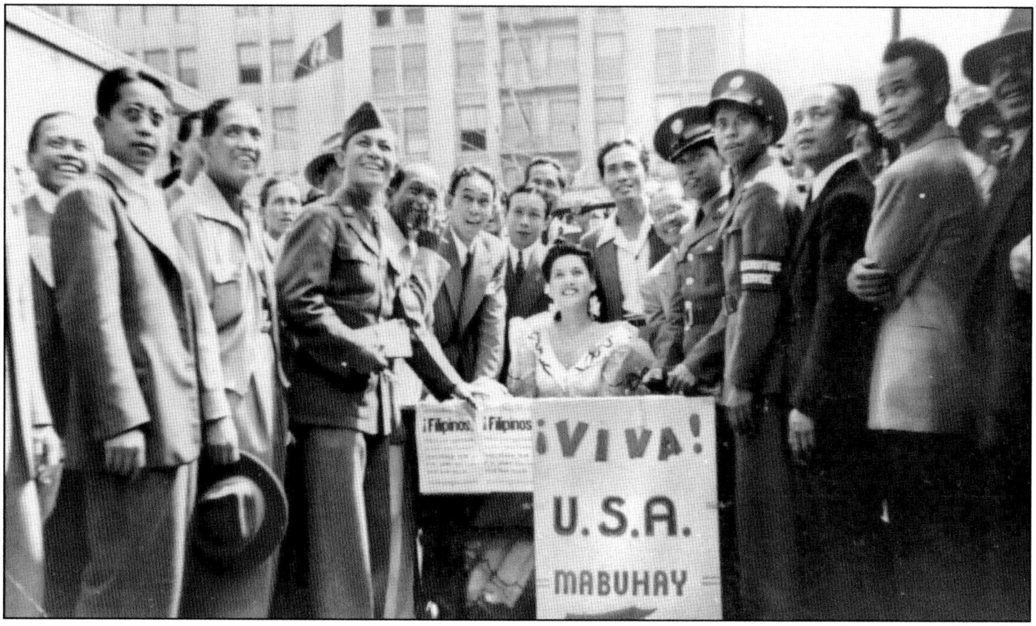

Filipino servicemen and friends gather in downtown Los Angeles to celebrate the end of World War II in 1945. America granted citizenship to some Filipinos who fought with American soldiers during the war but rescinded its promise to these veterans to receive benefits. (Courtesy of Shades of L.A. Archives/Los Angeles Public Library.)

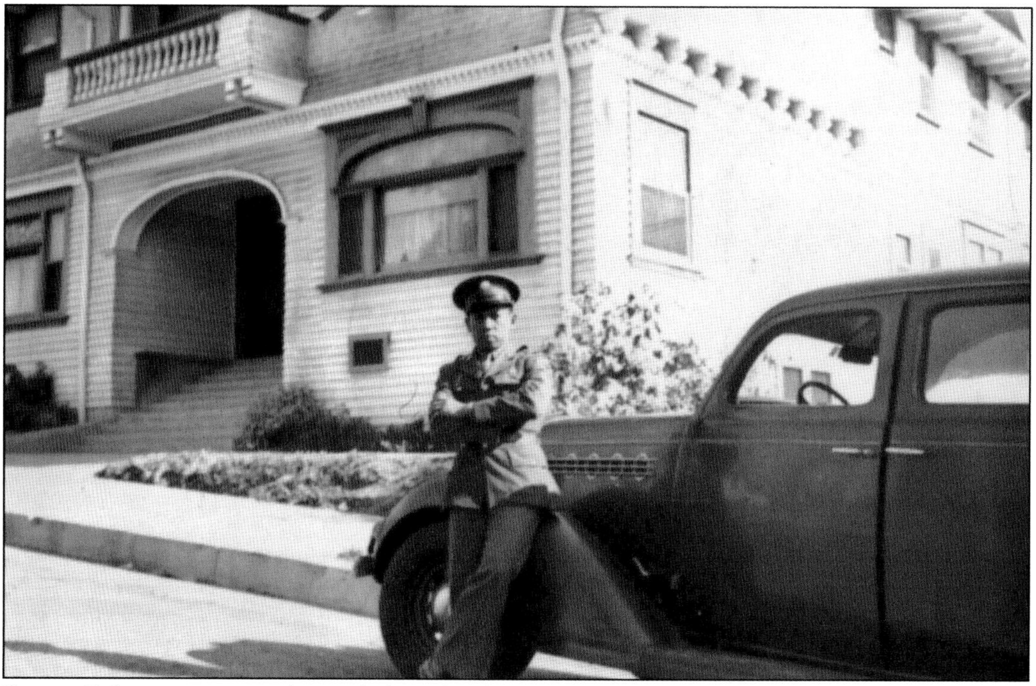

Severo Gubatan is seen in front of a boardinghouse on Bunker Hill while on military furlough in the early 1940s. Upon completion of his military service, he returned to Los Angeles and raised a family. (Courtesy of Gerald Gubatan.)

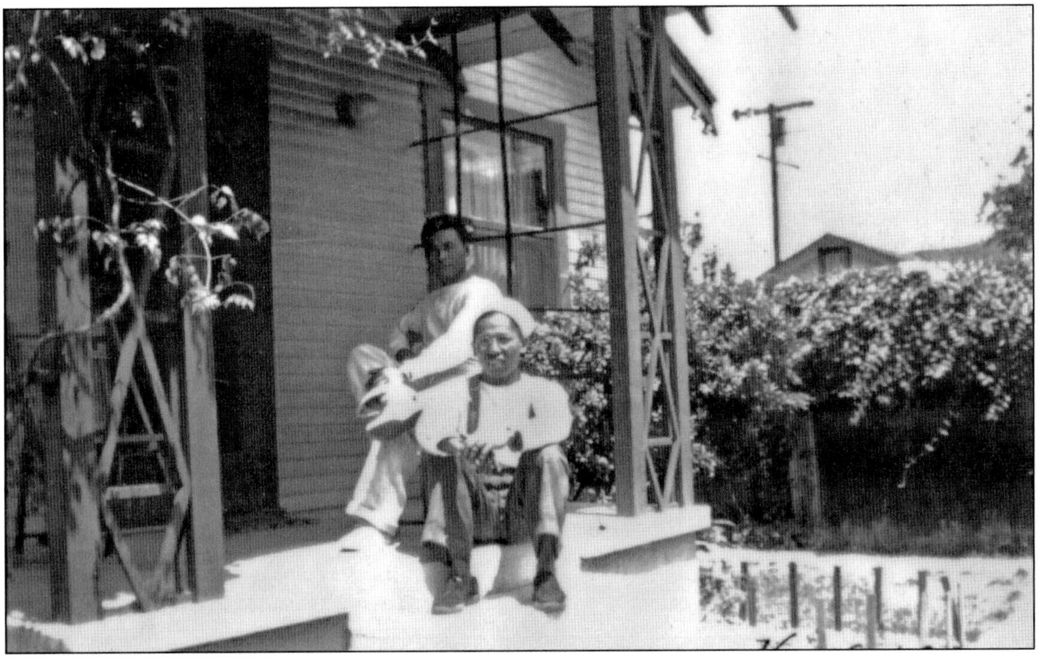

Severo Gubatan (front) and friend Eddie Ferrer are seen in front of a rented bungalow in Los Angeles during the late 1940s. Bungalows offered the freedom to have visitors, play music, host parties, and cook native foods. By the 1940s, many Filipinos lived in and around Boylston to Temple Streets; Centennial to San Pedro Streets; Sixth to Boylston Streets; and Burlington at Temple Streets, where small houses and bungalows could be rented. (Courtesy of Gerald Gubatan.)

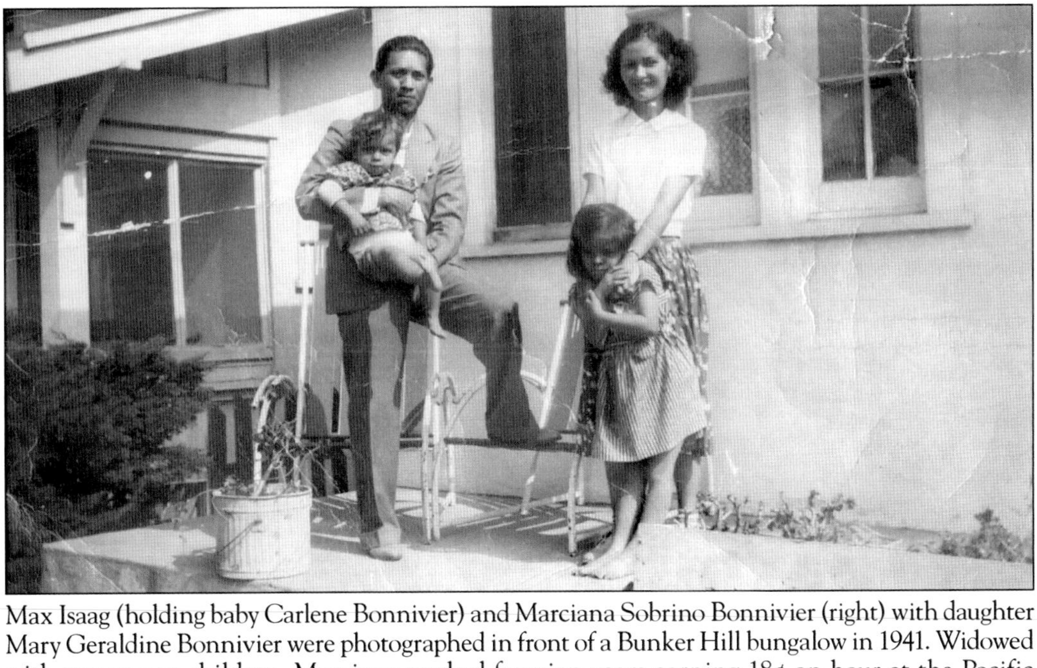

Max Isaag (holding baby Carlene Bonnivier) and Marciana Sobrino Bonnivier (right) with daughter Mary Geraldine Bonnivier were photographed in front of a Bunker Hill bungalow in 1941. Widowed with two young children, Marciana worked for nine years earning 18¢ an hour at the Pacific Enameling and Plating Company in Los Angeles. (Courtesy of Carlene Sobrino Bonnivier.)

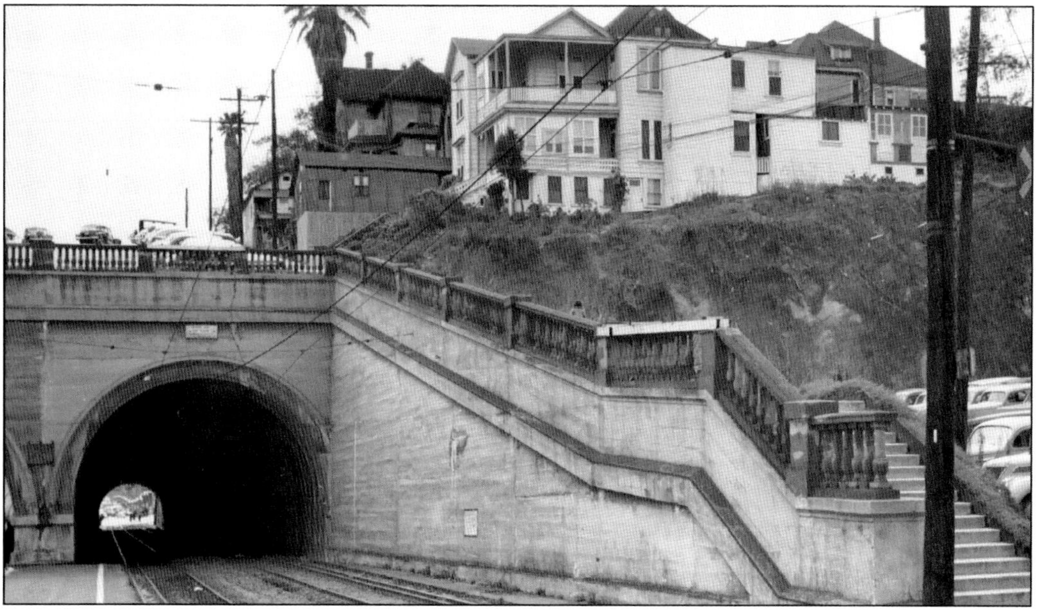

This 1945 photograph looks south at Temple Street through the streetcar side of the Hill Street tunnel, which was bored through a part of Bunker Hill in 1909. The tunnel connects Hill Street from First Street to Temple Street. On the right is a staircase that leads to the residential area of Bunker Hill, where large Victorian homes were converted into affordable boardinghouses. (Courtesy of Security Pacific National Bank.)

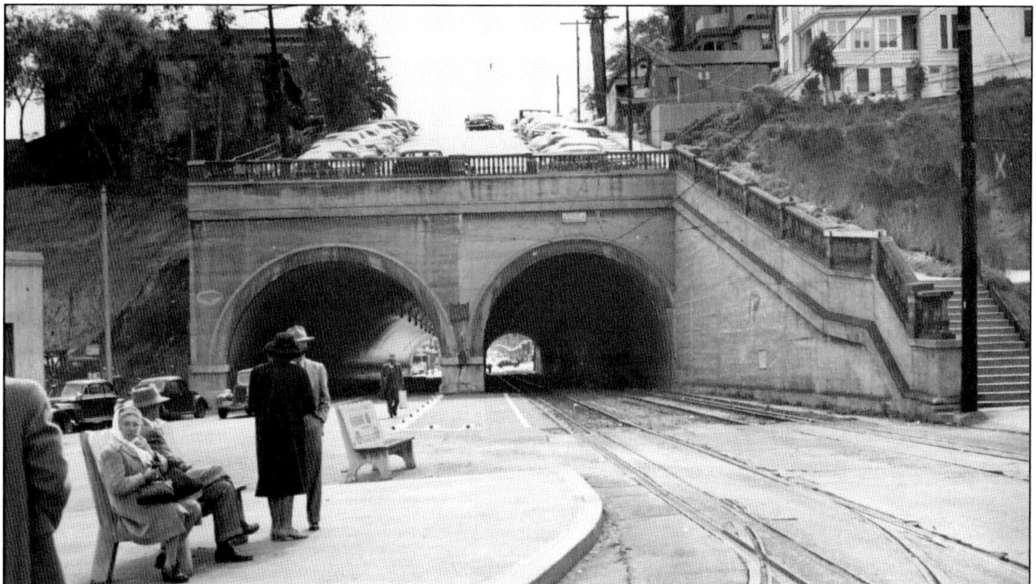

Another 1945 photograph looks south at Temple Street to Hill Street through a part of Bunker Hill. Streetcar traffic passed through the right tunnel, and automobiles passed through the left. By the late 1940s, many of the houses above on Bunker Hill were considered slum housing. As Filipinos were being displaced from the Little Tokyo area because of redevelopment and racial tensions, Bunker Hill became an affordable alternate place to relocate. (Courtesy of the Boris Leven Collection.)

A 1940s photograph of a slum apartment building on Bunker Hill shows the Los Angeles City Hall in the background. (Courtesy of Security Pacific National Bank.)

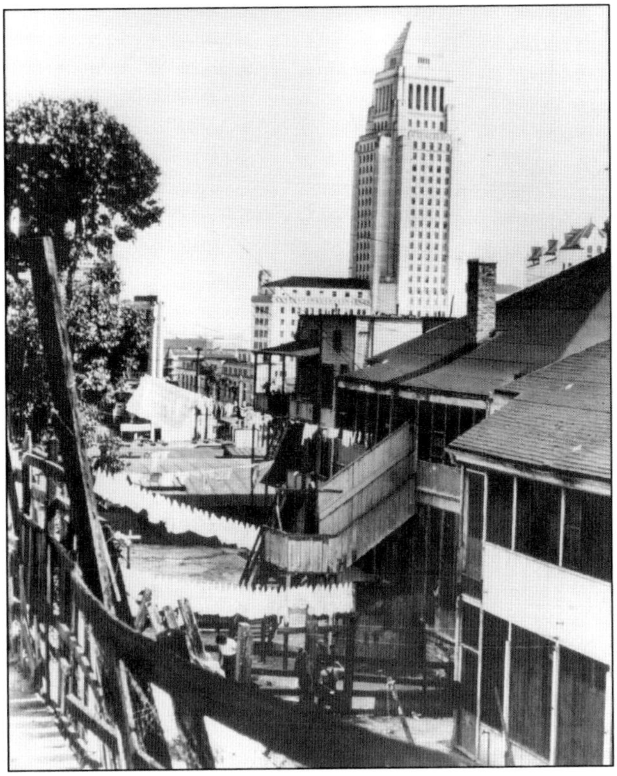

Pictured below is another 1940s slum apartment building on Bunker Hill. Crowded apartment buildings added to the complaints against Filipino occupants, who often shared an apartment with a group of friends to cover expenses and conserve funds. Neighbors often complained of foot traffic, music, and noise. (Courtesy of Security Pacific National Bank.)

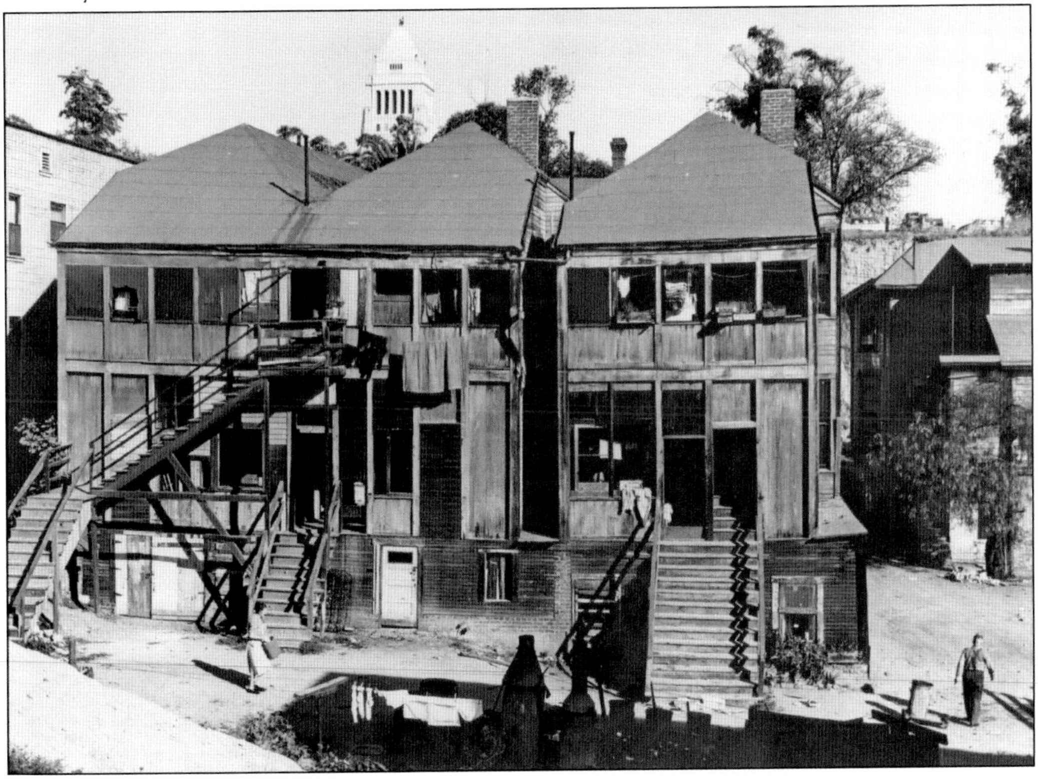

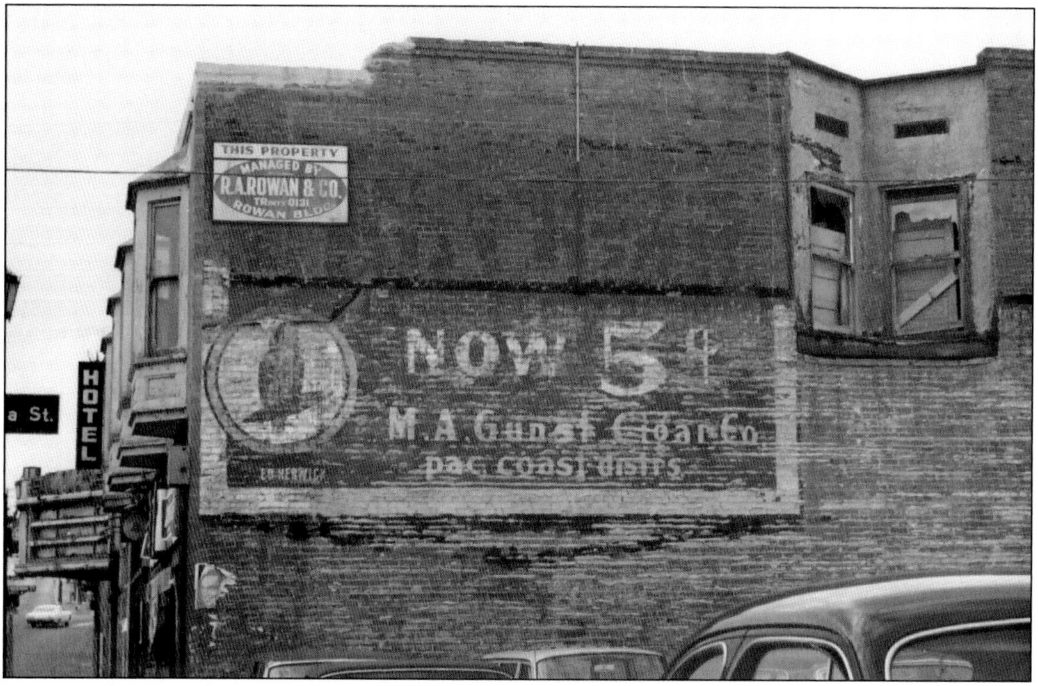

A 1950s photograph shows a hotel on Figueroa Street on Bunker Hill that was slated to be razed as part of a redevelopment project of the city. Filipinos residing in the hotel were again forced to relocate. (Courtesy of Security Pacific National Bank.)

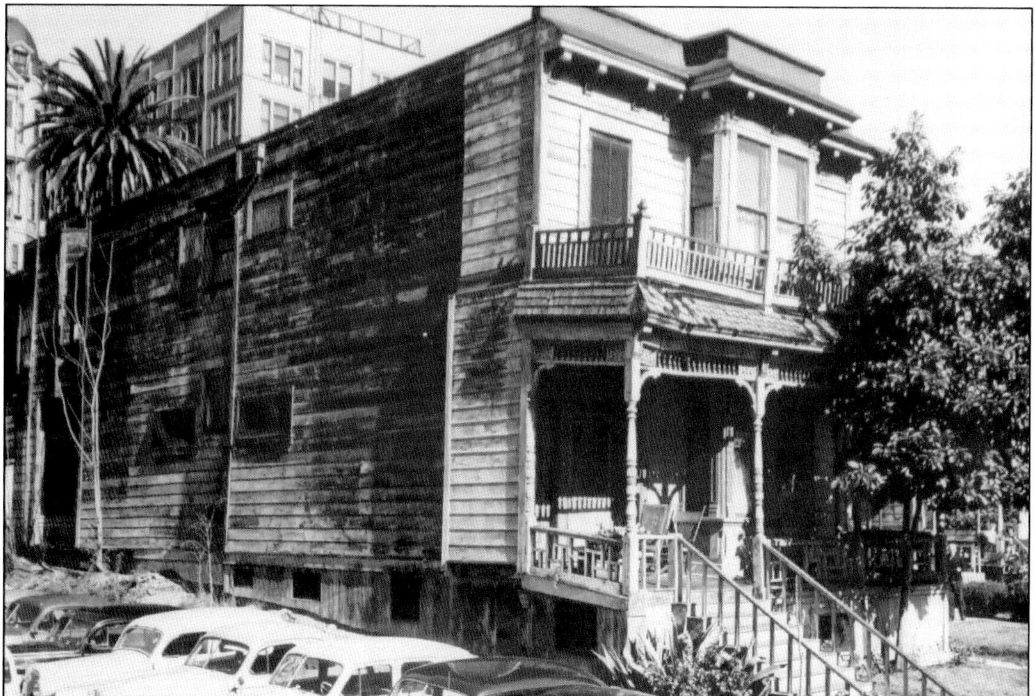

A typical slum apartment building on Bunker Hill with a Victorian facade is shown in this 1951 photograph. (Courtesy of Security Pacific National Bank.)

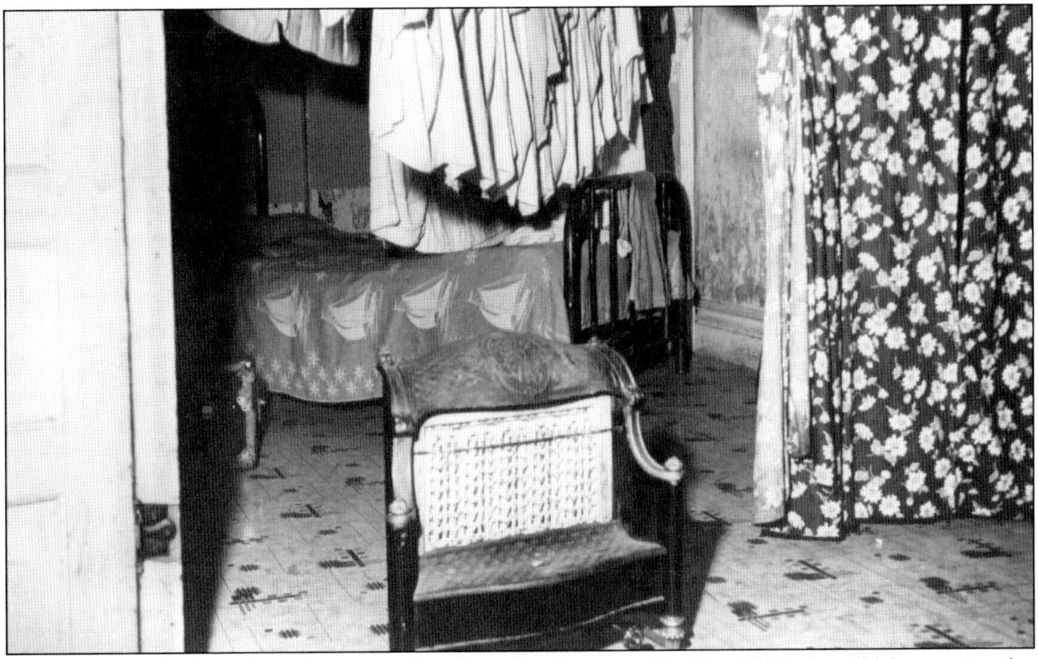

Pictured above is an interior view of a slum dwelling on Bunker Hill. An old heater in the foreground stands before the bedroom, which is portioned off by a flowery curtain. Two lines of laundry hang over the bed. Filipinos often shared small living quarters with five or more friends. (Courtesy of the Otto Rothschild Collection.)

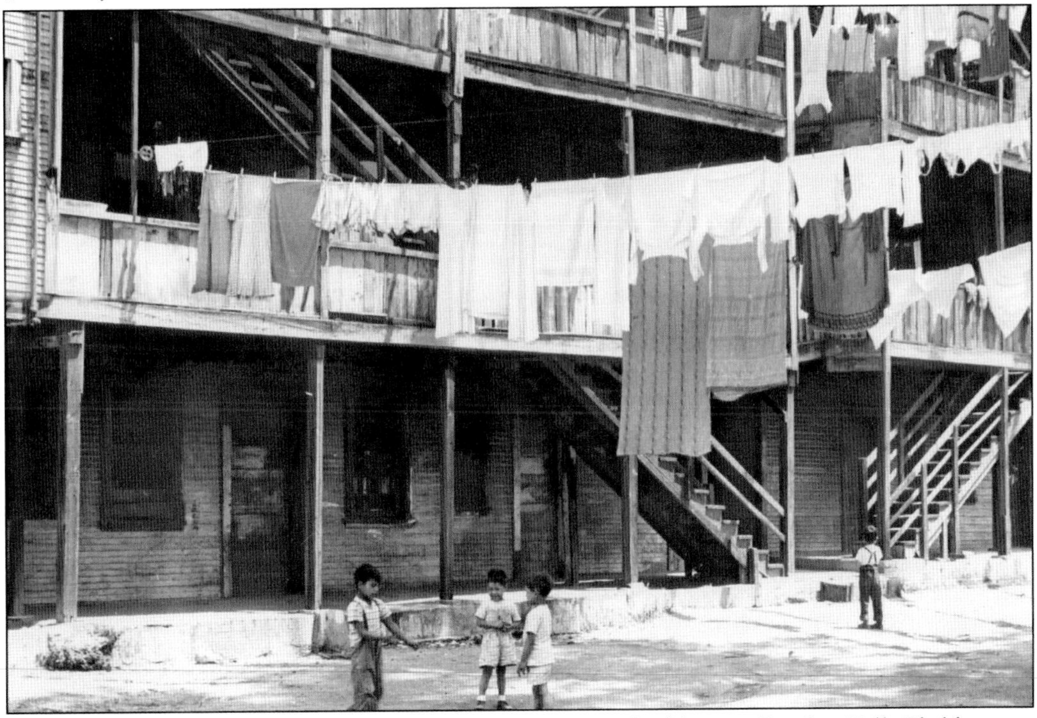

This 1950s photograph shows the rear of a slum apartment building on Bunker Hill. Children are seen playing under hanging laundry. (Courtesy of Security Pacific National Bank.)

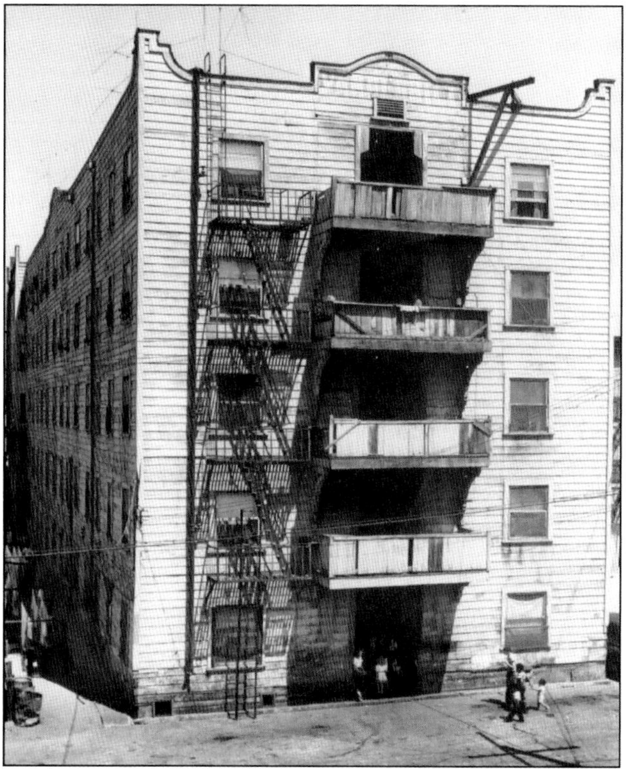

This exterior view of a five-story building with 71 units was located at 334 South Figueroa Street. Units consisted of three rooms, and rent ranged from $7 to $10.50 per week, depending on the number of people living in the unit. Residents shared four toilets and two baths on each floor. At the time of this 1952 photograph, 102 children lived in the building. (Courtesy of Security Pacific National Bank.)

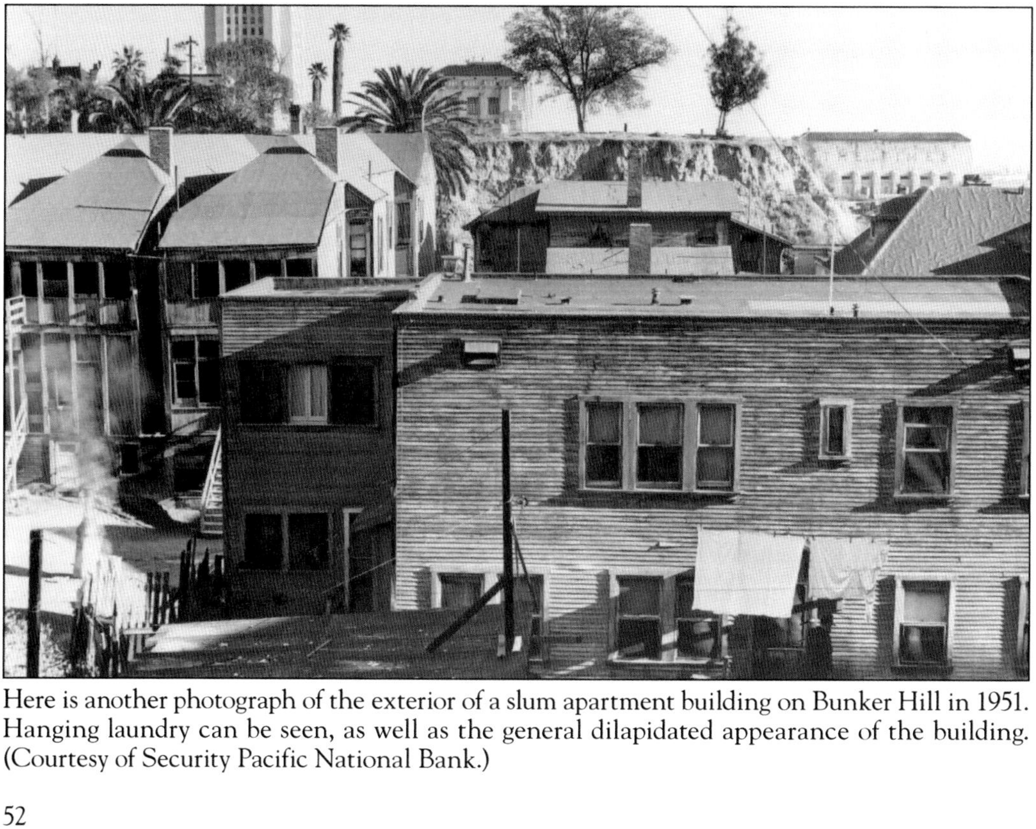

Here is another photograph of the exterior of a slum apartment building on Bunker Hill in 1951. Hanging laundry can be seen, as well as the general dilapidated appearance of the building. (Courtesy of Security Pacific National Bank.)

Toilet stalls labeled "Men" and "Wemen" were available to tenants outside of their units, usually located on each floor. (Courtesy of Security Pacific National Bank.)

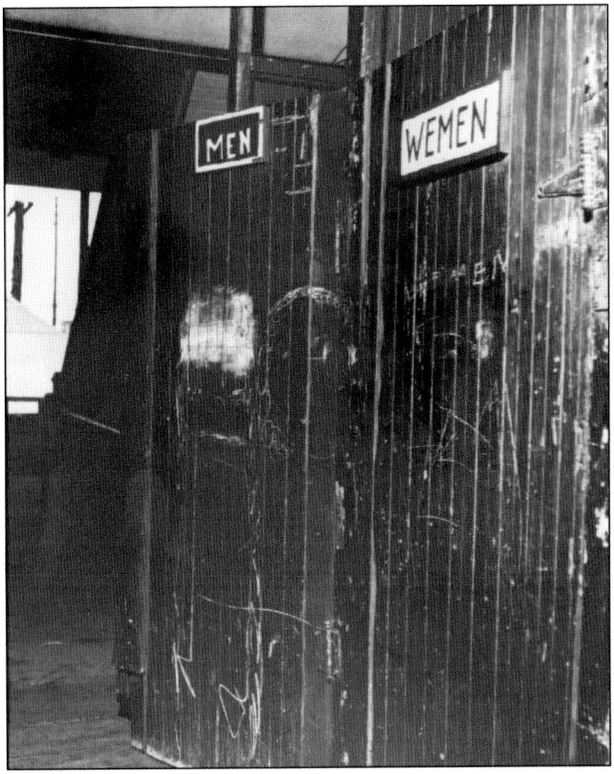

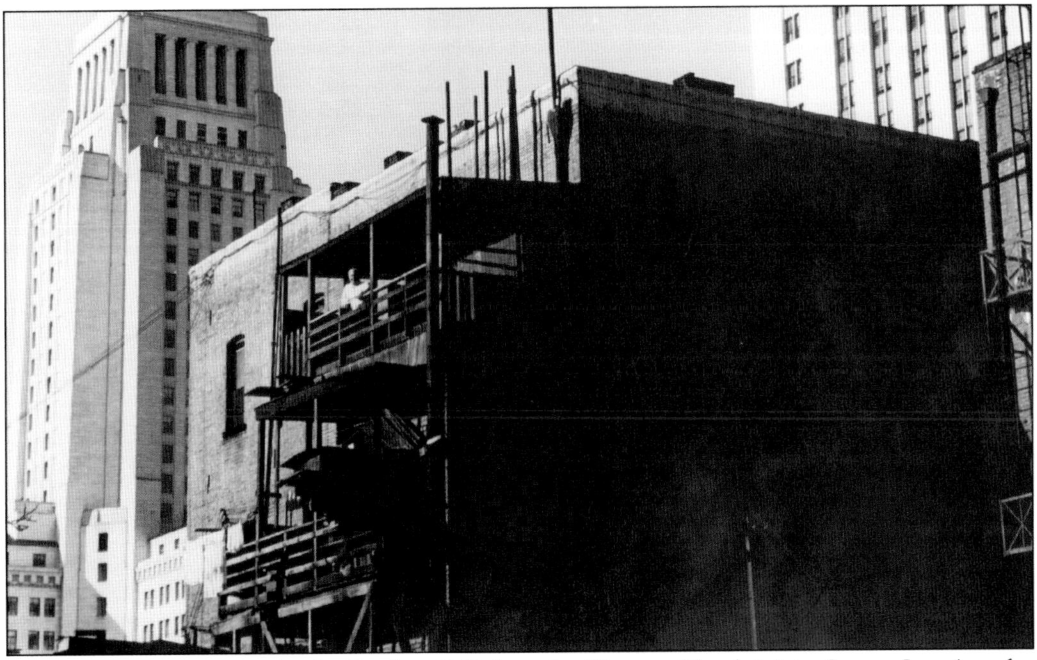

This is a 1951 photograph of a Bunker Hill slum dwelling on North Main Street. Los Angeles City Hall can be seen in the background, and the U.S. District Court can be seen across the street. This dwelling was razed in the late 1950s and was later replaced with the Los Angeles Mall. (Courtesy of Security Pacific National Bank.)

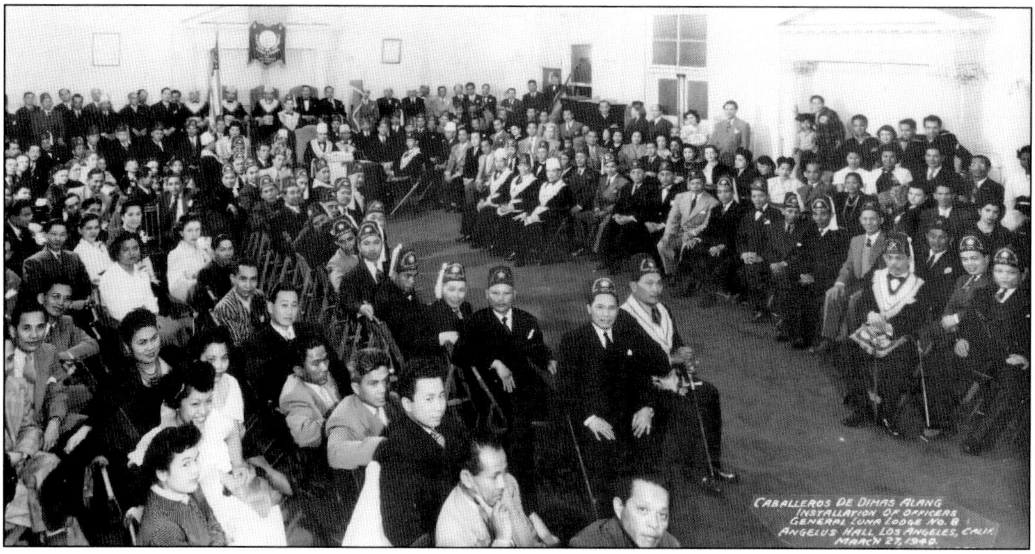

Caballeros de Dimas-Alang, Inc., General Lodge No. 8, is pictured at Angelus Hall in Los Angeles on March 27, 1949. Founded in Manila in 1906, the organization promoted Philippine liberation from the United States. By the mid-1930s, it had 26 lodges in California, including one in Los Angeles. Fraternal in nature, it provided needy members with food, clothing, and funds for medical and burial expenses. (Courtesy of Gerald Gubatan.)

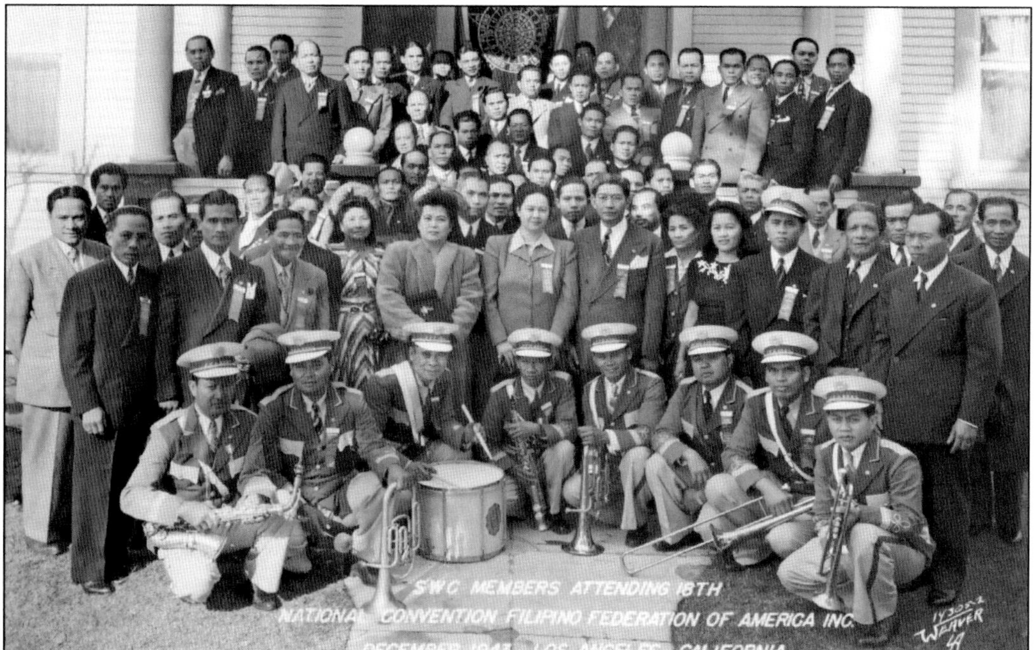

Members of the Filipino Federation of America, Inc., are shown in December 1943 at the federation's 18th national convention, held in Los Angeles. The federation was among several Filipino mutual aid organizations in Los Angeles that held annual grand events. Other mutual aid organizations included the Filipino Mercantile Association, Filipino Brotherhood Association, Filipino American Christian Fellowship, and the Pangasinan Association, to name a few. (Courtesy of the Filipino Federation of America, Inc.)

Three

TEMPLE-BEVERLY CORRIDOR

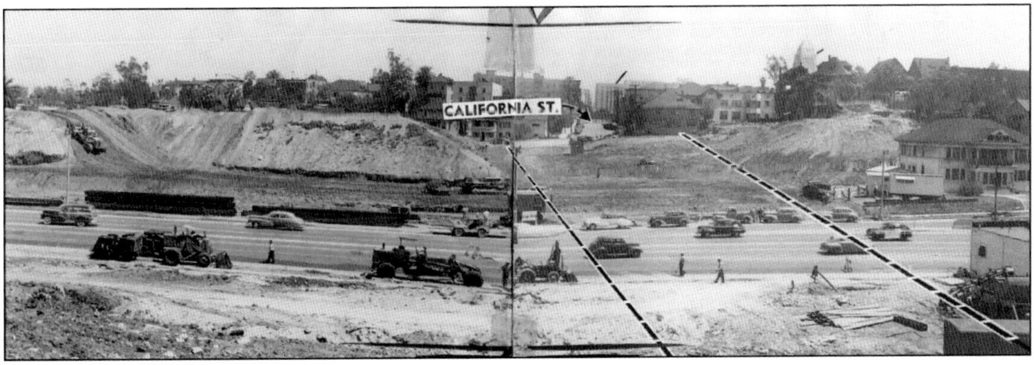

A 1948 view of Bunker Hill shows workmen pushing construction along North Figueroa Street between Sunset and Temple Streets. Sections of Bunker Hill are seen being cut away to make way for the construction of the Hollywood Freeway and the four-level bridge. This view shows Bunker Hill almost completely removed. The outlines indicate the area where the Hollywood Freeway will be built. Once again, Filipino neighborhoods were being shifted, and residents were forced to relocate to make way for urban renewal and redevelopment projects. (Courtesy of the *Herald-Examiner* Collection.)

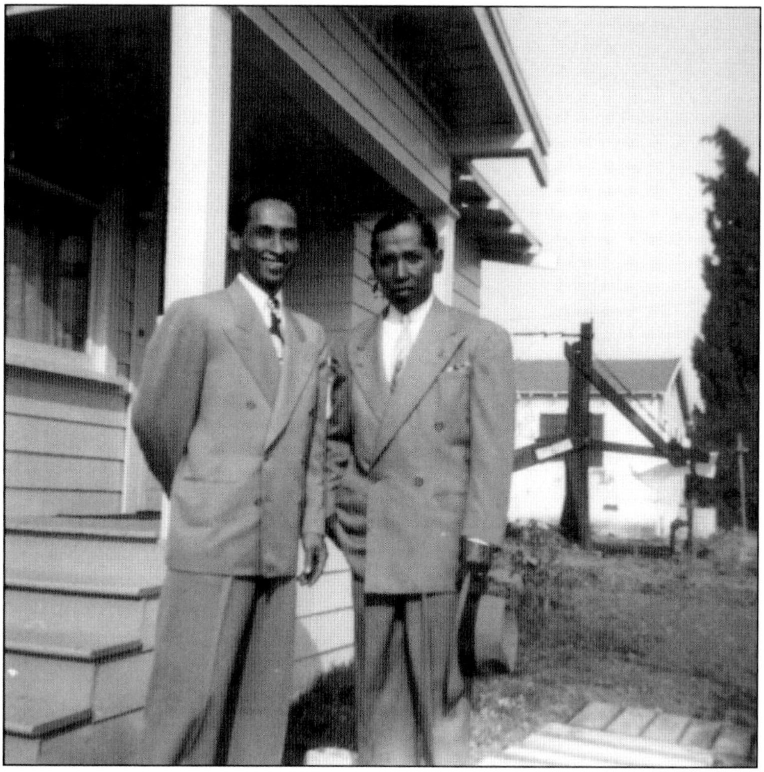

Severo Gubatan (right) and a friend are pictured in the Temple-Beaudry area, which was bordered by Temple Street to the north, Olive Street to the east, Third Street to the south, and Fremont Avenue to the west. The War Brides Act of 1945 allowed Filipino wives of U.S. military men and others to immigrate to the United States, resulting in families settling in and around the Temple-Beverly corridor. (Courtesy of Gerald Gubatan.)

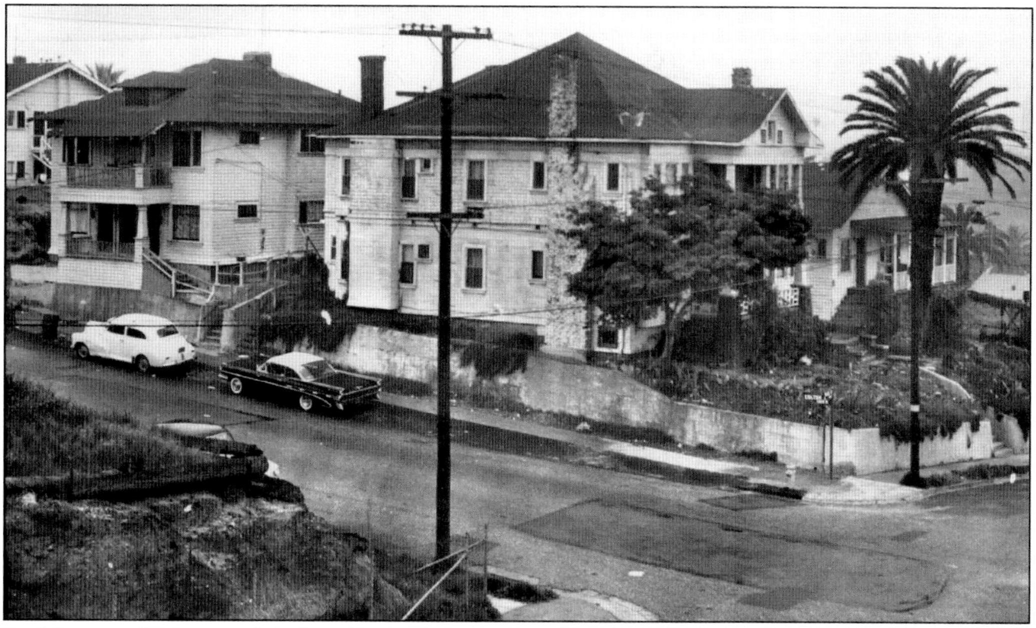

Buildings on Toluca and Colton Streets are seen in this 1962 photograph, which looks southeast toward First Street in the Temple-Beaudry area. One of the oldest areas in the city and considered as one of the most run-down, it was slated to be destroyed as part of the Temple Redevelopment Project. Filipino families who had settled in certain sections of the area were forced to relocate as a result of the redevelopment. (Courtesy of the *Herald-Examiner* Collection.)

Mary Geraldine Sobrino sits on the steps of a rented bungalow at 330 North Temple Street in 1952. Temple Street can be seen running along the left side of the bungalow. (Courtesy of Carlene Sobrino Bonnivier.)

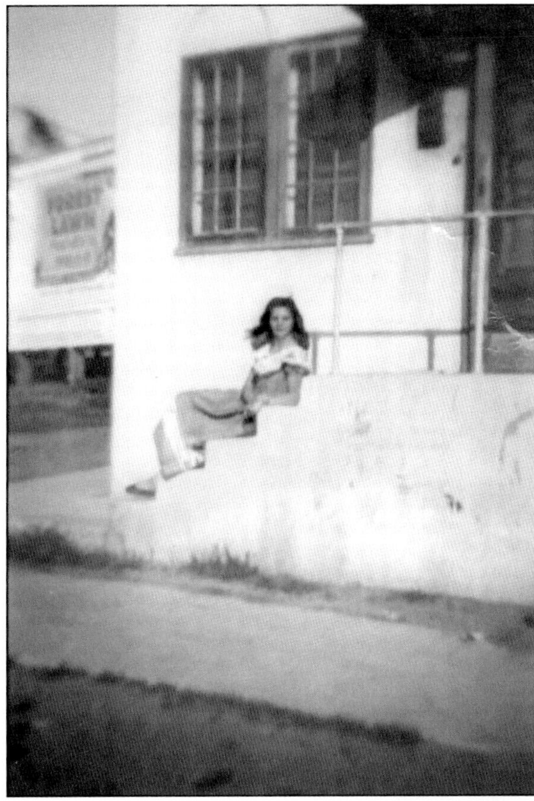

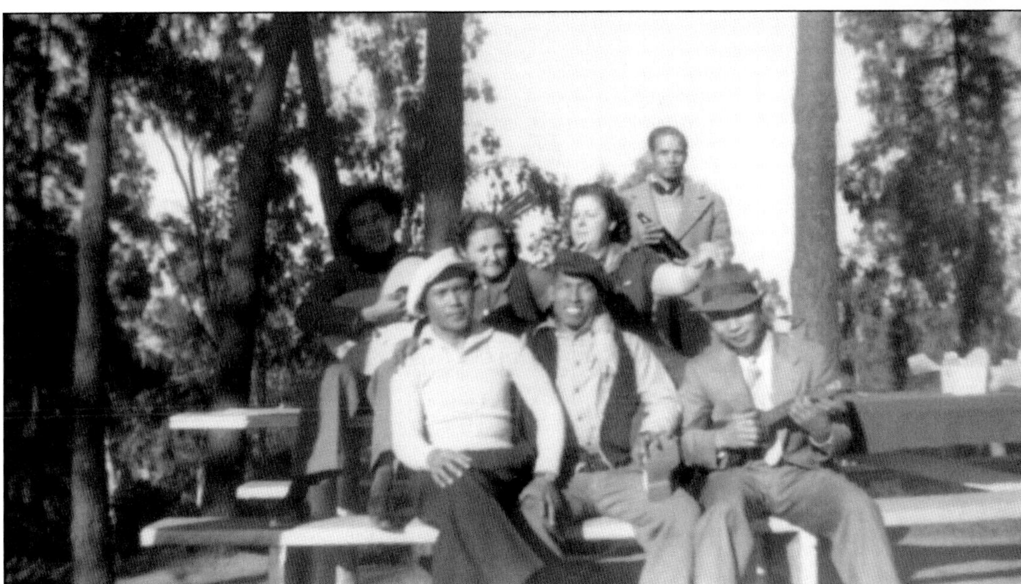

Severo Gubatan (first row, center) is seen with friends at Echo Park in the 1940s. Echo Park was a popular gathering place for Filipinos because of its close proximity to downtown Los Angeles and residences in and around the Temple-Beaudry area and Temple-Beverly corridor. Echo Park was also host to several Filipino sports teams that competed in baseball, volleyball, and tennis games. (Courtesy of Gerald Gubatan.)

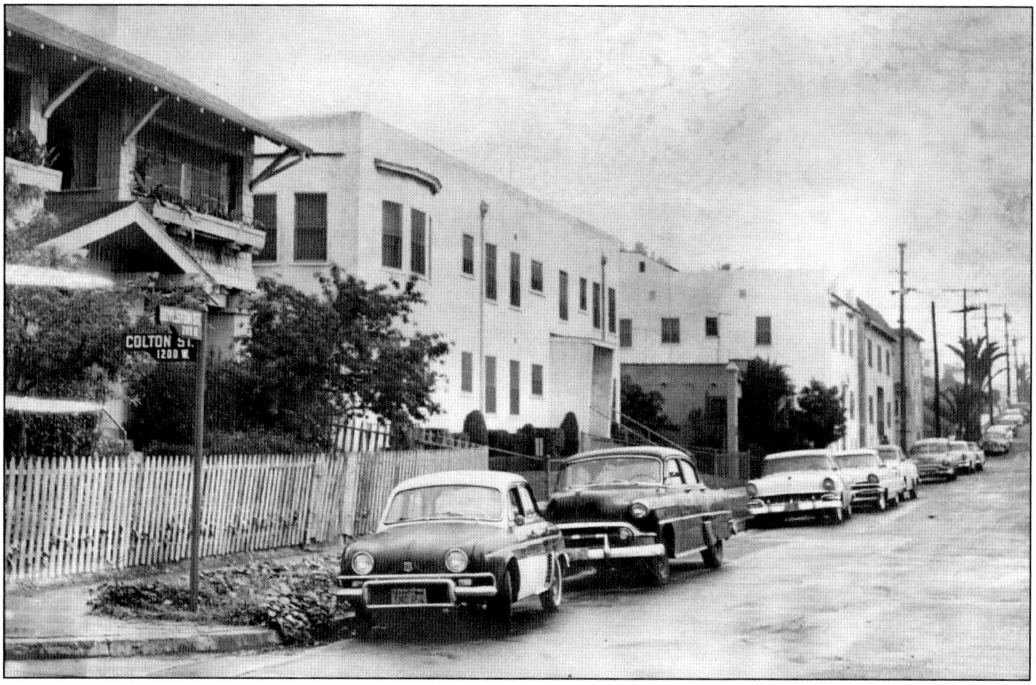

A 1962 photograph shows apartment buildings in the Temple-Beaudry area slated to be destroyed during the Temple Redevelopment Project. The view is on Boylston and Colton Streets, looking north toward Temple Street. (Courtesy of the *Herald-Examiner* Collection.)

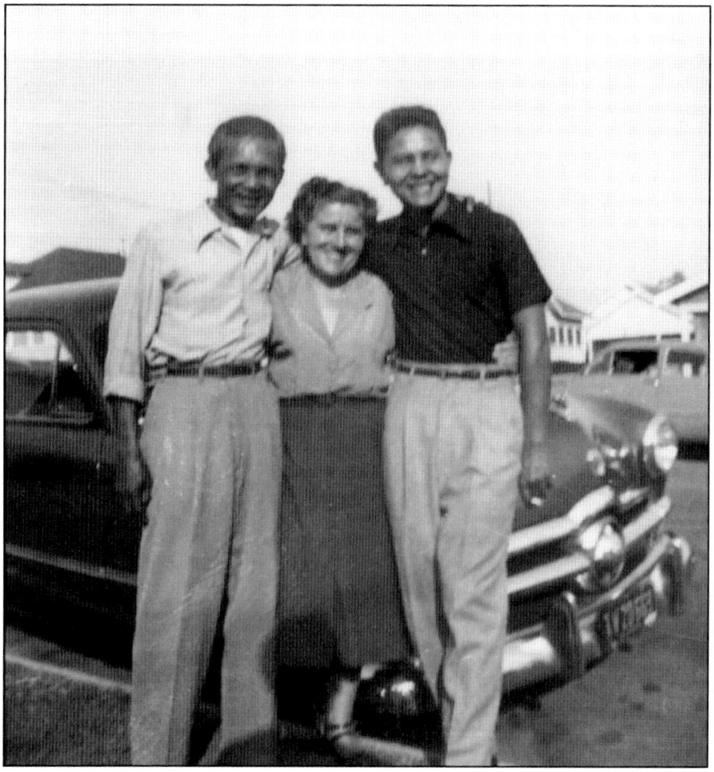

A Filipino American family is seen here in the Temple-Beaudry area. From left to right are Richard Dionzon, Molly Lofink Dionzon, and Kenny Dionzon. Richard Dionzon was an active participant in Filipino community organizations in Los Angeles, devoting his life to involvement with the Filipino Optimist Club and Filipino American Senior Citizens program. (Courtesy of Kenny Dionzon.)

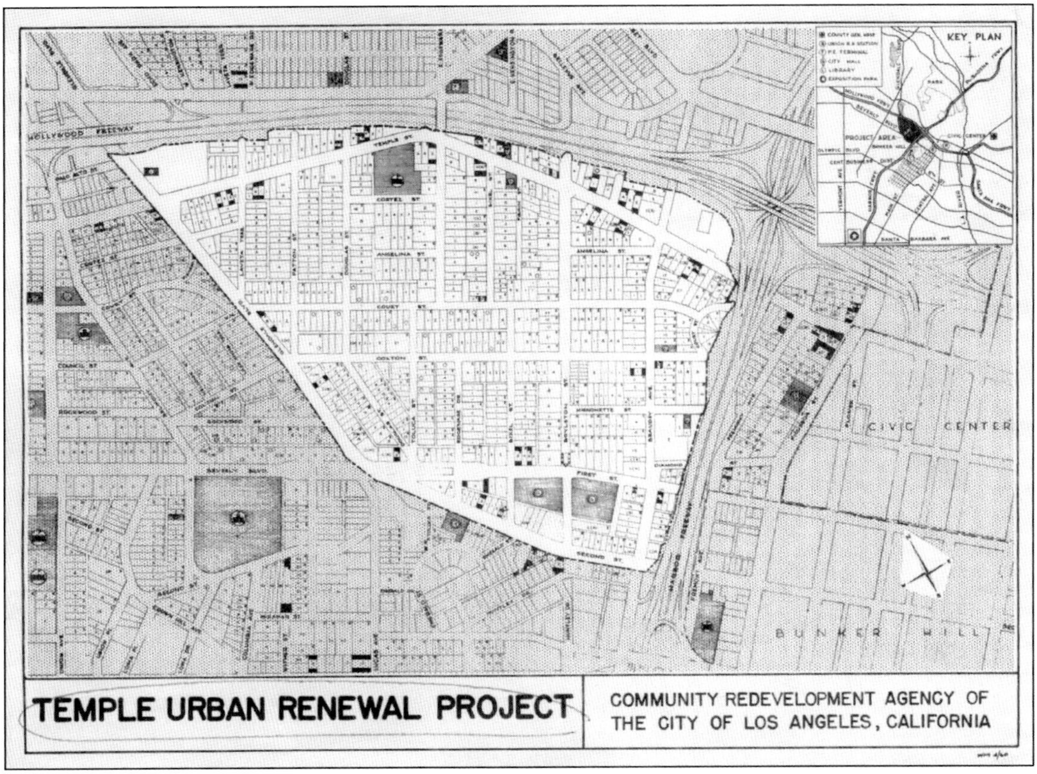

Pictured above is a 1962 map of the area to be redeveloped in the Temple Urban Renewal Project, according to the Community Redevelopment Agency of the City of Los Angeles. The boundaries of the redevelopment included the Hollywood Freeway to Second Street and Glendale Boulevard to the Harbor Freeway, which included the Temple-Beaudry area. (Courtesy of the *Herald-Examiner* Collection.)

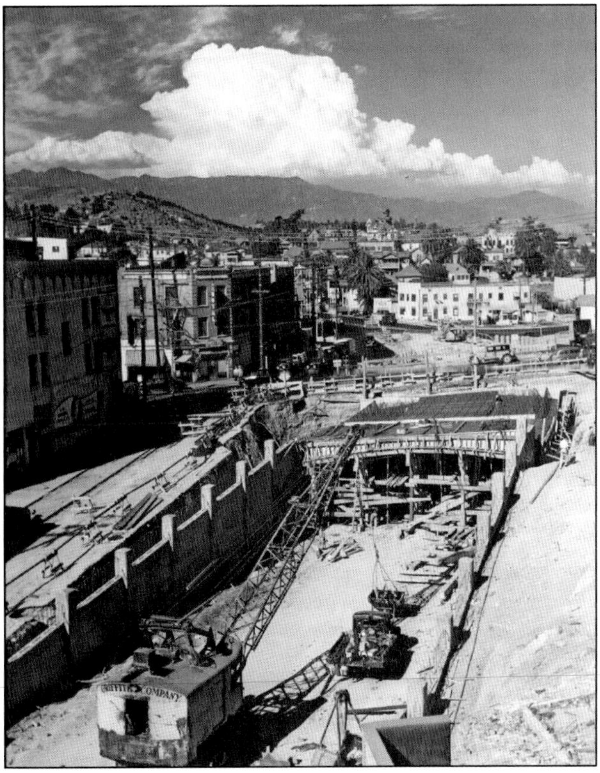

Construction of an underpass at the intersection of Figueroa and Flower Streets is seen in this 1939 photograph. The intersection is being paved to allow traffic flow. In the foreground is Figueroa Street, which will run under Temple Street. The underpass would be a link to the Arroyo Seco Highway. (Courtesy of Los Angeles Public Library.)

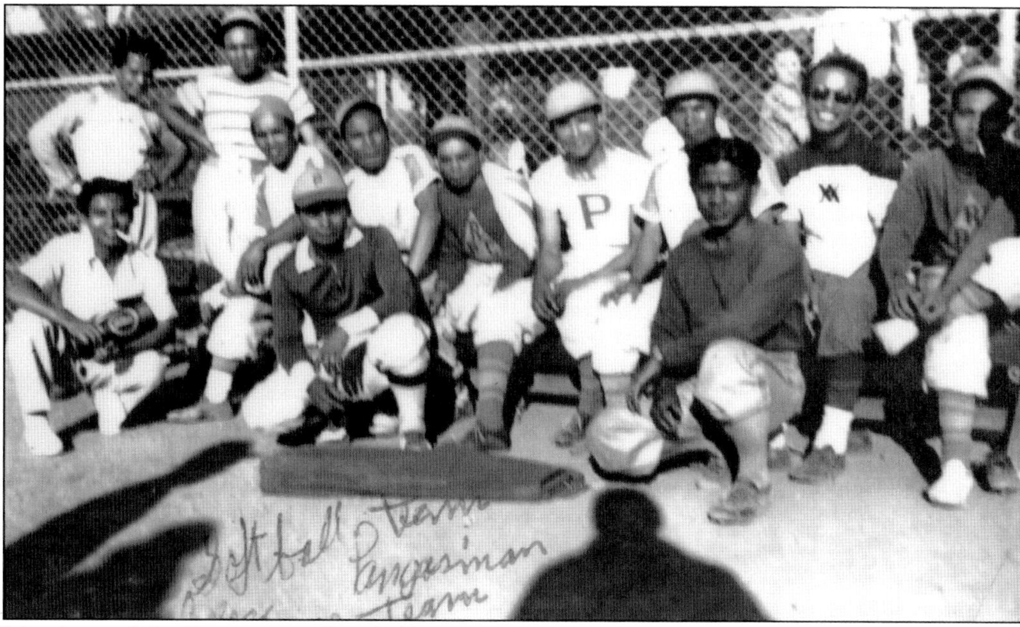

Members of the Pangasinan baseball team are pictured at Echo Park in the 1940s. Filipino associations, including the Ilocus Sur, Filipino Patriotic, La Union, Catholic Filipino Club, and Sons of Cebu, each had a baseball team. Other associations such as the Filipino Youth, Tanay Club, Filipino Christian Fellowship, Sequijor, and the Filipino Federation of America, Inc., had teams in track and field, volleyball, Ping-Pong, and golf. (Courtesy of Gerald Gubatan.)

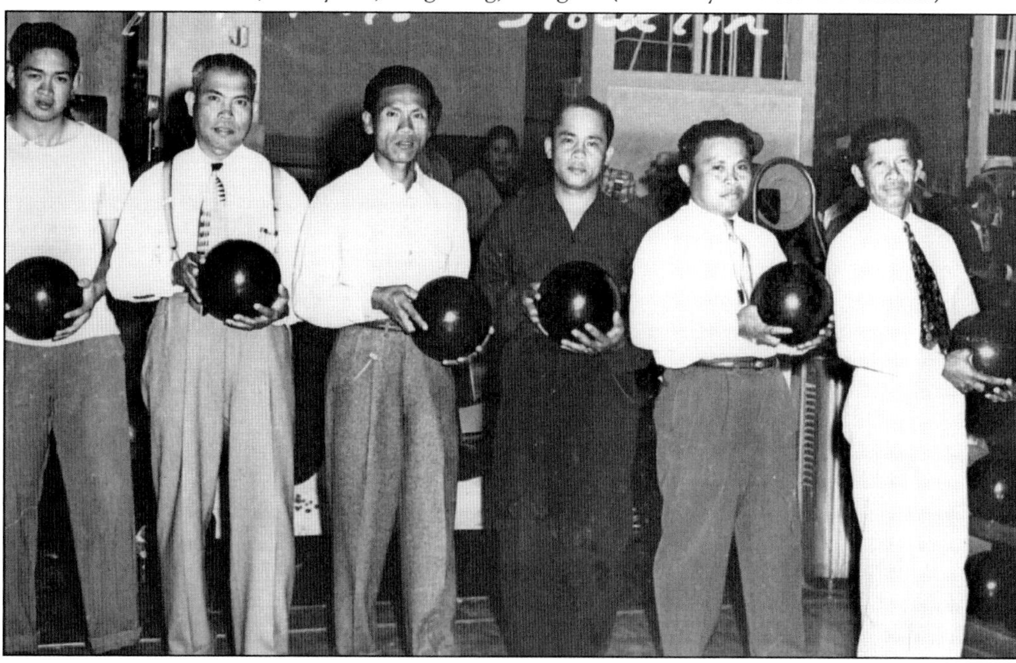

The Filipino Federation of America, Inc.'s Los Angeles bowling team competed in bowling games against other federation lodges. This photograph, taken on July 8, 1948, shows the Los Angeles team, which played the federation's Stockton, California, bowling team. (Courtesy of the Filipino Federation of America, Inc.)

Carlene Sobrino Bonnivier (first row, second from right, facing camera) celebrates her first Holy Communion in 1949 at Our Lady of Loretto grammar school, located at 258 North Union Avenue in the Temple-Beverly corridor. There were several churches in the Temple-Beverly corridor that were predominately Filipino, such as Praise Christian Fellowship, Filipino Christian Church, Iglesia ni Cristo, and St. Columban Catholic Church. (Courtesy of Carlene Sobrino Bonnivier.)

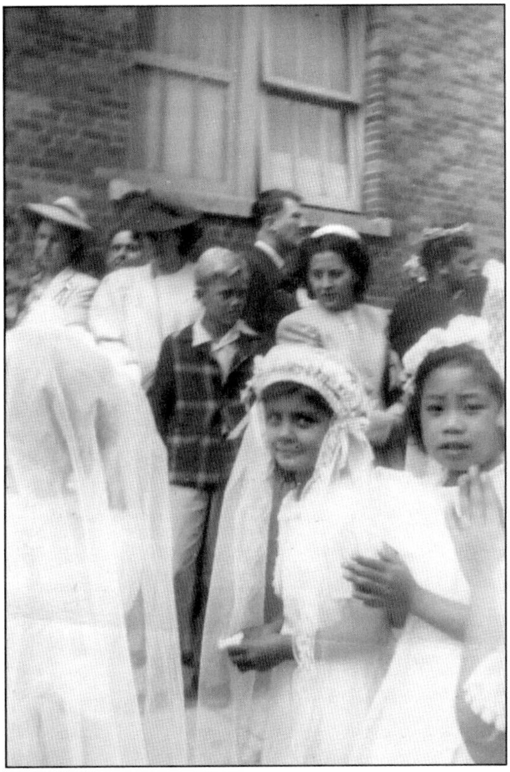

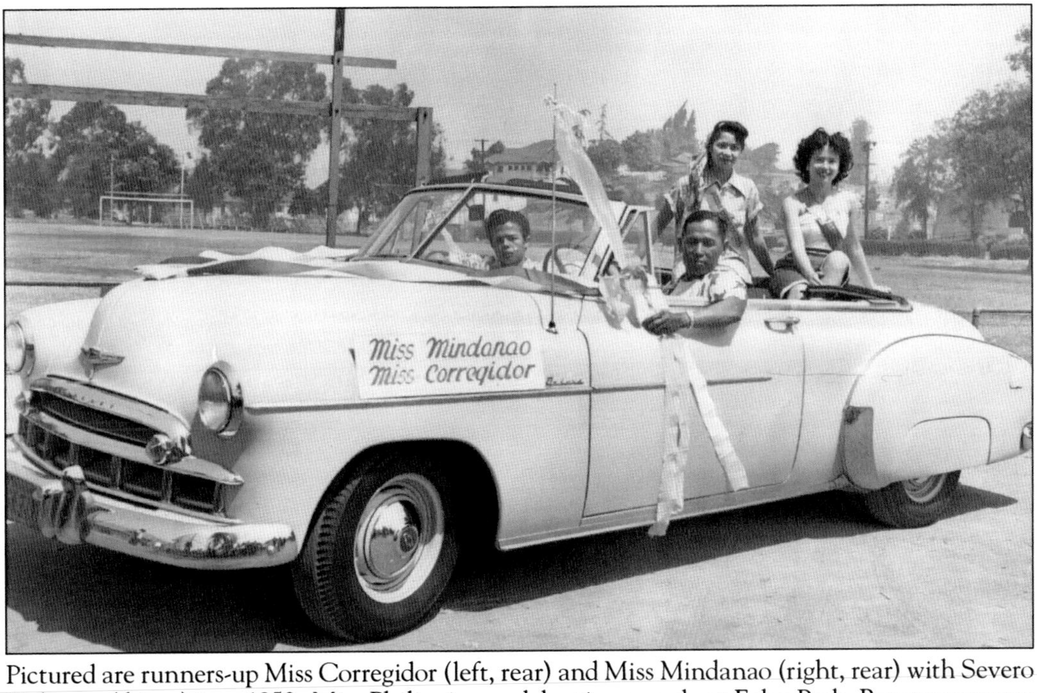

Pictured are runners-up Miss Corregidor (left, rear) and Miss Mindanao (right, rear) with Severo Gubatan (driver) in a 1950s Miss Philippines celebration parade at Echo Park. Beauty pageants such as the Miss Philippines pageant were annual fund-raising events sponsored by Filipino organizations in Los Angeles. (Courtesy of Gerald Gubatan.)

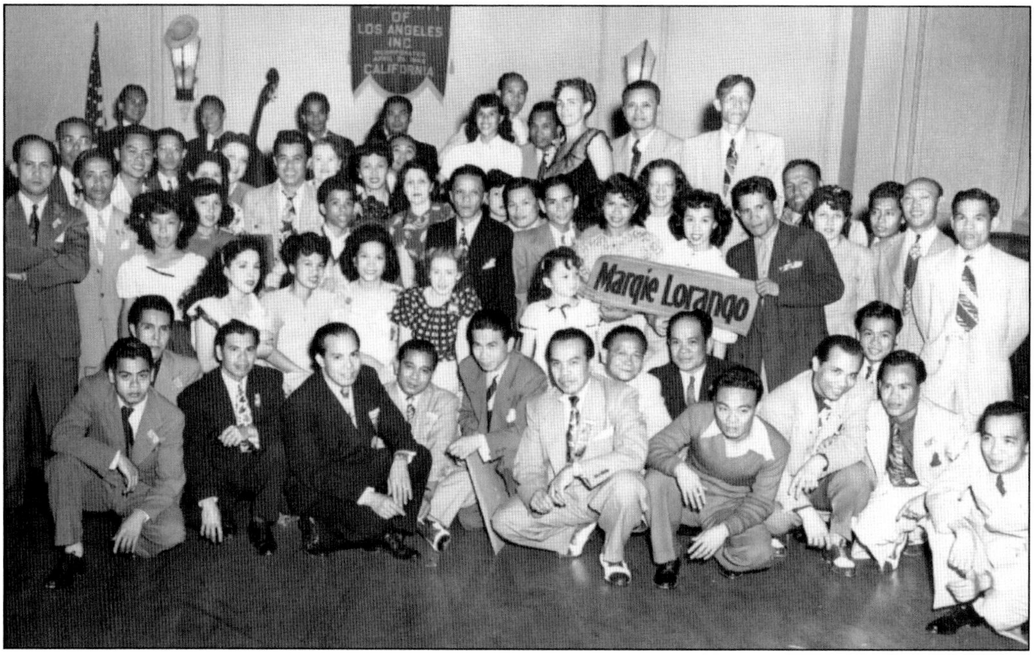

Members belonging to the Pangasinan Association of Los Angeles support Margie Lorango, a Miss Philippines beauty pageant winner who was crowned at a formal coronation celebration as part of the Los Angeles Filipino community's fund-raising efforts. The photograph dates to the 1950s. (Courtesy of Gerald Gubatan.)

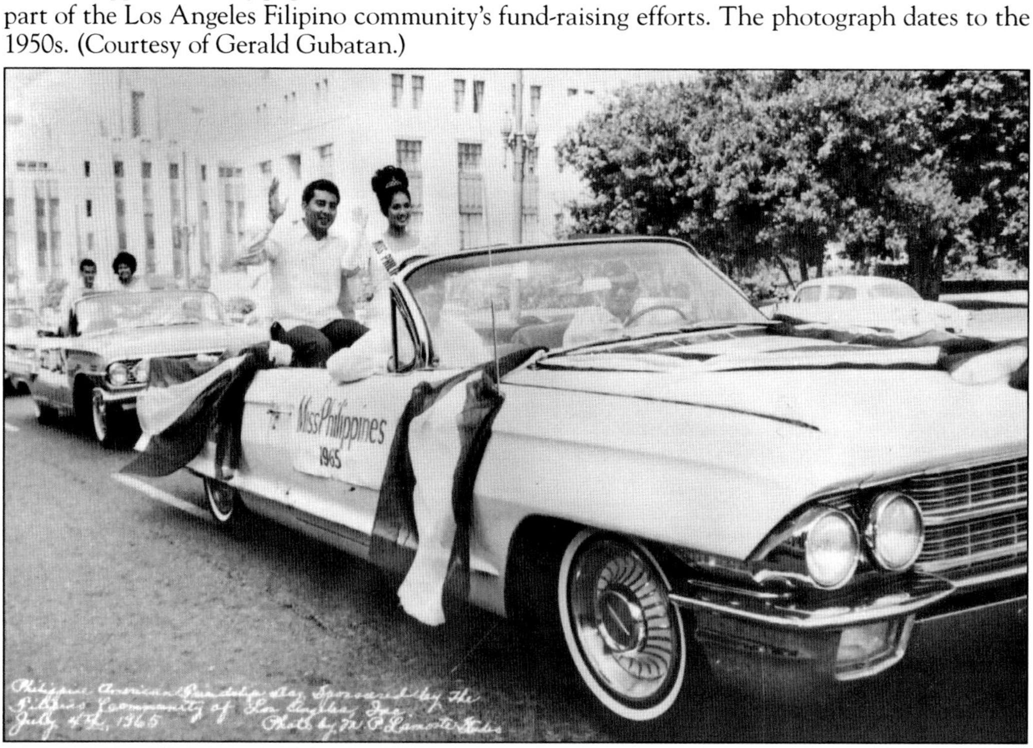

Another Miss Philippines celebration parade, sponsored by the Filipino Community of Los Angeles, is seen in 1965. The parade was part of a Fourth of July celebration held at Los Angeles City Hall in downtown. (Courtesy of Shades of L.A. Archives/Los Angeles Public Library.)

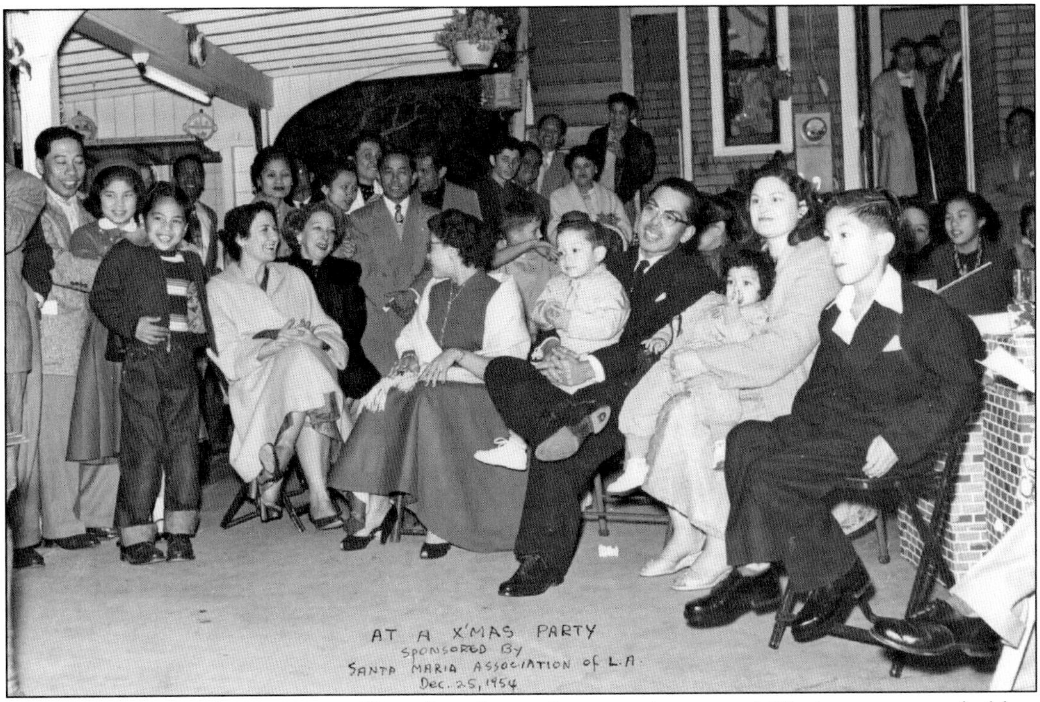

The Santa Maria Association of Los Angeles is shown at its annual Christmas party, held at the home of Rafael and Alfreda Pena on Union Street in 1954. Filipino Americans from towns and provinces in various parts of the Philippines formed their own organizations, such as the Pangasinan, Cebu, and Bohol Associations. These organizations promoted community involvement and socialization among families by holding monthly meetings, annual events, and celebrations, and they provided assistance to members in need. (Courtesy of Juliet Lagmay-Akiaten.)

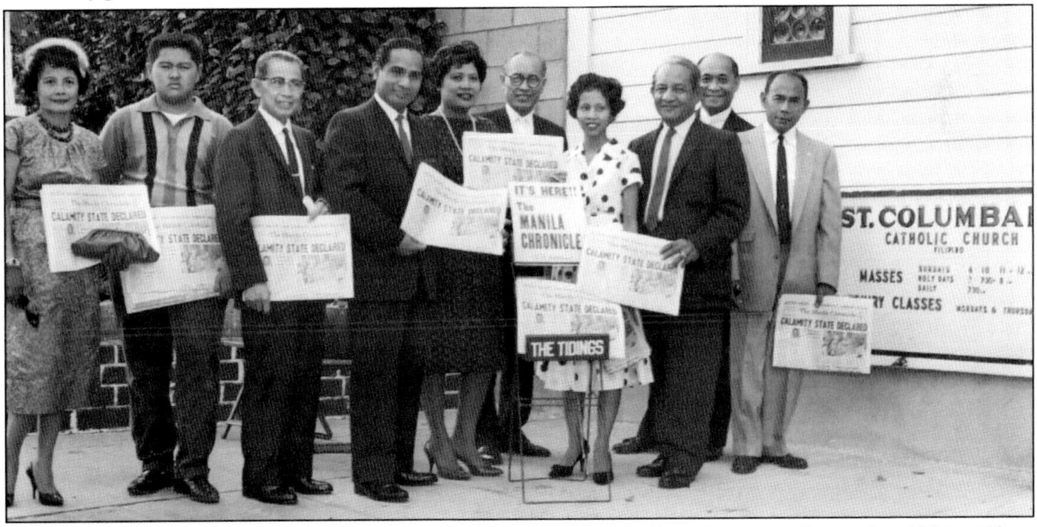

Members of the St. Columban Catholic Church pose for this photograph in the 1950s. They are holding up a *Manila Chronicle* newspaper with the headline reading, "Calamity State Declared." Located at 125 South Loma Drive, the church purchased an old fire station in 1947 and converted it into the first Filipino-owned Catholic church in America. (Courtesy of Juliet Lagmay-Akiaten.)

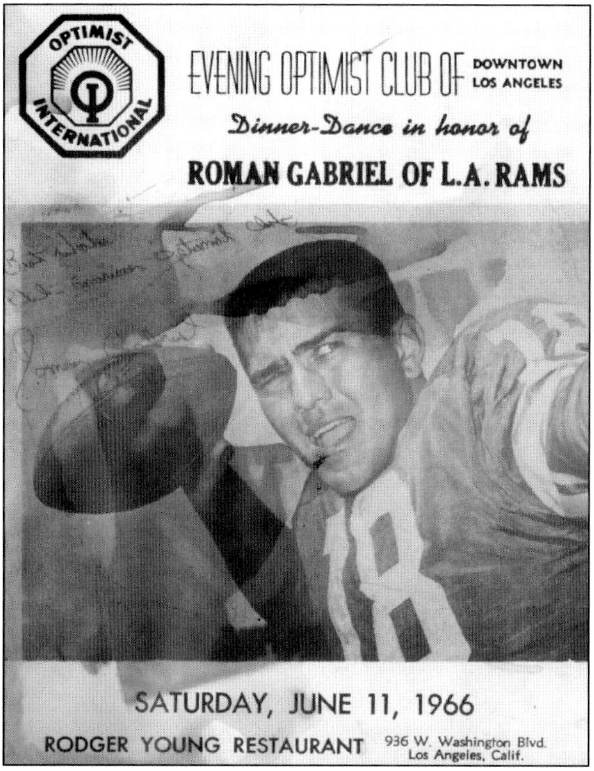

A 1966 brochure of the Filipino Optimist Club of Downtown Los Angeles honors Filipino American Roman Gabriel, who played quarterback for the Los Angeles Rams from 1962 through 1972. (Courtesy of Kenny Dionzon.)

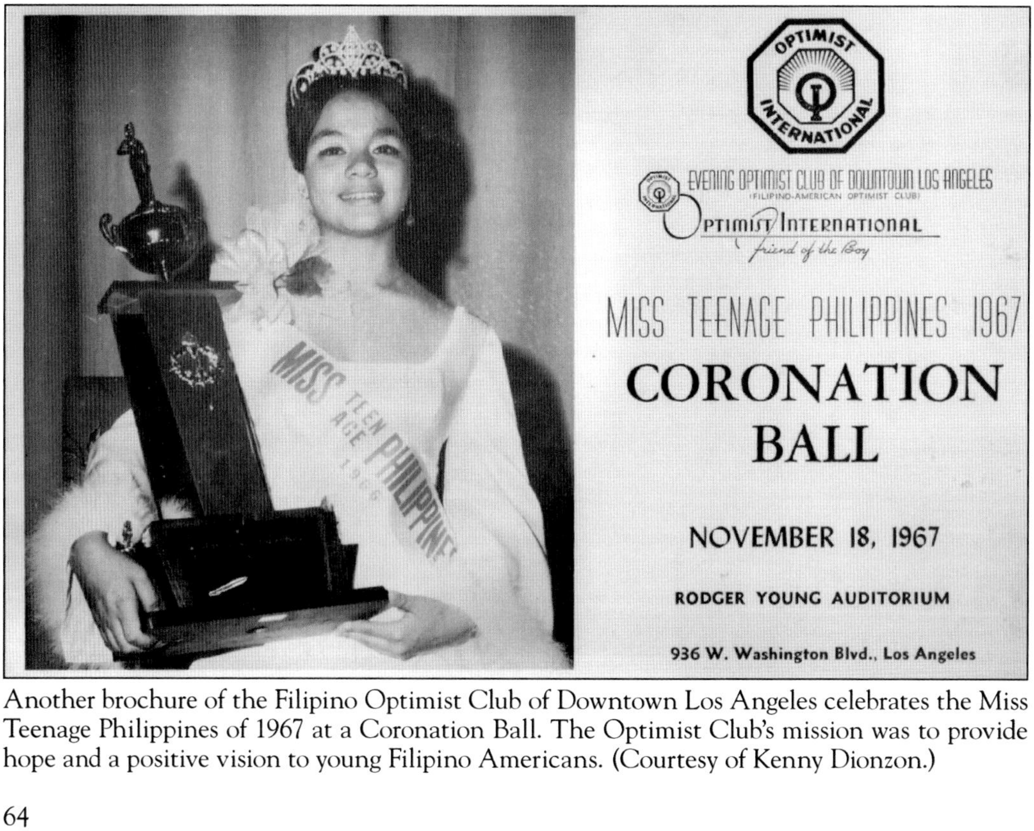

Another brochure of the Filipino Optimist Club of Downtown Los Angeles celebrates the Miss Teenage Philippines of 1967 at a Coronation Ball. The Optimist Club's mission was to provide hope and a positive vision to young Filipino Americans. (Courtesy of Kenny Dionzon.)

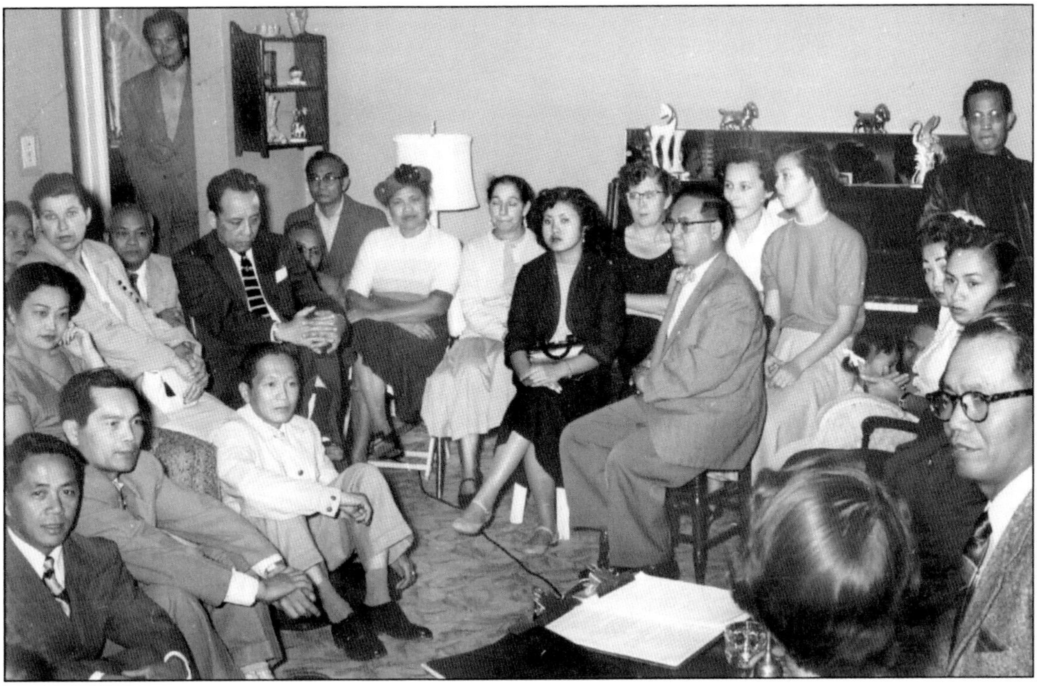

A Santa Maria Association monthly meeting was held at a member's home in the Temple-Beverly corridor in the 1960s. Monthly meetings and events kept members connected with each other and fostered community spirit among new immigrants. (Courtesy of Juliet Lagmay-Akiaten.)

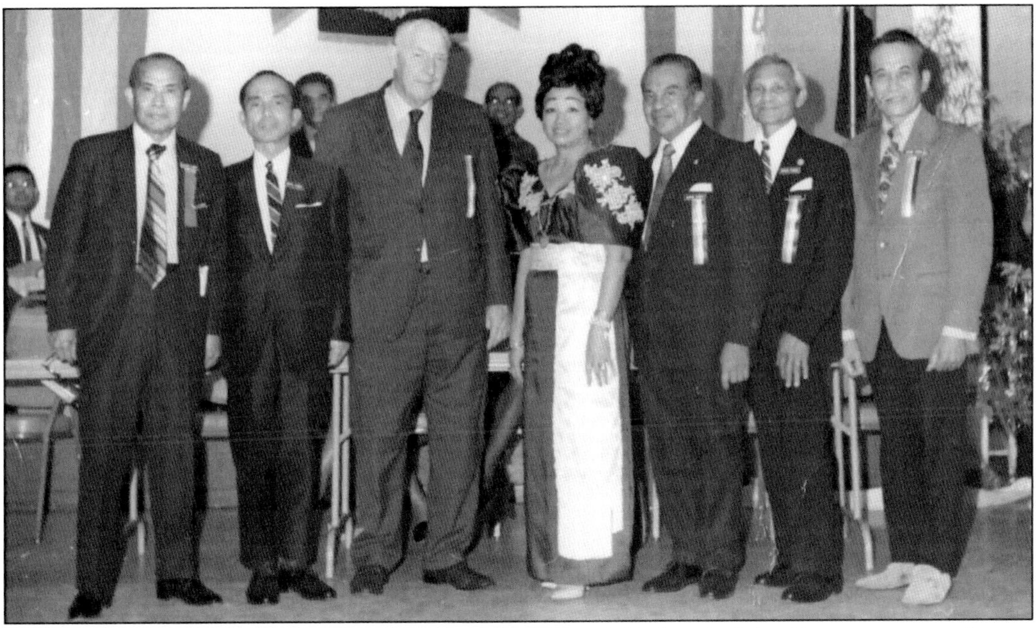

A 1970s photograph includes Tom Murphy (third from left), head of the Community on Aging; Amparo Domingo (fourth from left); and Richard Dionzon (sixth from left) at an awards event sponsored by the American Legion in Los Angeles. The event was held to recognize individuals for their leadership and support of the Filipino American senior citizens program. (Courtesy of Kenny Dionzon.)

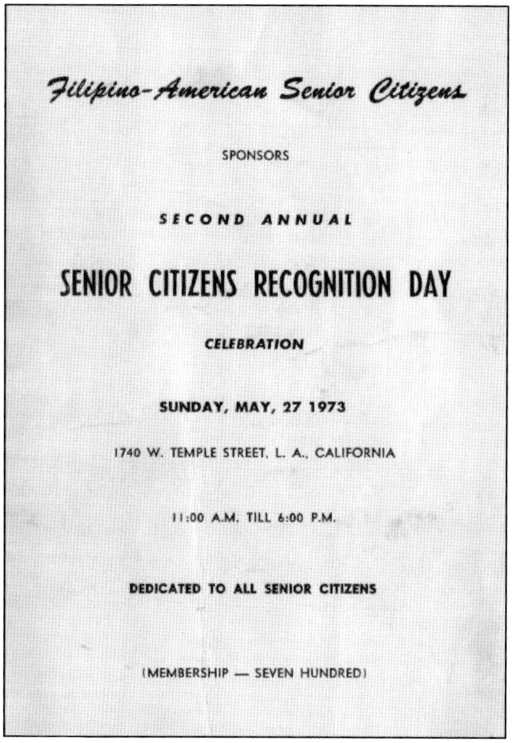
Filipino-American Senior Citizens

SPONSORS

SECOND ANNUAL

SENIOR CITIZENS RECOGNITION DAY

CELEBRATION

SUNDAY, MAY, 27 1973

1740 W. TEMPLE STREET, L. A., CALIFORNIA

11:00 A.M. TILL 6:00 P.M.

DEDICATED TO ALL SENIOR CITIZENS

(MEMBERSHIP — SEVEN HUNDRED)

Filipino American senior citizens were celebrated at the second annual Senior Citizens Recognition Day in 1973. The program enhanced the lives of the elderly by providing lunch programs and by promoting social events, and more. (Courtesy of Kenny Dionzon.)

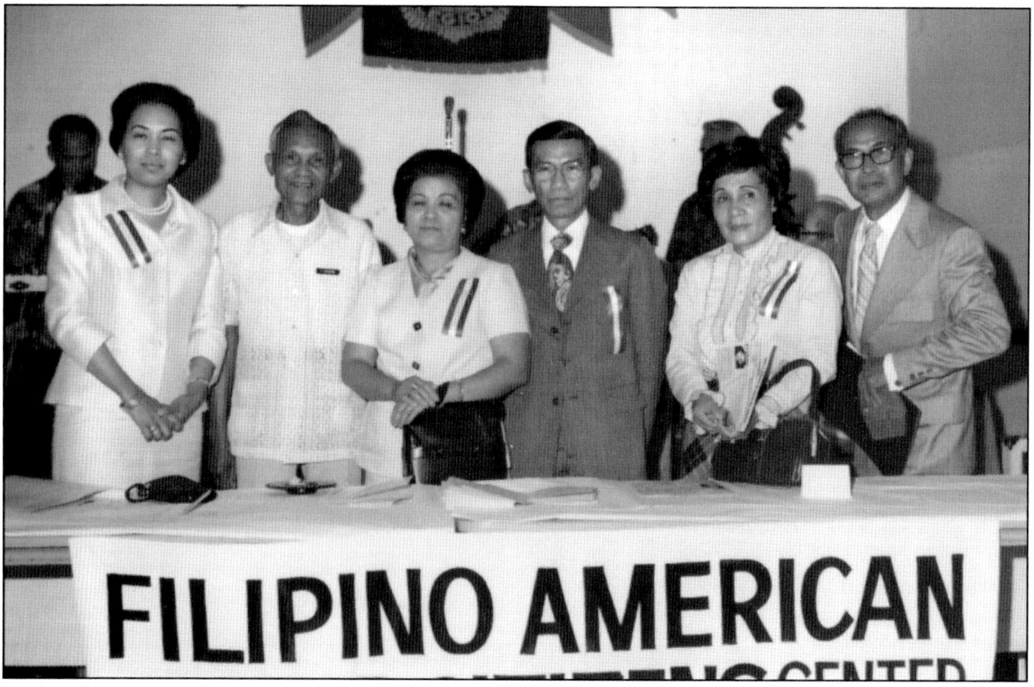

Richard Dionzon (second from left) and Remedios Geaga (fifth from left) are seen with other program members and leaders in this 1970s photograph. They were acknowledged for their efforts and contributions to the Filipino Senior Citizens program in Los Angeles. (Courtesy of Kenny Dionzon.)

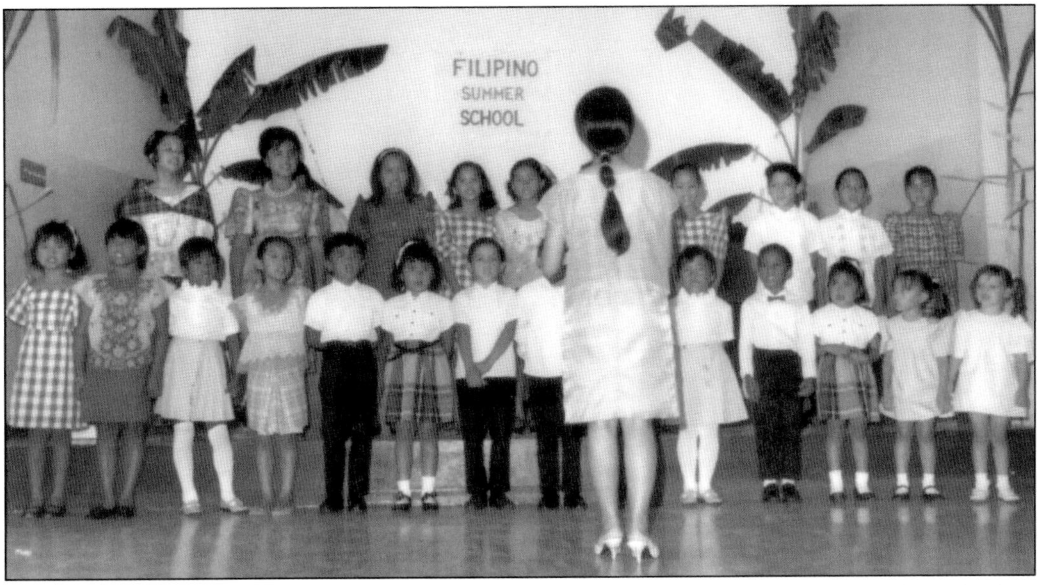

Joselyn Geaga-Rosenthal teaches one of the first Filipino American summer schools in the late 1960s in the section of Los Angeles now designated as Historic Filipinotown. (Courtesy of Joselyn Geaga-Rosenthal.)

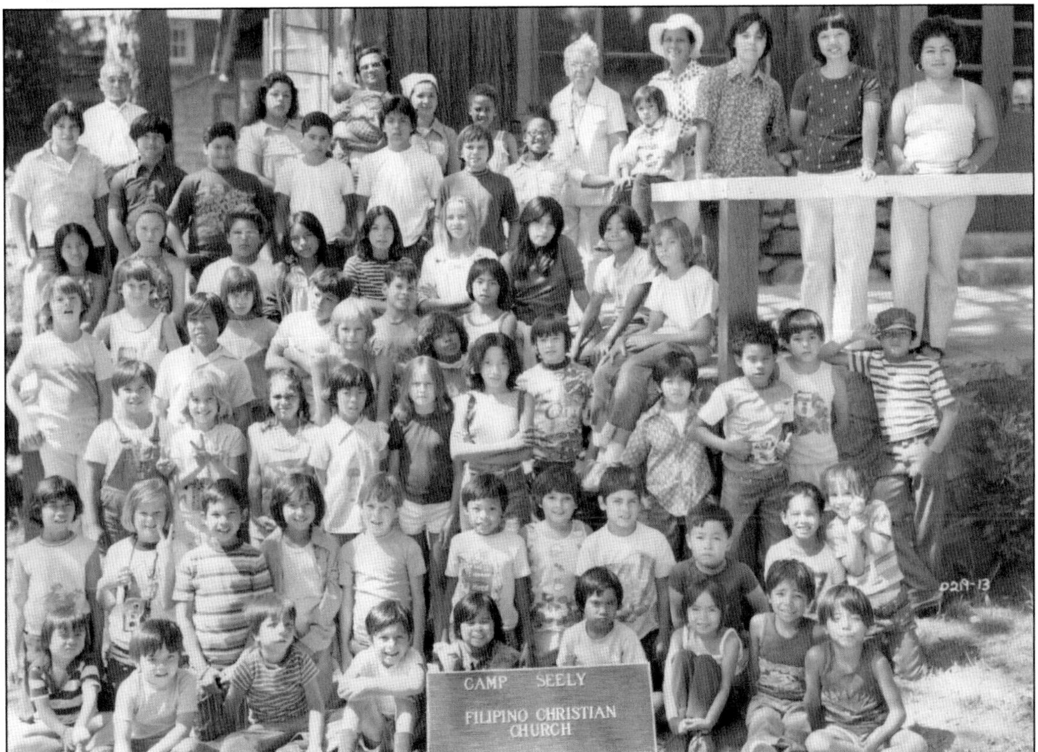

Pictured is a 1976 Filipino Christian Church–sponsored Camp Seely event for the youth members of the church. At its inception, the church was dedicated to developing and fostering the spiritual and religious side of Filipinos' lives. (Courtesy of the Filipino Christian Church.)

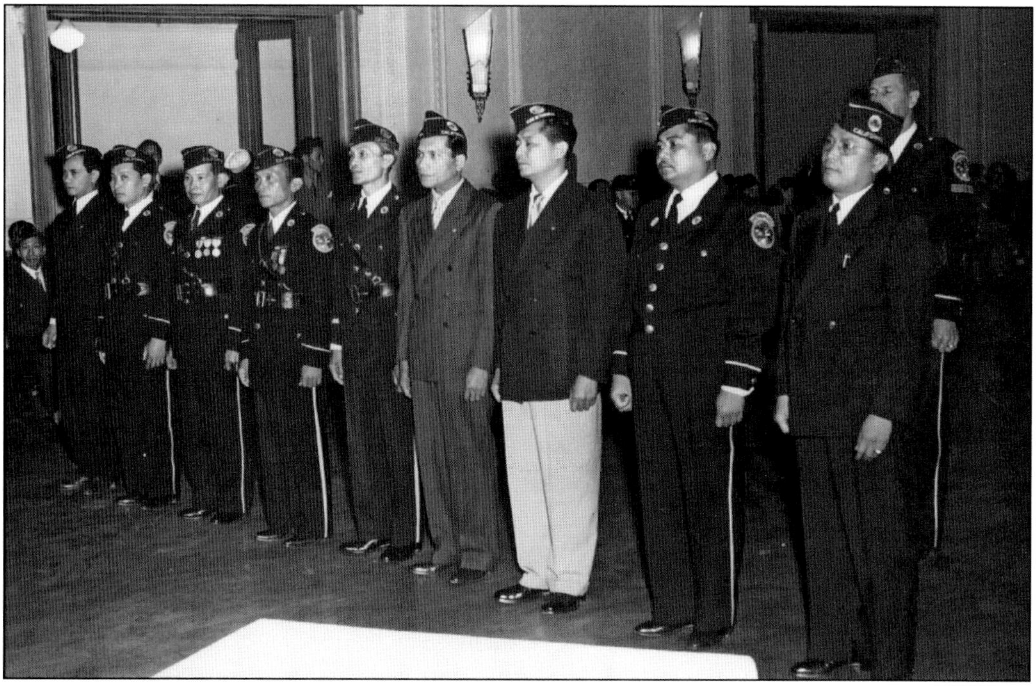

Veteran members of Manila Post 464 attend an installation of officers in Los Angeles in the 1960s. One member is identified as Vincent Calzado (first row, fourth from right). (Courtesy of Kenny Dionzon.)

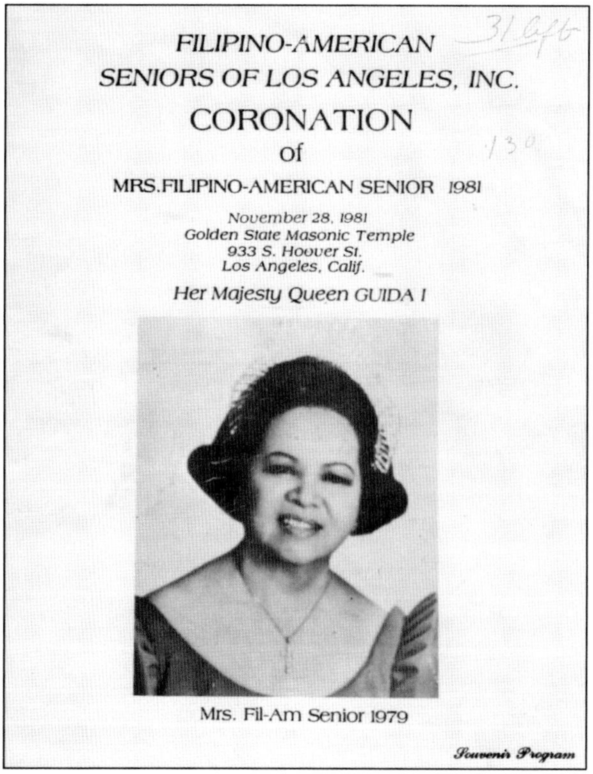

Filipino-American Seniors of Los Angeles, Inc., celebrates the coronation of Mrs. Filipino-American Senior of 1981, one of the many events sponsored by the organization for the benefit and well-being of Filipino seniors. (Courtesy of Kenny Dionzon.)

Four

COMMUNITY SPIRIT

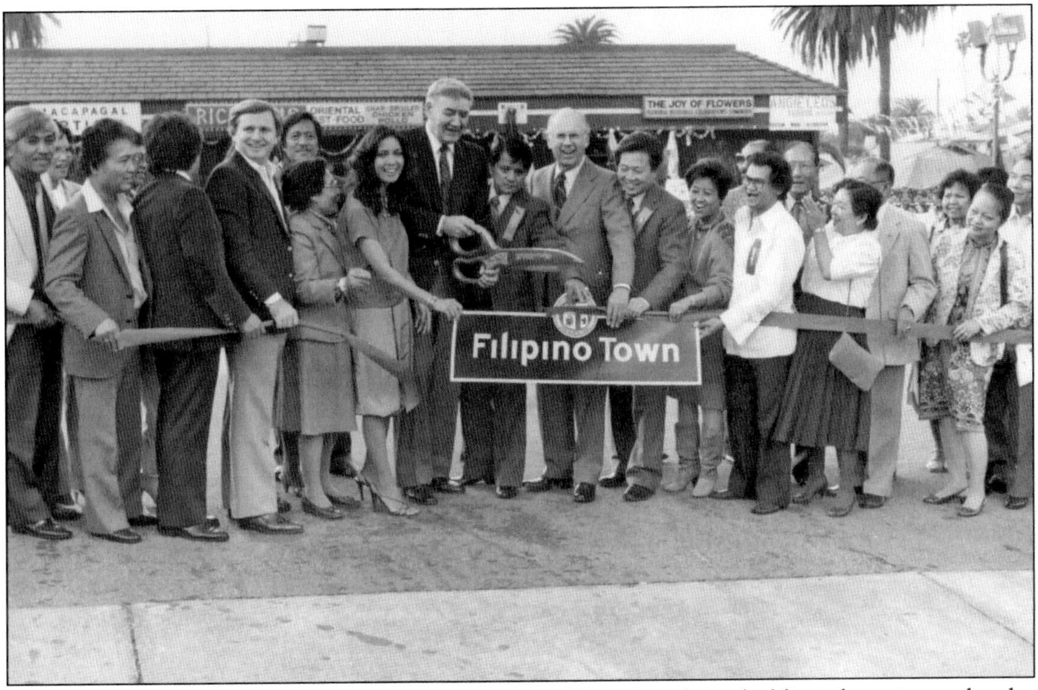

Councilman John Ferraro of District 4 of the city of Los Angeles is holding the scissors that he used to cut the ceremonial ribbon signifying the birth of Filipino Town. The two-day celebration, called Pasko Sa Nayon: A Filipino Town is Born, was held on December 8–9, 1984, at the Filipinas Plaza, located on the corner of Temple and Carondelet Streets in the Temple-Beverly corridor. Los Angeles city officials, Filipino community leaders, and residents of the area joined together at the celebration in support of community efforts to have a designated Filipino Town. The celebration provided free food, entertainment, and guest speakers. Pictured from left to right are Ben Aniceto, Dan Alura, Gene Galang, assemblyman Mike Roos, Remedios Geaga, Cora Ugalde-Yellen, councilman John Ferraro, FACLA president Greg Cruz, supervisor Kenneth Hahn, Edgar O. Yap, Dr. Arliene Rosas, Cesar Patulot, Vis Bayan, Cecile Ochoa, and Mr. and Mrs. Almario Hermosura. (Courtesy of Jonathan Yap.)

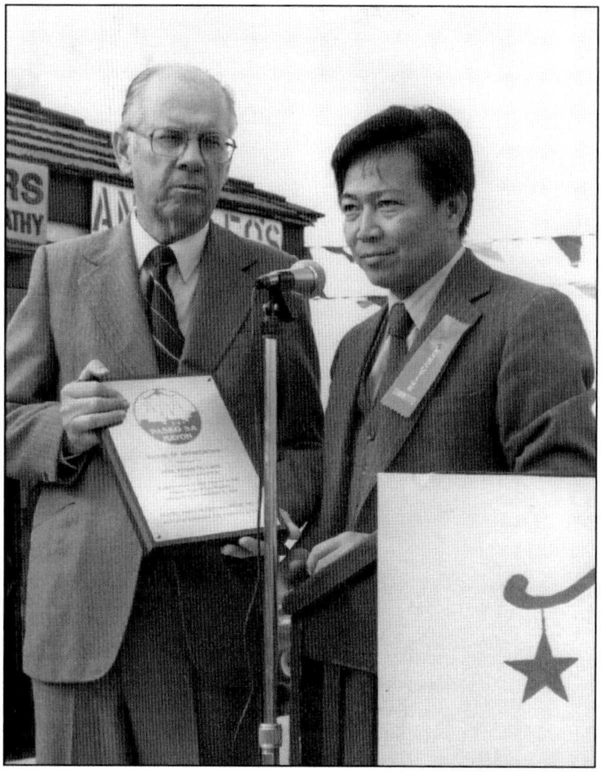

Supervisor Kenneth Hahn (left) was presented an award of appreciation by community leader Edgar O. Yap for his support of the Filipino community in its effort to have a designated Filipino Town. The award was presented during the two-day celebration of Pasko Sa Nayon: A Filipino Town is Born, which was held on December 8–9, 1984, at the Filipinas Plaza. (Courtesy of Jonathan Yap.)

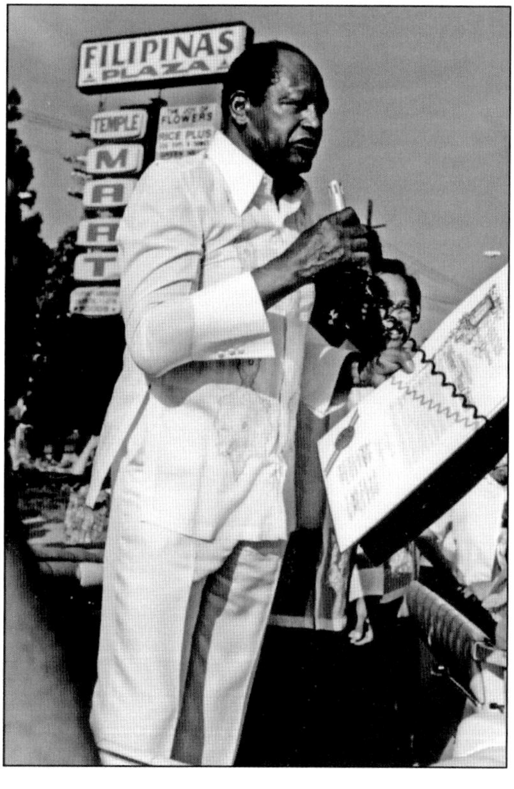

Los Angeles mayor Tom Bradley is pictured in 1986 at a ceremony held at the Filipinas Plaza during the Filipino Heritage Festival, which was sponsored by the Bayanihan Jaycees of Los Angeles. Bradley participated in the Heritage Festival's parade, as well as in many Filipino community events and celebrations during his terms in office (1973–1993). (Courtesy of Jonathan Yap.)

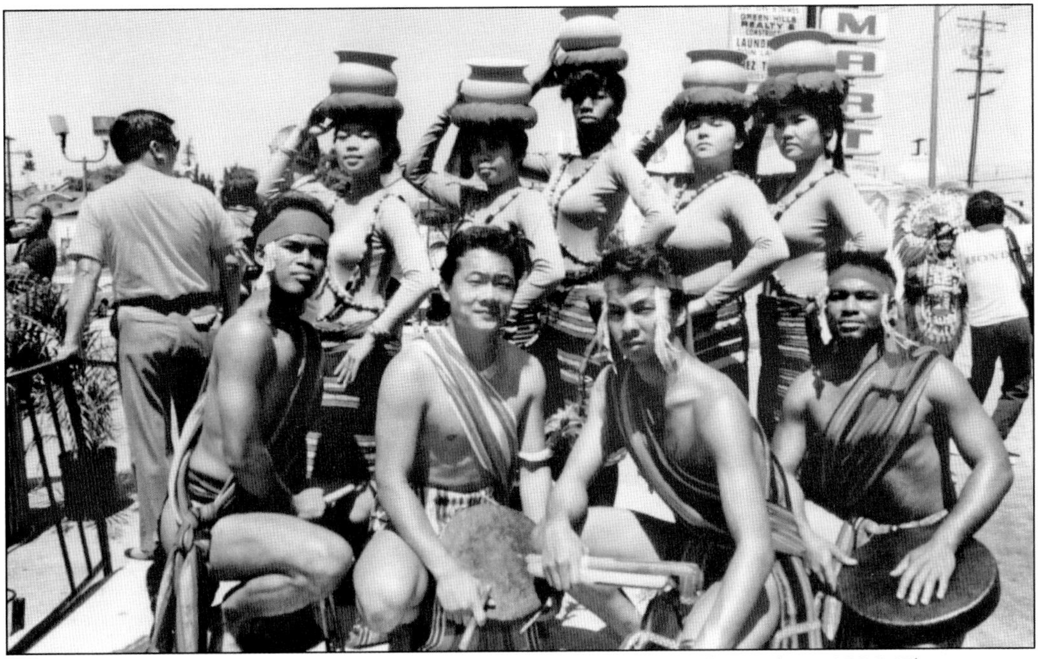

Pictured are Filipino folk dancers at the Filipino Heritage Festival parade in 1986. There are six different tribes that live in the mountains of the central Cordillera region of Northern Luzon, also known as the "Philippine Skyland." The collective name used for the mountain people is Igorot. The Igorots are known for their dances to cure sickness, to have success in battle, and to ward off back luck, as well as dances for bountiful harvests and for favorable weather. In the Takiling dance, men chant and dance while beating brass gongs (*gangsa*) and displaying their ability to use shields and hunting gear. One male folk dancer is identified as Joel Jacinto (first row, second from left). (Courtesy of Jonathan Yap.)

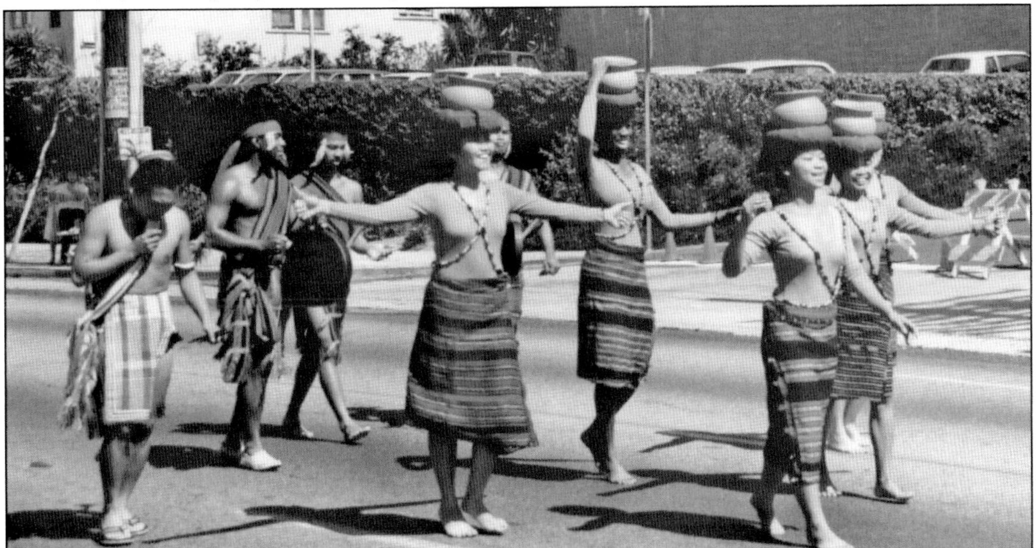

Women folk dancers are pictured at the Filipino Heritage Festival parade in 1986 carrying jars and baskets on their heads. This dance is based on women gathering food and water. (Courtesy of Jonathan Yap.)

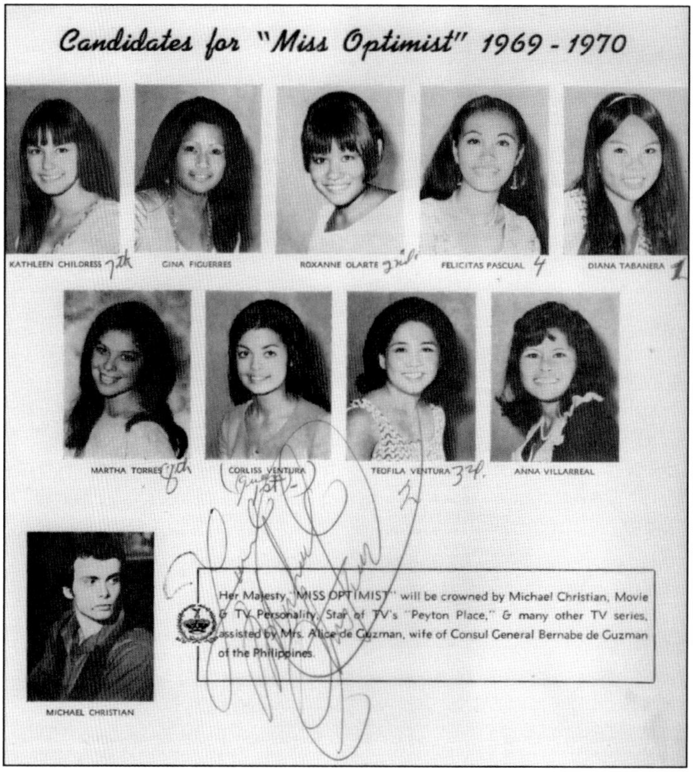

Pictured are the candidates for the title of Miss Optimist of 1969–1970, sponsored by the Filipino Optimist Club of Los Angeles. The winner was to be crowned by actor Michael Christian, who is pictured on this autographed photograph of the candidates. The Optimist Club held many fund-raising events, all in the spirit of fostering hope and vision to the community's young Filipino Americans and its seniors. Other fund-raising events included the Miss Teenage Philippines contest; Mrs. Filipino-American contest; oratorical and debate events; and occasions honoring noteworthy individuals in the community. (Courtesy of Kenny Dionzon.)

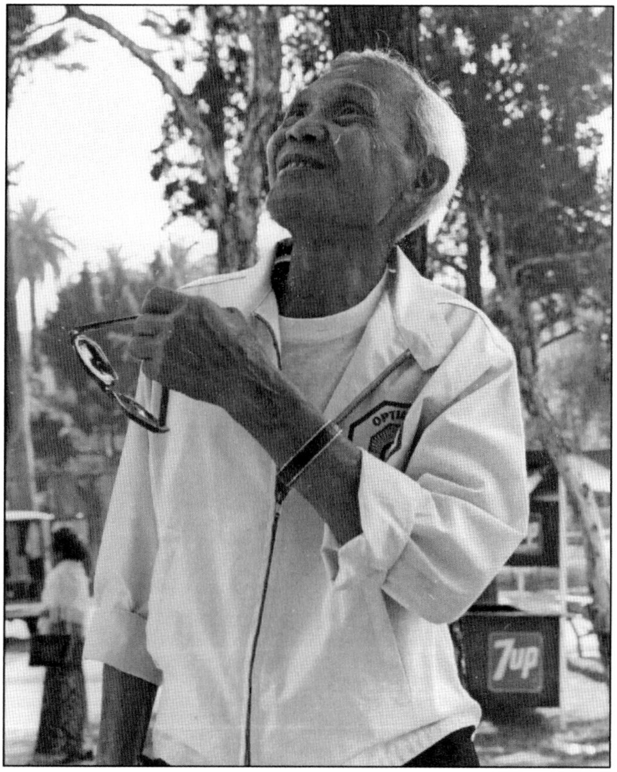

Pictured is Richard Dionzon at Echo Park attending a fund-raising event sponsored by the Filipino Optimist Club of Los Angeles in the early 1990s. Dionzon was an active member of the club for several years, devoting the remainder of his retired years in furtherance of the organization's mission to foster hope and vision to its young people and to promote well-being among its seniors. (Courtesy of Kenny Dionzon.)

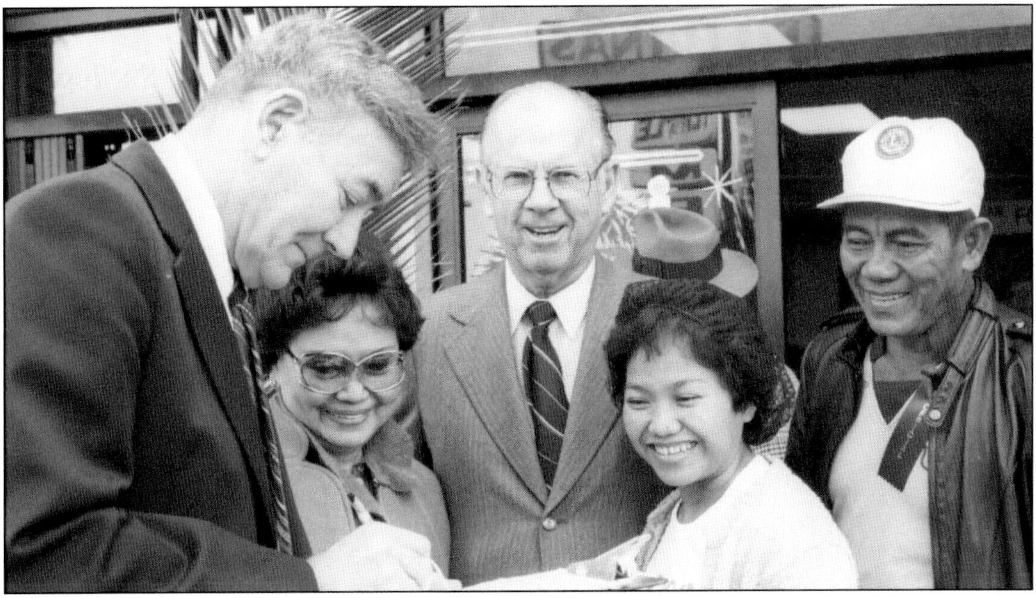

Councilman John Ferraro of District 4 of the City of Los Angeles (far left) signs a petition for the release of Satur Ocampo, a former Manila newsman, addressed to President Ferdinand Marcos of the Philippines. The petition was being circulated around the Filipino community in Los Angeles in the early 1980s. Ocampo was arrested on charges of subversion during the imposition of martial law in 1972. Also pictured are, from left to right, Connie Guerrero, Los Angeles supervisor Kenneth Hahn, Minerva Mabini, and Frank Burcellis. (Courtesy of Jonathan Yap.)

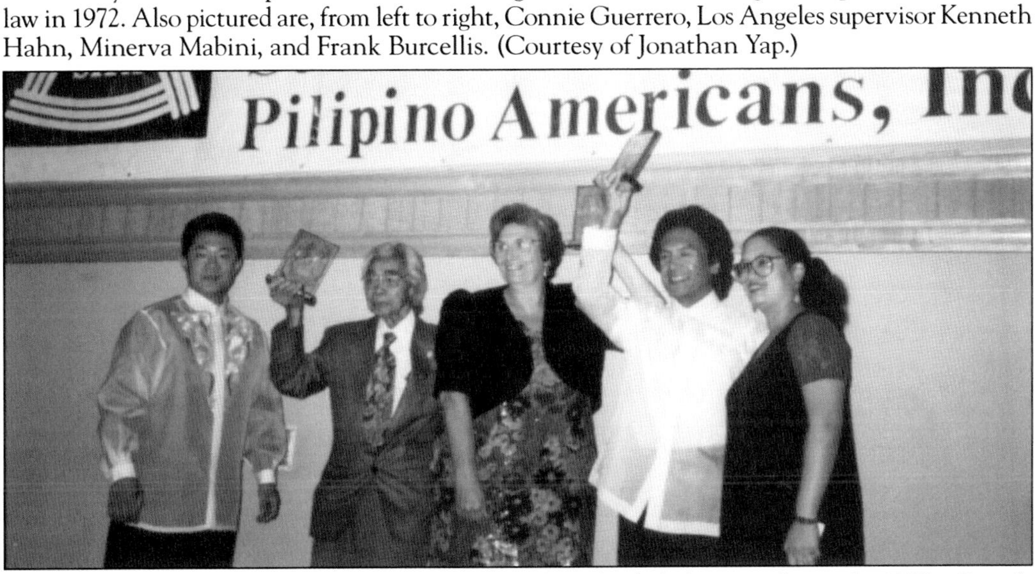

Founded by Roy Morales, Alan Kumamoto, and Paul Chikahisa in the early 1970s, Search to Involve Pilipino Americans, Inc., (SIPA) is a nonprofit organization providing health and human services, as well as community economic development and cultural programs to diverse multi-ethnic youth and families, including Filipino Americans, throughout Los Angeles County. SIPA is one of the most involved organizations in the Filipino community today. Pictured is a late-1990s SIPA event with, from left to right, executive director of SIPA Joel Jacinto; Philip Vera Cruz; Philip's wife, Deborah Vollmer; Sylvester ?; and Aileen Almeria. Past executive directors who have helped shape and carry out the mission of the organization's founders include Jeannie Abella, Liza Javier, and Meg Malpaya Thornton. (Courtesy of Ann Morales.)

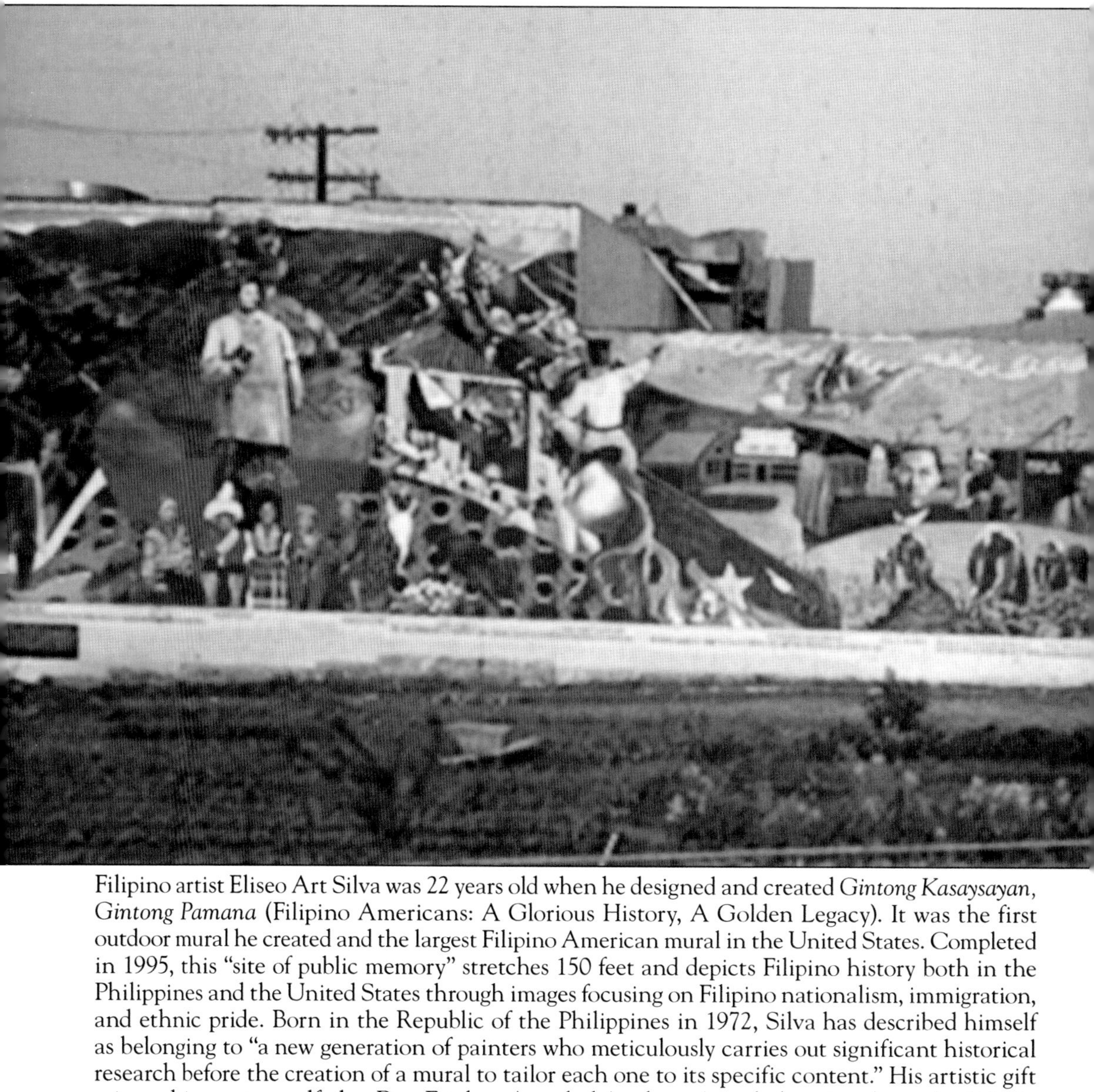

Filipino artist Eliseo Art Silva was 22 years old when he designed and created *Gintong Kasaysayan, Gintong Pamana* (Filipino Americans: A Glorious History, A Golden Legacy). It was the first outdoor mural he created and the largest Filipino American mural in the United States. Completed in 1995, this "site of public memory" stretches 150 feet and depicts Filipino history both in the Philippines and the United States through images focusing on Filipino nationalism, immigration, and ethnic pride. Born in the Republic of the Philippines in 1972, Silva has described himself as belonging to "a new generation of painters who meticulously carries out significant historical research before the creation of a mural to tailor each one to its specific content." His artistic gift mirrors his great-grandfather Don Esteban Arambulo's talent. Arambulo painted murals of idyllic scenes on glass doorways in the family's 19th-century, two-story, ancestral home in Calamba, Laguna. Silva began to draw at the age of four, and by nine, he was painting in oil and acrylic.

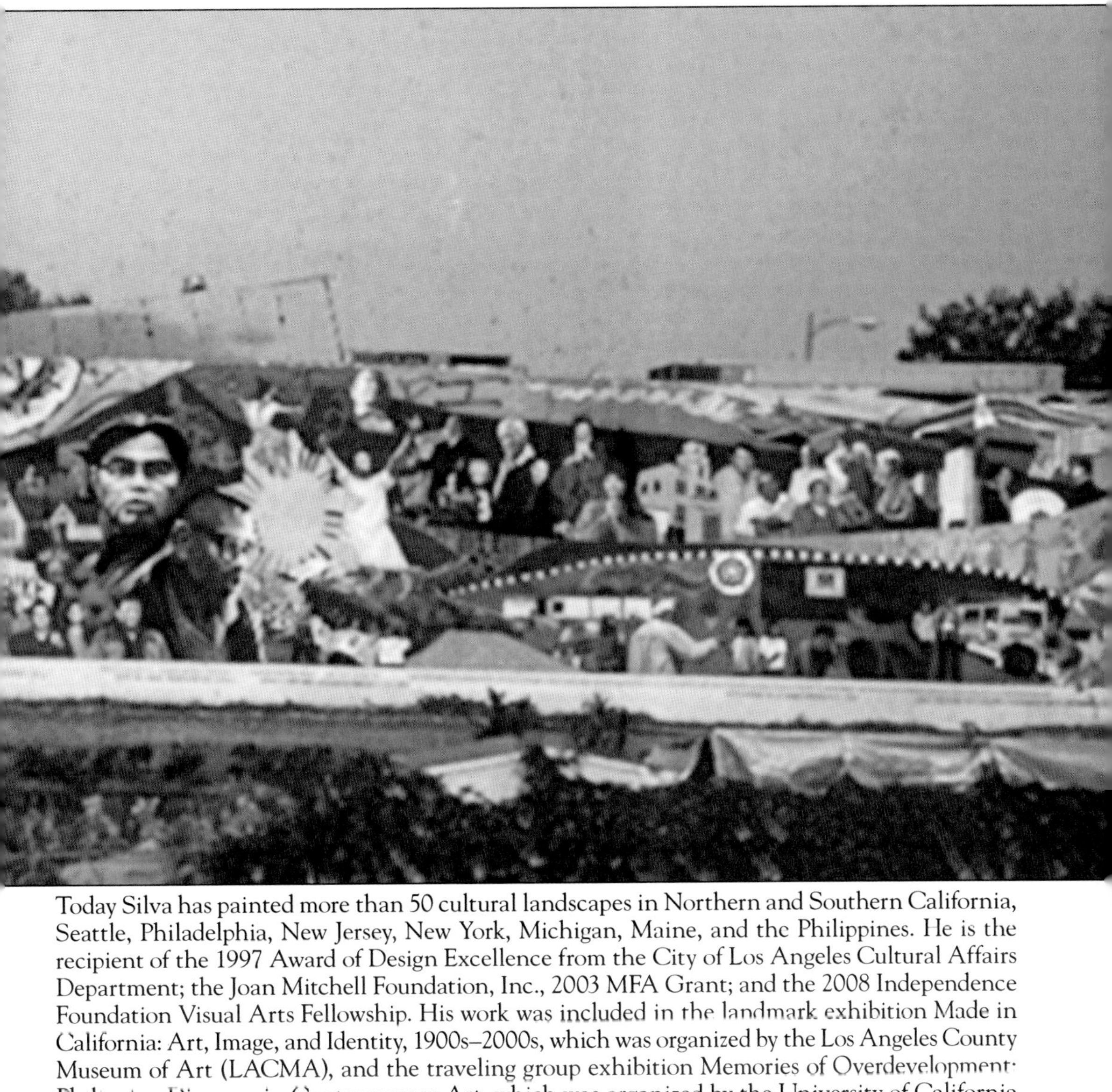

Today Silva has painted more than 50 cultural landscapes in Northern and Southern California, Seattle, Philadelphia, New Jersey, New York, Michigan, Maine, and the Philippines. He is the recipient of the 1997 Award of Design Excellence from the City of Los Angeles Cultural Affairs Department; the Joan Mitchell Foundation, Inc., 2003 MFA Grant; and the 2008 Independence Foundation Visual Arts Fellowship. His work was included in the landmark exhibition Made in California: Art, Image, and Identity, 1900s–2000s, which was organized by the Los Angeles County Museum of Art (LACMA), and the traveling group exhibition Memories of Overdevelopment: Philippine Diaspora in Contemporary Art, which was organized by the University of California Irvine and the Plug-In Gallery in Canada, and was shown in various cities in Canada and the United States from 1997 to 1999 in commemoration of the centennial of the 1896 Philippine Revolution. (Courtesy of Eliseo Art Silva.)

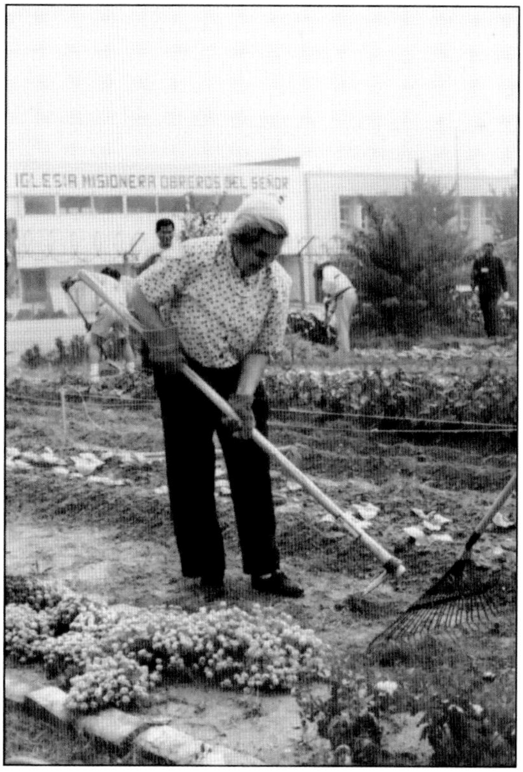

Pictured is Helen Summers Brown in the late 1990s. She is one of the founders of the Filipino American Library. Here she tends a vegetable garden in the park that hosts the *Gintong Kasaysayan, Gintong Pamana* mural. Filipino community residents and individuals created the vegetable garden by diligently sowing and harvesting it. (Courtesy of Carol Kimbrough.)

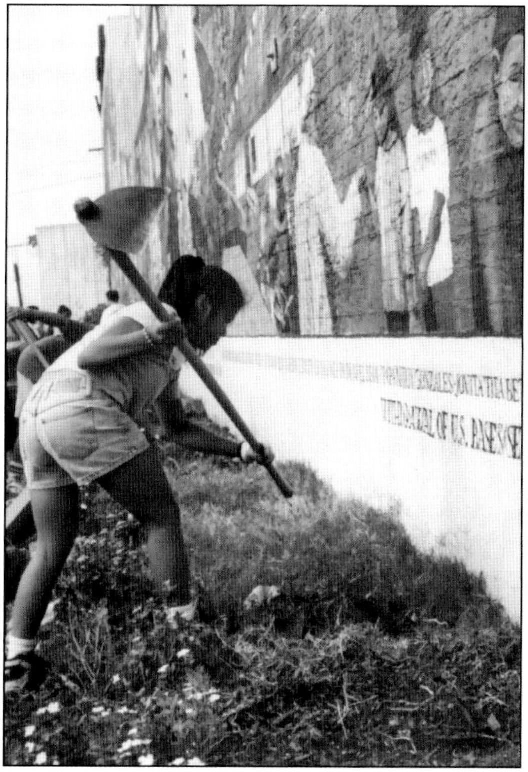

After vegetable gardening efforts waned, the park became a weed garden and had to be cleared annually. Pictured is a female University of California–Los Angeles (UCLA) student in 2000 with a hoe, clearing weeds that framed the base of the mural. (Courtesy of Carol Kimbrough.)

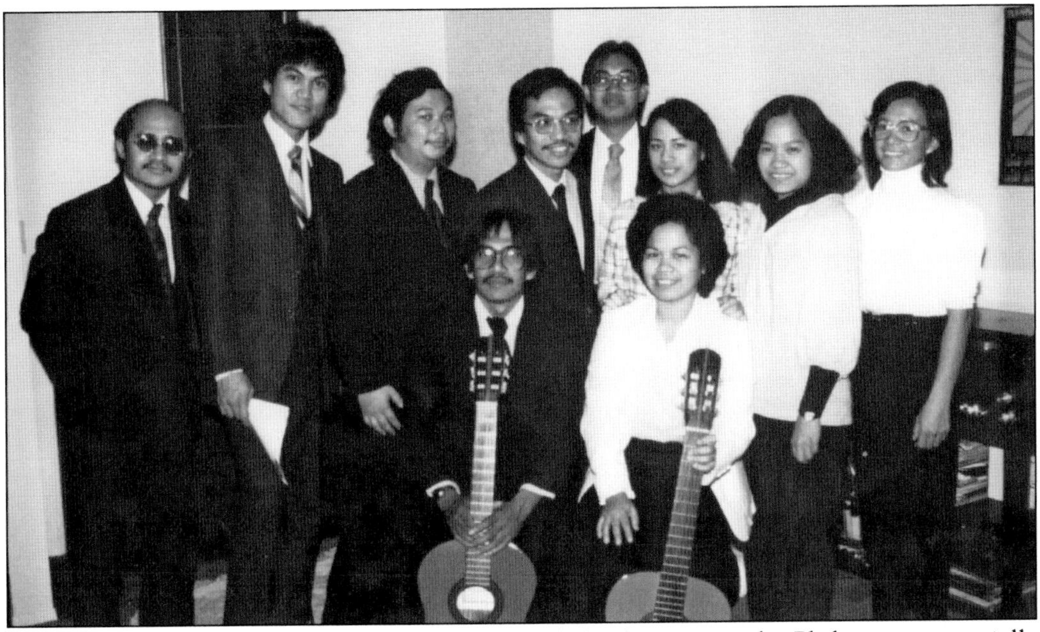

Christmas carolers in the 1980s raised money to help the poor in the Philippines, especially families of political prisoners who were the sole breadwinners of their families. Money raised was sent through church agencies working with nonprofit organizations in the Philippines. The carolers visited homes in various parts of Los Angeles, Orange, and Ventura Counties, singing traditional Christmas songs in English and Tagalog. (Courtesy of Carol Kimbrough.)

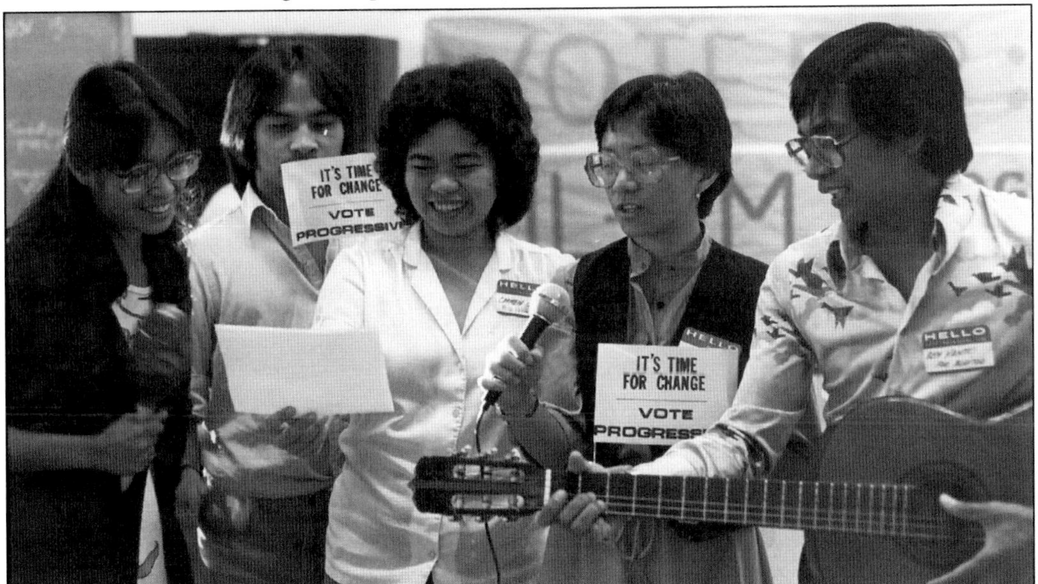

Pictured are Filipino community activists in the late 1970s who ran for office on a progressive slate led by attorney Bert Mendoza, challenging the then-incumbent Filipino American Community of Los Angeles (FACLA) president Antonio "Tony" San Jose. FACLA elections were in need of outside supervision, and Los Angeles councilmember Jackie Goldberg assigned one of her staff to monitor the elections. Pictured from left to right are Maria Abadesco, Jerry Espejo, Carol Kimbrough, Maribel Yanto, and Ben Yanto. (Courtesy of Carol Kimbrough.)

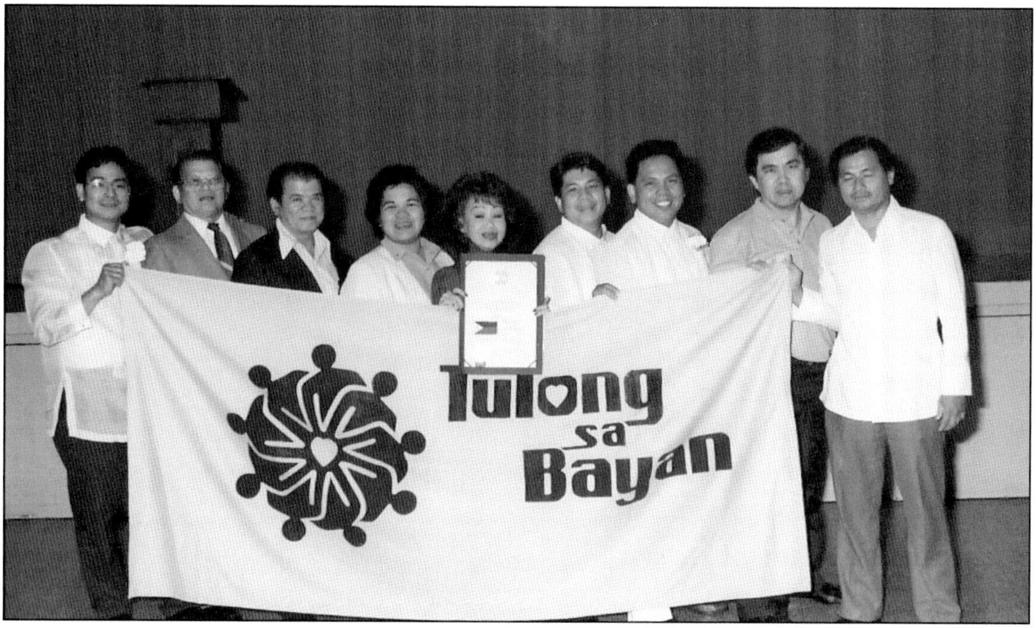

The Tulong Sa Bayan (Aid to the Philippines) group was formed in 1986. Its main cause was to provide monetary and in-kind support to the Philippines, especially to areas hard hit by natural disasters. Pictured is an installation dinner for new officers; they were recognized by the Philippine government and by Los Angeles County supervisor Gloria Molina. (Courtesy of Carol Kimbrough.)

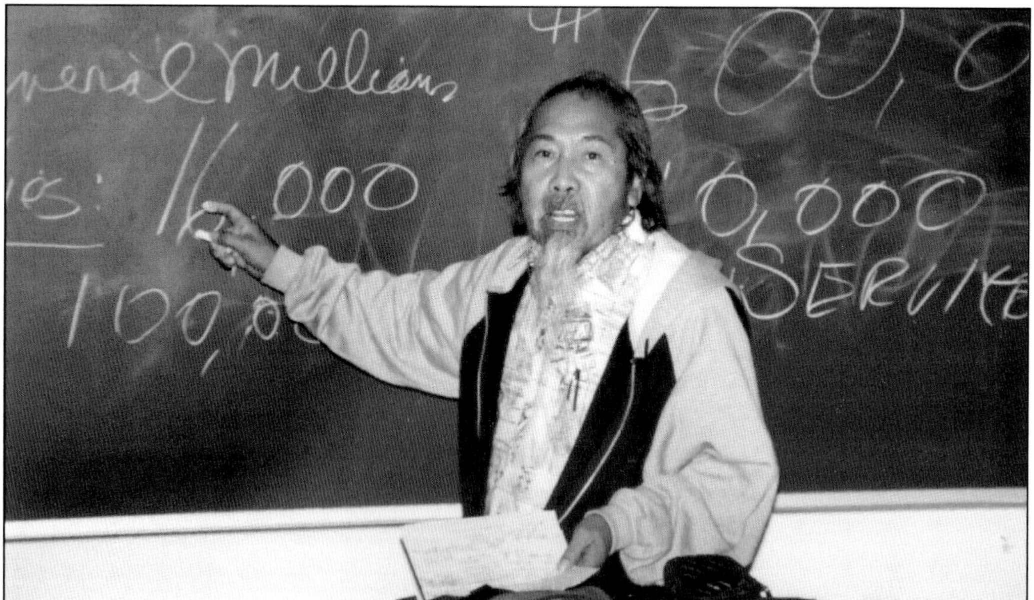

Pictured is Roy Morales in the 1990s. Morales was an extraordinary Filipino community activist who cofounded several nonprofit organizations in Los Angeles and devised a tour of Los Angeles's Little Manila for his Pilipino American Experience classes, which he taught at several local campuses for more than 15 years. He authored the book *Makibaka: The Pilipino American Struggle*. *Makibaka* means "to fight." (Courtesy of Ann Morales.)

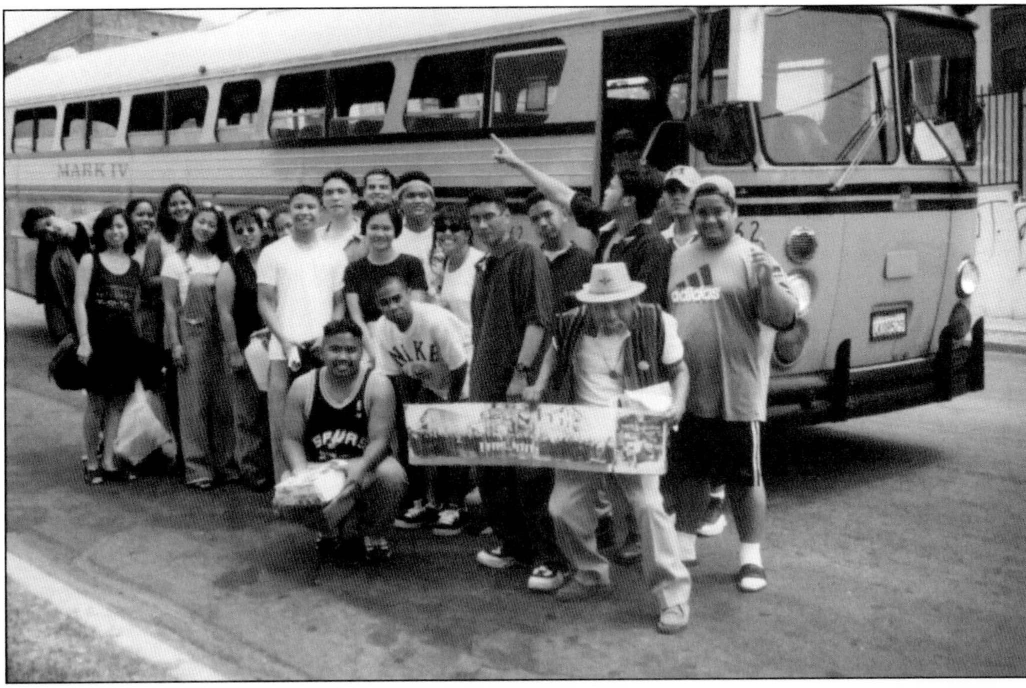

Above, Roy Morales (front, holding photograph) is seen in the 1990s leading one of his Pilipino American Experience classes on the "Little Manila" tour in Los Angeles. At right is Gerald Gubatan (right) with Roy Morales in front of the mural *Gintong Kasaysayan, Gintong Pamana* during the Little Manila tour. (Both, courtesy of Ann Morales.)

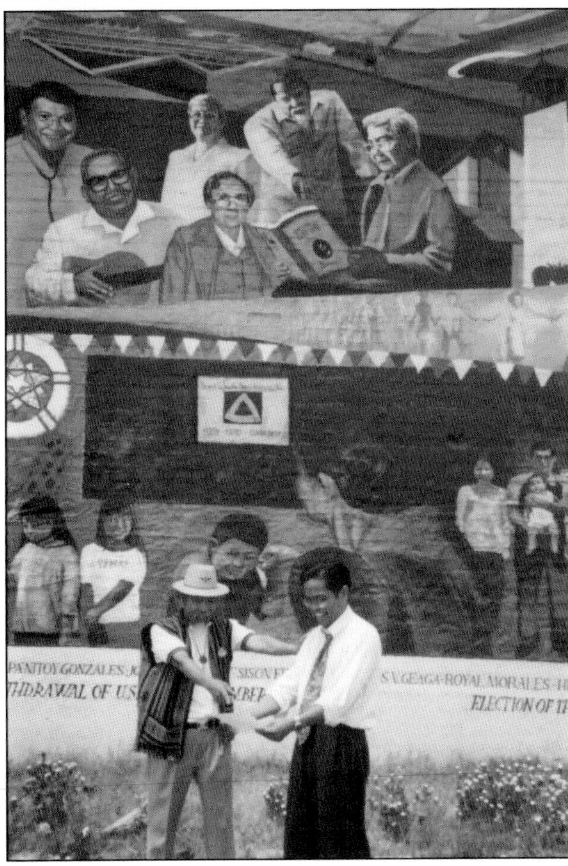

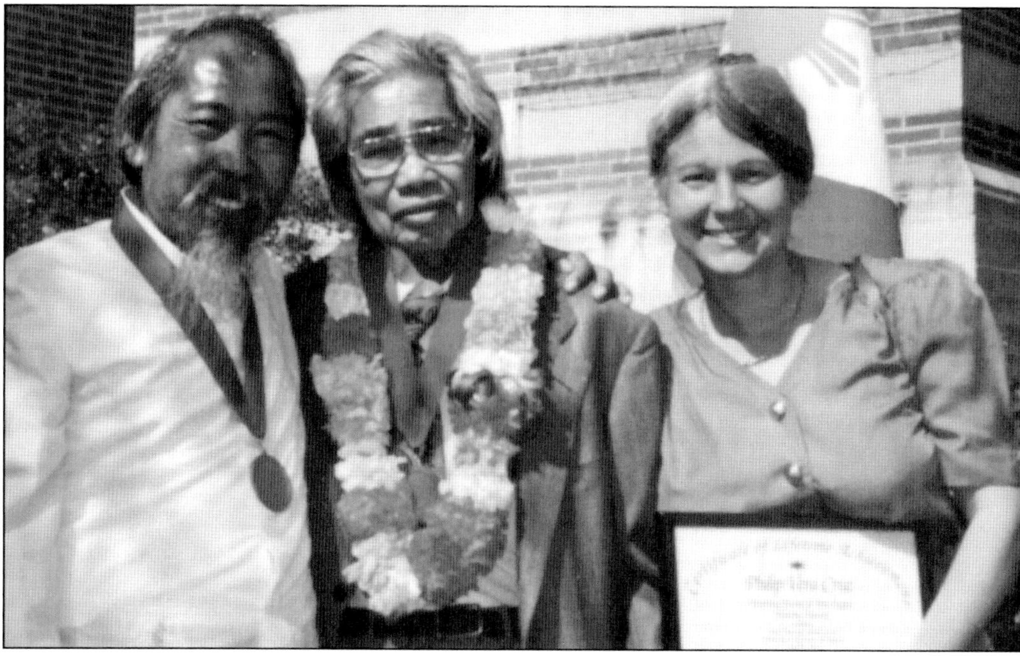

Pictured in the late 1990s are, from left to right, community activist Roy Morales; Philip Vera Cruz, vice president of United Farm Workers Association; and Philip's wife, Deborah A. Vollmer. Philip was awarded a Certificate of Lifetime Achievement for his years of work as a Filipino American labor leader and farm worker. (Courtesy of Ann Morales.)

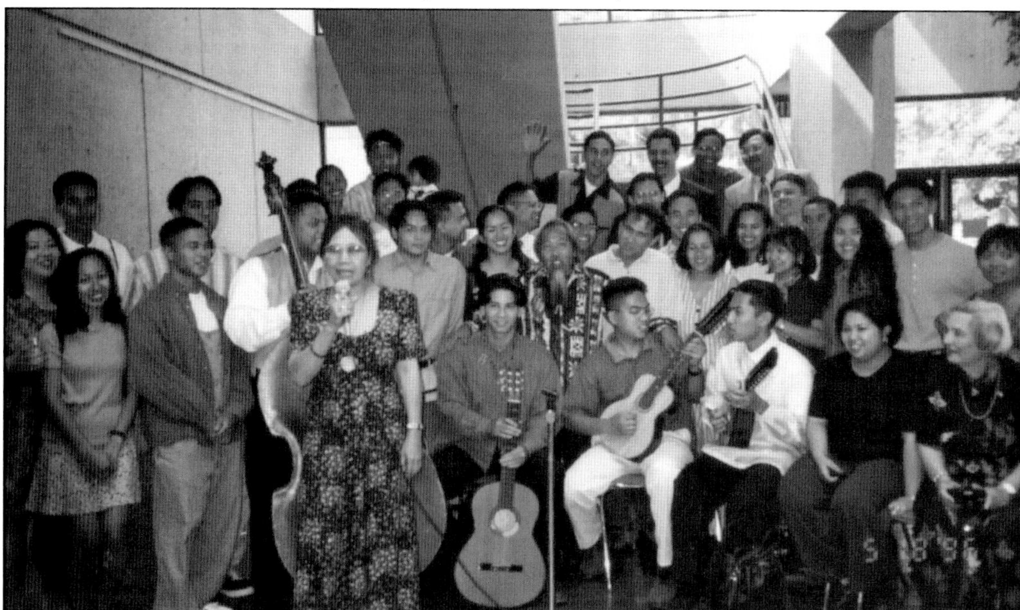

Family, friends, and students celebrate Roy Morales's retirement at an event held at UCLA and sponsored by UCLA Asian American Studies Center, Pilipino Alumni Association of UCLA, and the UCLA Alumni Association in 1996. For two decades, Roy Morales taught a class entitled Pilipino American Experience, incorporating a visual tour using vintage photographs of the original Little Manila and Bunker Hill areas. (Courtesy of Ann Morales.)

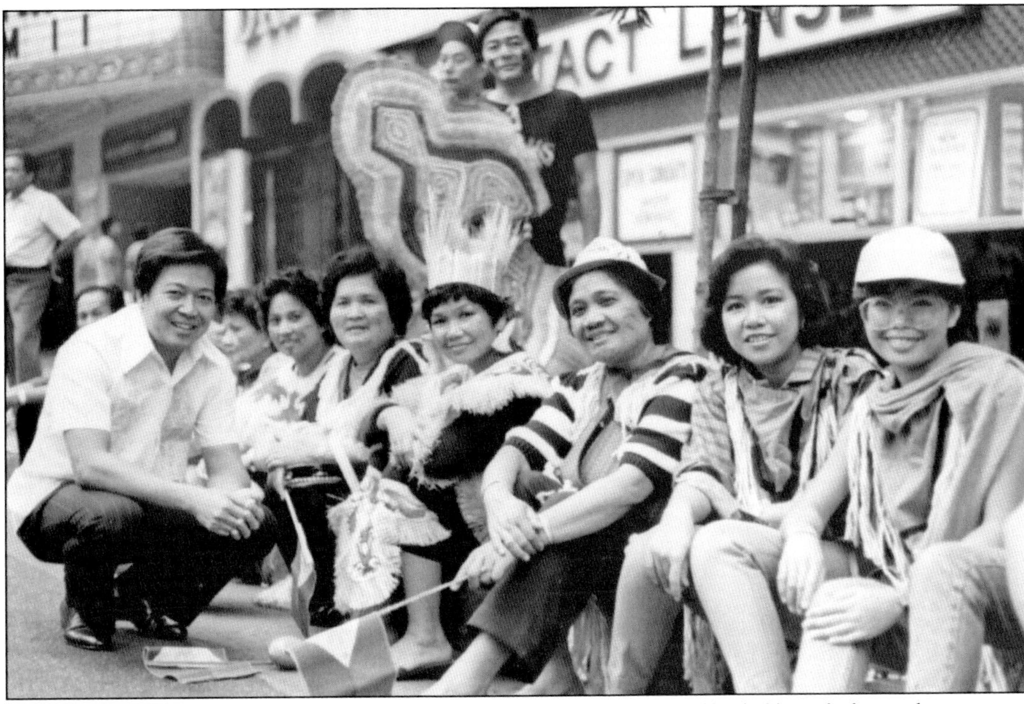

Pictured is Filipino community leader and activist Edgar O. Yap (far left) with festival spectators at the Filipino Heritage Festival, which was sponsored by the Bayanihan Jaycees of Los Angeles in the late 1980s. Held in the Temple-Beverly corridor, the festival included a parade and street dancers, and featured a queen of the festival. (Courtesy of Jonathan Yap.)

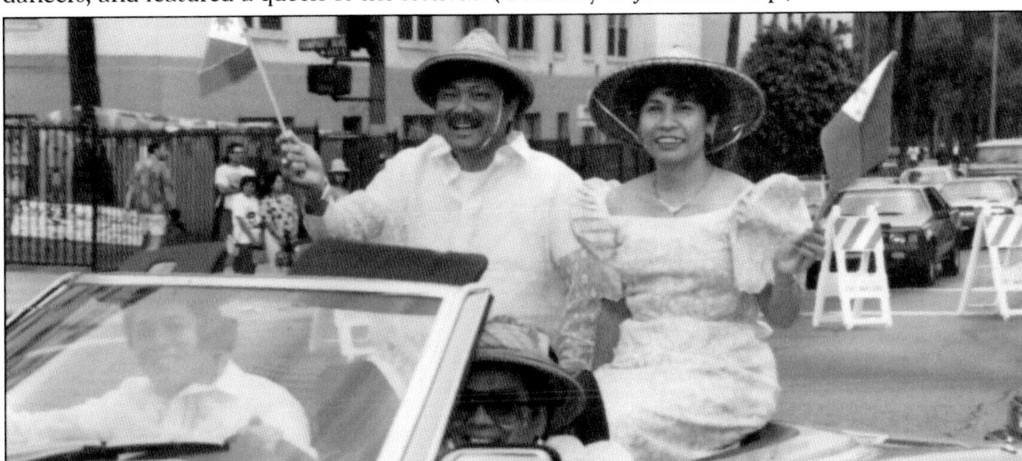

Filipino community leaders Valente and Cecile Ramos are seen here in the late 1980s at the Filipino Heritage Festival. A highlight of the festival's parade is the "Hermano and Hermana" of the festival—a title given to those who have significantly contributed to the enrichment of the lives of Filipinos in the community while keeping Filipino cultural traditions and values alive. The Ramoses were bestowed the titles. Valente and Cecile founded VGR and Associates, which developed the Burlington School in 1974, Luzon Plaza, and the Villa Ramos, Mountain View Terrace, and Manila Terrace apartments in Historic Filipinotown. (Courtesy of Cecile Ramos.)

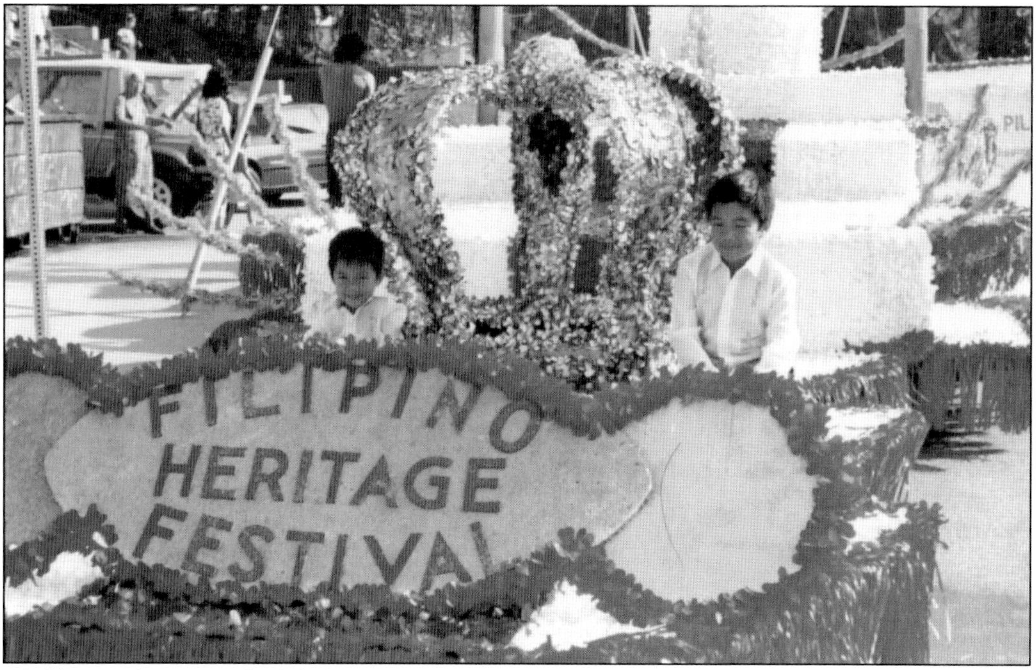

Children ride on a colorful, decorated float at the Los Angeles Filipino Heritage Festival in the 1980s. The festival was celebrated in the Temple-Beverly corridor. (Courtesy of Joselyn Geaga-Rosenthal.)

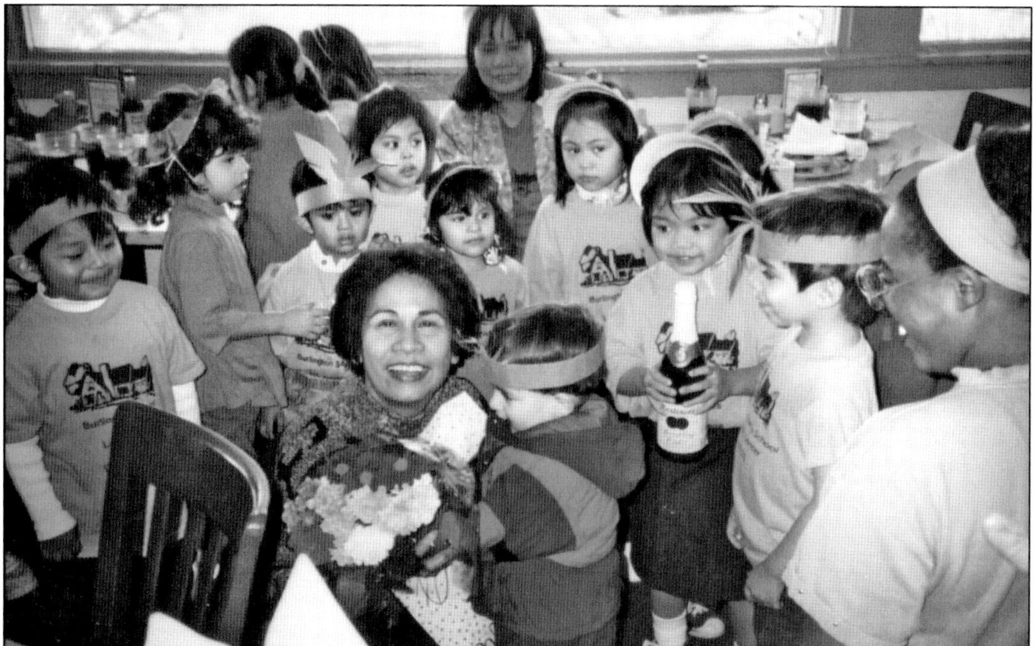
Pictured is Cecile Ramos, founder and school administrator of the Burlington School, with young preschool and grade-school children in the 1990s. Founded in 1974, the Burlington School is a private child care center, preschool, and grade school. It incorporates Filipino history, language, and culture as part of its curriculum. (Courtesy of Cecile Ramos.)

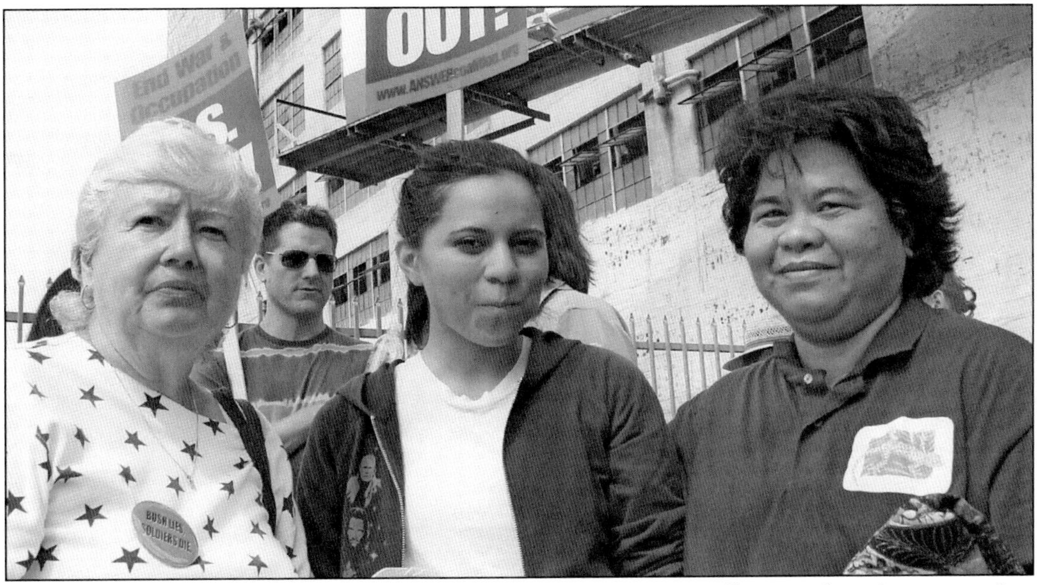

Three generations of community activists are seen at a peace rally staged in downtown Los Angeles in 2003. Suzanne Kimbrough (left) is a longtime resident of Echo Park and is active with the Echo Park Neighborhood Council and Improvement Association. She is the grandmother of Sarah Ojeda Kimbrough, a student, (center) and mother-in-law of Carol Kimbrough (right), a lecturer at California State University–Fullerton in the Asian American studies program and a former field deputy to Los Angeles councilmember Jackie Goldberg of District 13. (Courtesy of Carol Kimbrough.)

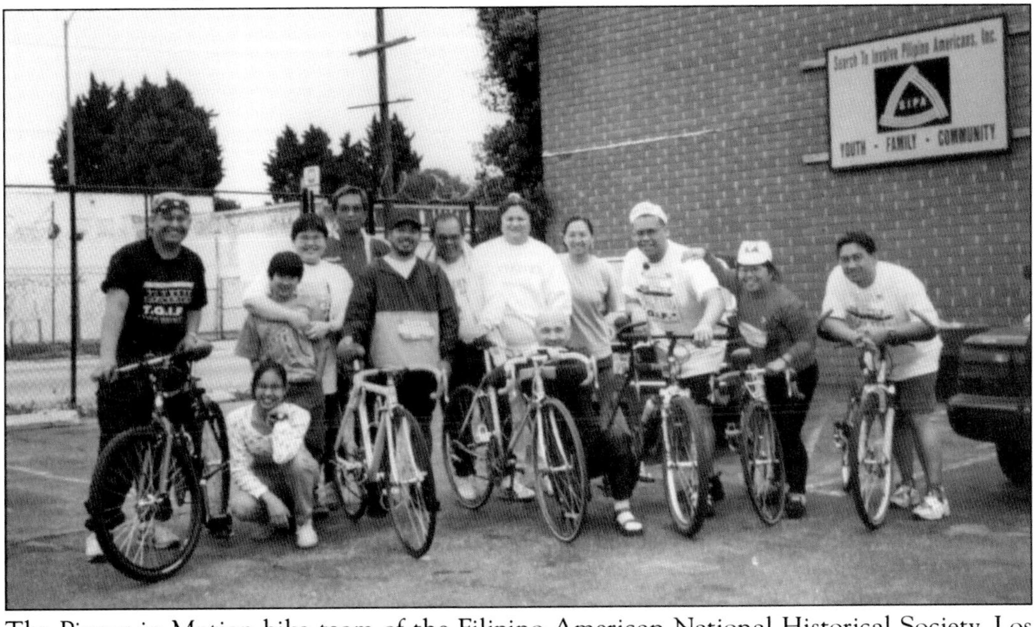

The Pinoys in Motion bike team of the Filipino American National Historical Society, Los Angeles Chapter, participated in the 1998 Los Angeles Marathon bike tour. From left to right are Johann Diel, Corina de la Cruz, Carlo de la Cruz, Prosy Abarquez-Delacruz, Enrique B. de la Cruz, Raul Ebio, Sam Balucas, Meg Malpaya Thornton, Anna Gonzalez, Gil Ayuyao Ray Japor, Nora Custodio, and Florante Ibanez. (Courtesy of Prosy Abarquez-Delacruz.)

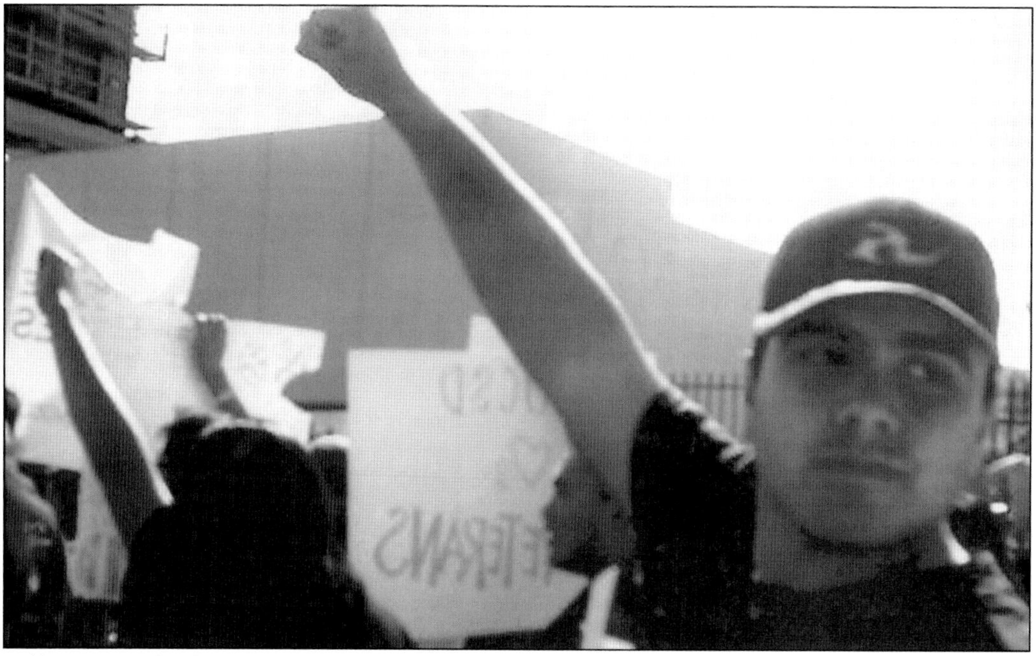

Following in the footsteps of his mother, Filipina community activist Carol Kimbrough, Daniel Kimbrough shows his support for justice for the Filipino veterans of World War II. In this photograph, Daniel is a participant in a rally held in downtown Los Angeles to support legislation that would give Filipino veterans the benefits promised them in 1942 but rescinded in 1946. (Courtesy of Carol Kimbrough.)

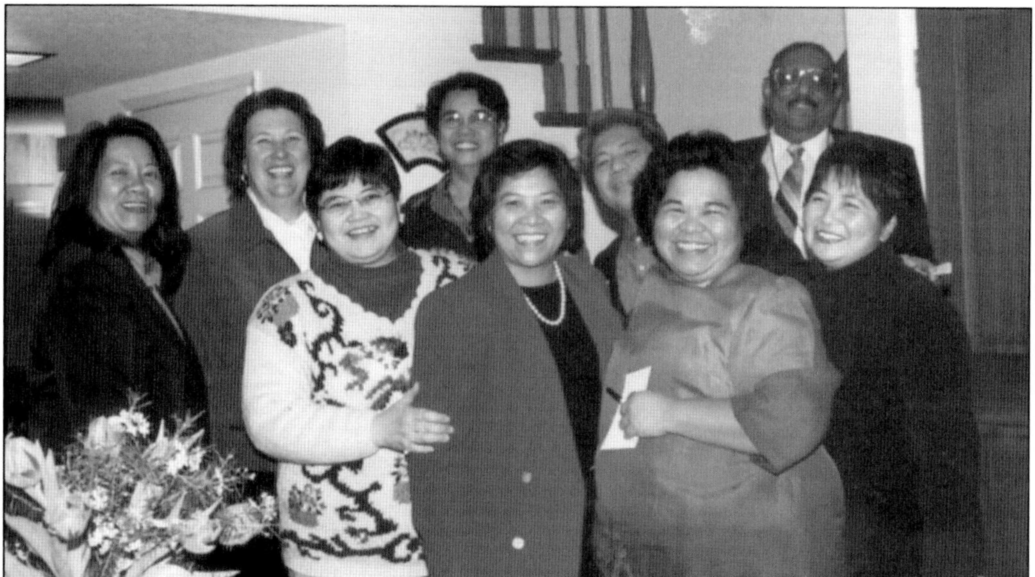

A fund-raising event for Los Angeles councilmember Jackie Goldberg was held at the home of Edmund Soo Hoo in Los Angeles. The group called themselves PAJAK (Pilipino Americans for Jackie Goldberg). Pictured from left to right are (first row) Prosy Abarquez-Delacruz, Susan Araneta, Carol Kimbrough, and Annie Villero; (second row) Rose Ibanez, Jackie Goldberg, Ruby De Vera, Jerry Villero, and John Mills. (Courtesy of Carol Kimbrough.)

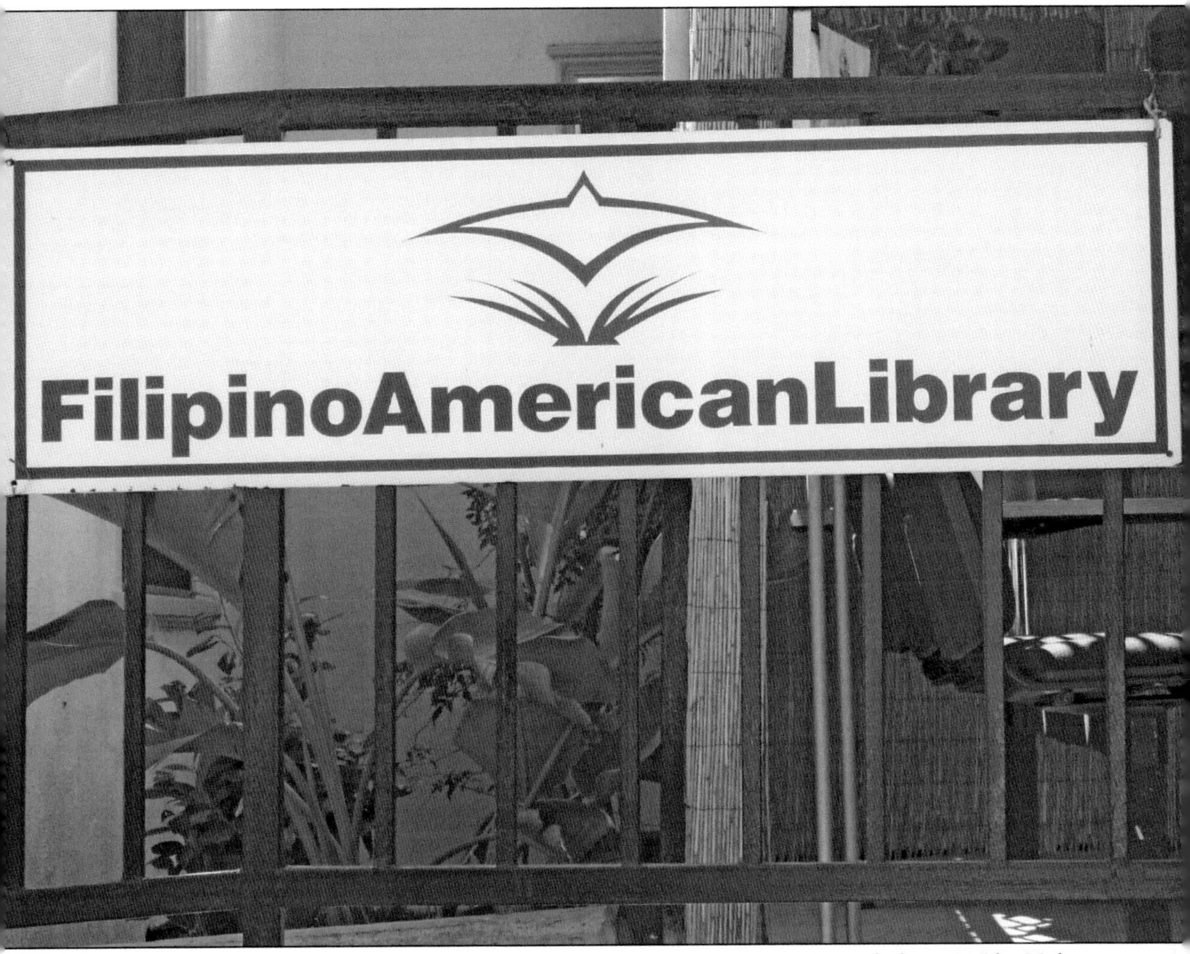

The Filipino American Library is the first Filipino library in America. Founded in 1985 by Helen Summers Brown, with the help of Roy Morales, the library was originally named the Pilipino American Reading Room and Library. In 1989, it was administered by the Pamana Foundation, and in 1999, the Filipino American Heritage Institute, a nonprofit cultural and educational organization dedicated to preserving the Filipino American heritage, assumed the administration of the library. Its mission is to "actively promote the history, culture, and professional achievements of Filipinos and Filipino Americans through the book collection, leadership development, and cultural programming." The library offers extensive information on Filipino history, Filipino American culture, education, and community issues and events. It has a collection of thousands of titles, including books, pamphlets, periodicals, and dissertations. In the main reading room, there are designated shelves containing books on World War II, Jose Rizal, Philippine arts and culture, and martial arts, as well as bilingual English-Tagalog books. (Courtesy of the author.)

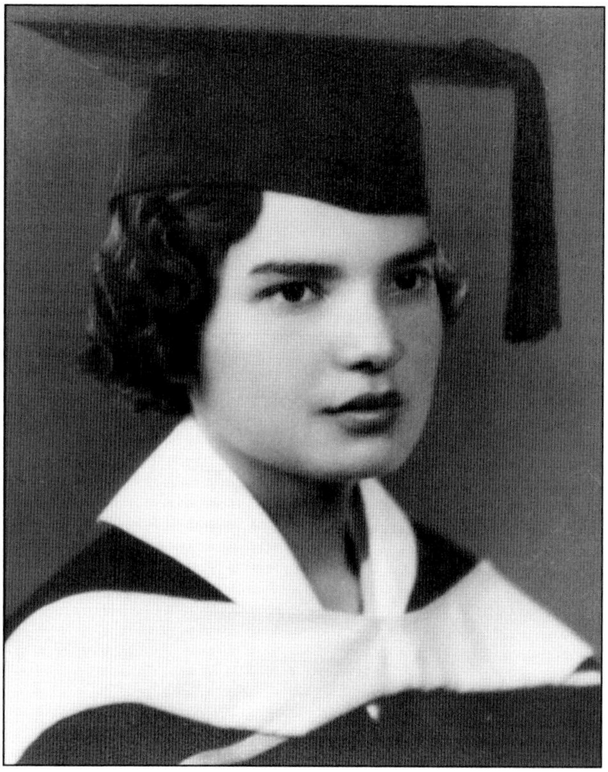

This graduation portrait of Helen Summers Brown was taken in the 1930s. Affectionately called "Auntie Helen," she founded the Filipino American Library. When she inherited her father's extensive library collection, she continued to add to it by collecting any and all books, pamphlets, newsletters, newspaper clippings, and souvenir programs from annual balls and galas of various Filipino organizations. Her private collection became well known among both the Los Angeles school district and the Filipino community, resulting in its recognition as one of the primary sources on Filipino matters. (Courtesy of the Filipino American Library.)

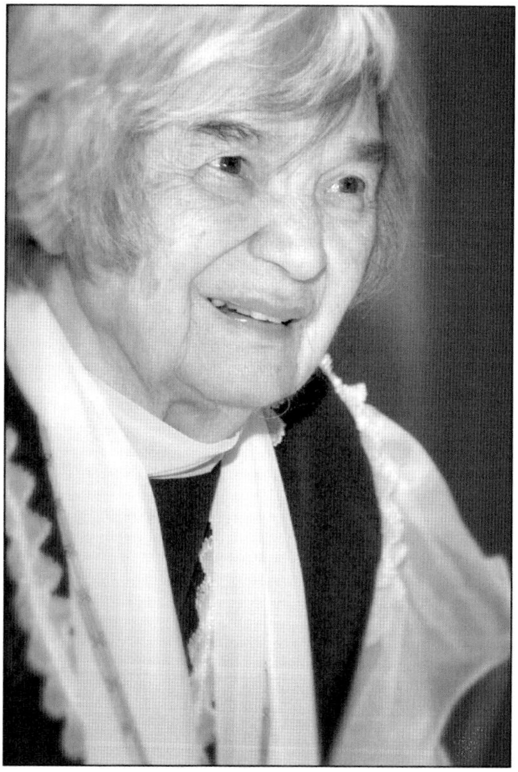

Pictured in the 21st century, Helen is in her 90s and is enjoying retirement, but she is occasionally seen in and around Historic Filipinotown. (Courtesy of the Filipino American Library.)

In 2008, the Filipino American Library got a decorative ethnic makeover with the addition of bamboo, installed at the entrance and in the back of the building. (Courtesy of Steven De La Vega.)

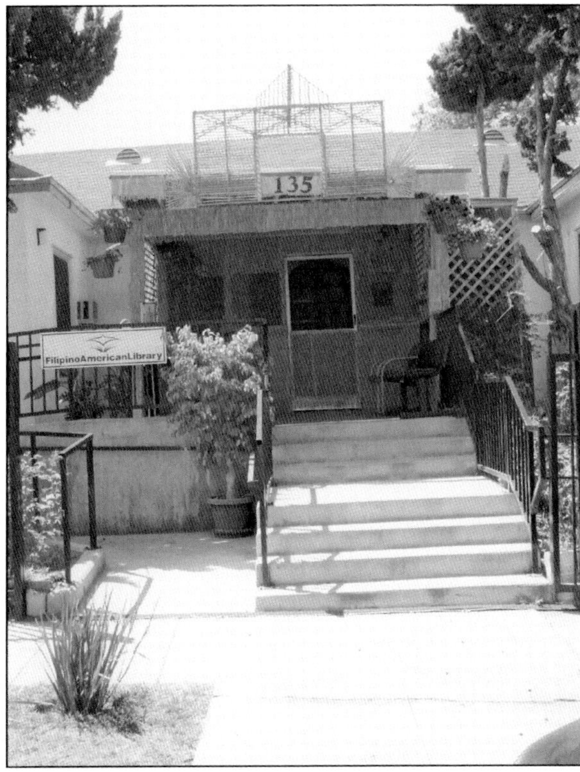

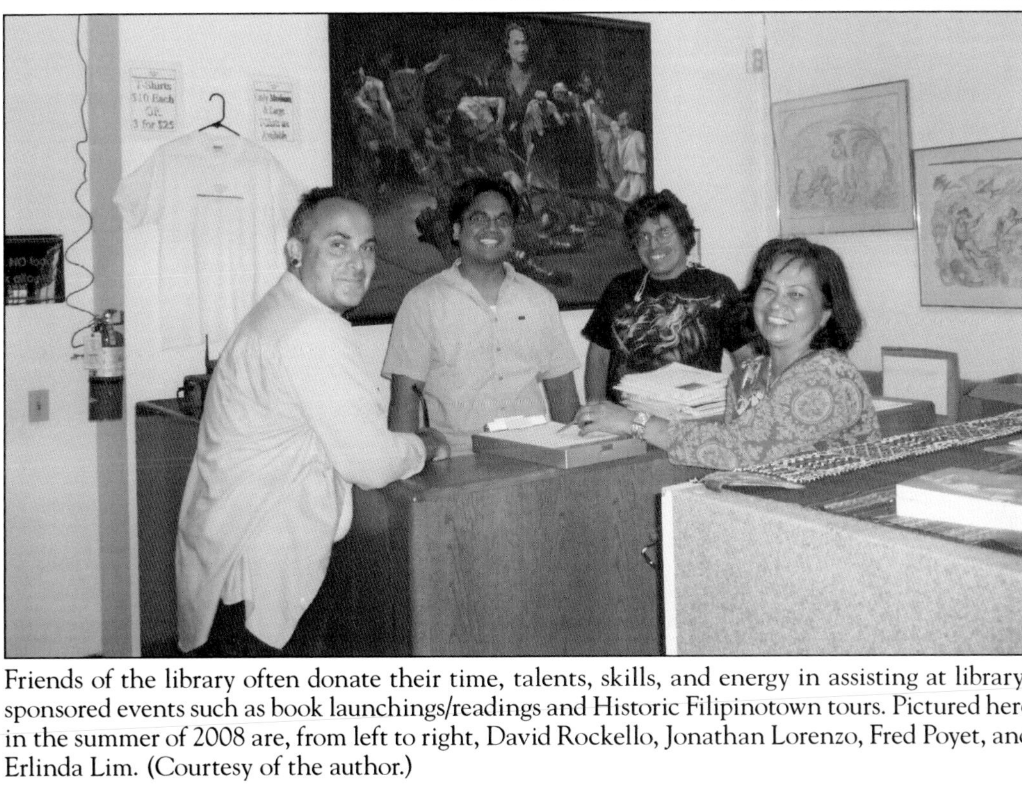

Friends of the library often donate their time, talents, skills, and energy in assisting at library-sponsored events such as book launchings/readings and Historic Filipinotown tours. Pictured here in the summer of 2008 are, from left to right, David Rockello, Jonathan Lorenzo, Fred Poyet, and Erlinda Lim. (Courtesy of the author.)

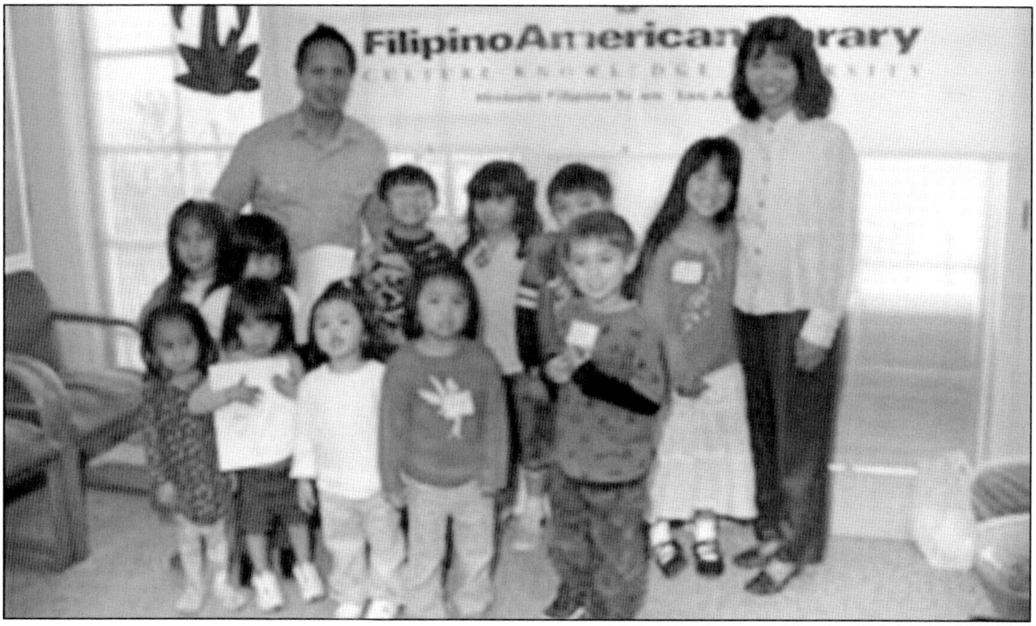

The Filipino American Library hosts a popular Children's Reading Program coordinated by Celeste B. Diaz, the Filipino American Library's librarian. Children are introduced to works by Filipino authors and illustrators. The program promotes the value of diversity to children through the reading of Filipino books, storytelling, and participation in art and culture-themed learning projects. (Courtesy of Florante Ibanez.)

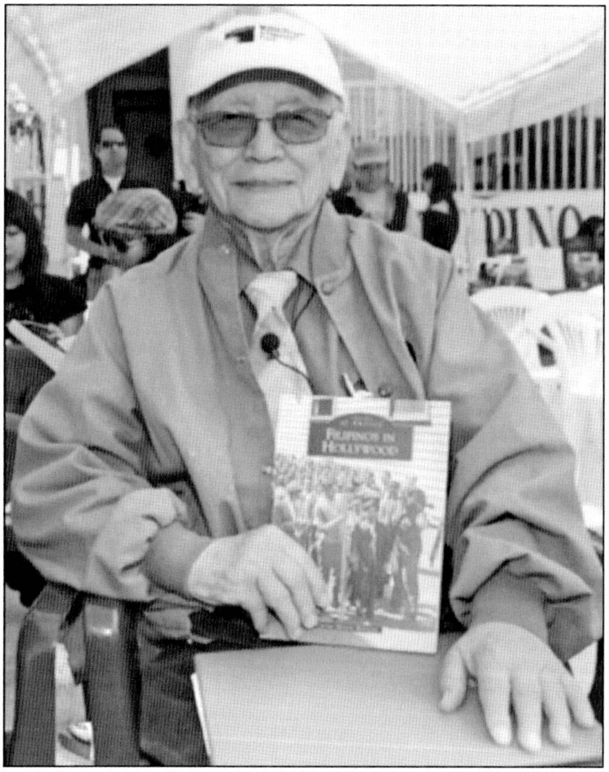

With the generous support of community sponsors, the Filipino American Library hosts book launchings and readings. Pictured is 90-plus-year-old Ben Resella at the book launching of *Filipinos in Hollywood* in March 2008. Ben Resella is an award-winning scene designer for his work on various Hollywood sets. (Courtesy of Sthanlee B. Mirador.)

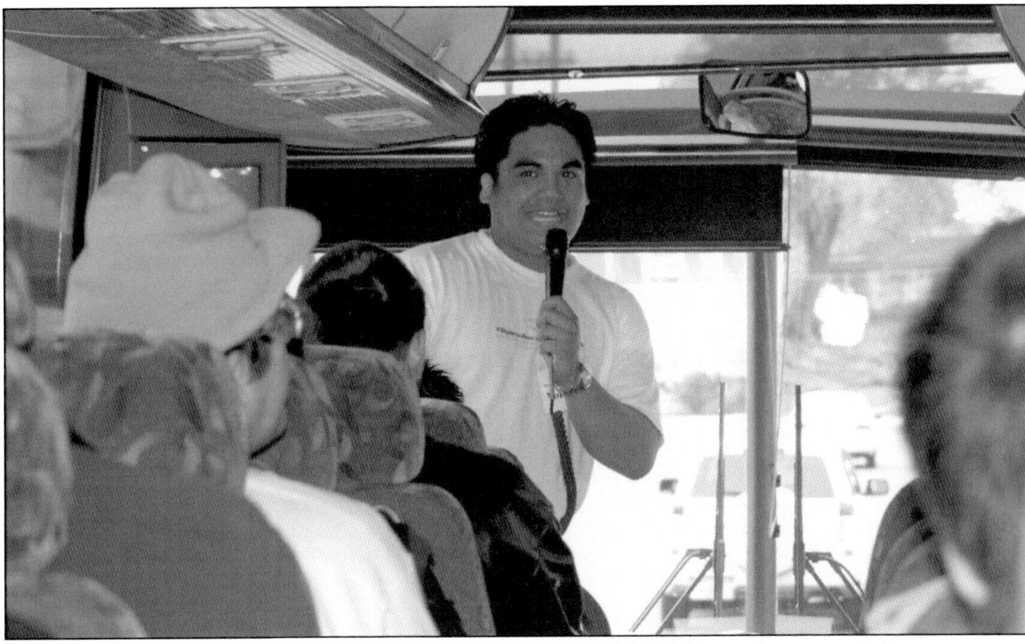

Jonathan Lorenzo (holding microphone), administrator of the Filipino American Library, narrates a Historic Filipinotown tour in 2007. Operating on donations, the library hosts free, narrated bus tours. The tour focuses on significant areas, sites, events, and individuals in and around the Temple-Beverly corridor, as well as the contributions key individuals have made in the community. The tour is in keeping with the spirit of Roy "Uncle Roy" Morales, who was the first to develop the tour of Little Manila and Historic Filipinotown, and who devoted most of his life in support of the Filipino American experience. (Courtesy of Florante Ibanez.)

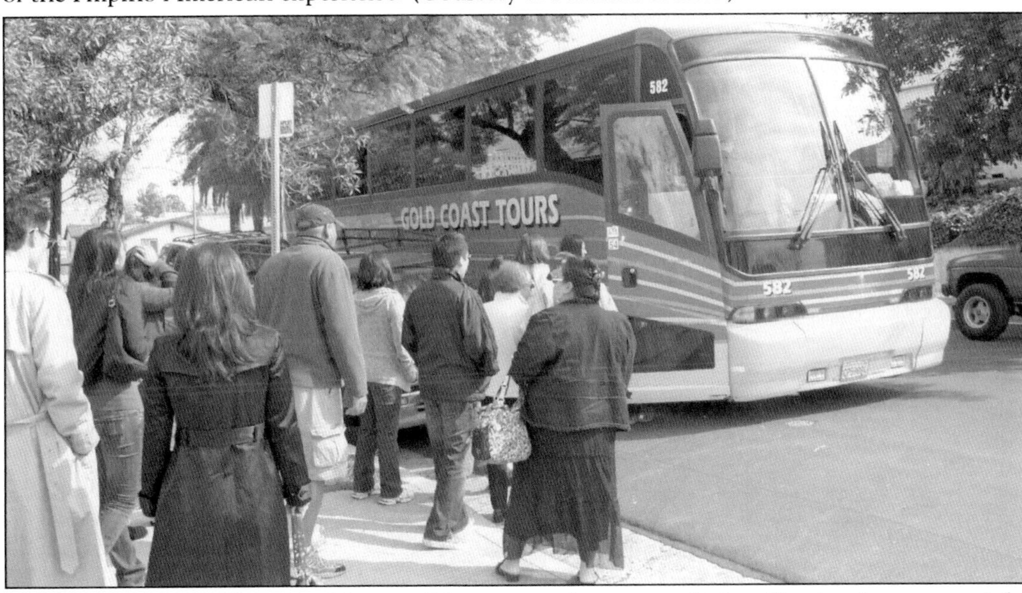

People are seen boarding the Historic Filipinotown bus tour, which will take them around the Temple-Beverly corridor. The tour's main goal is to answer the question, "What is Filipino about Historic Filipinotown?" The tour takes approximately one hour and concludes with a complimentary light lunch at the library. (Courtesy of Florante Ibanez.)

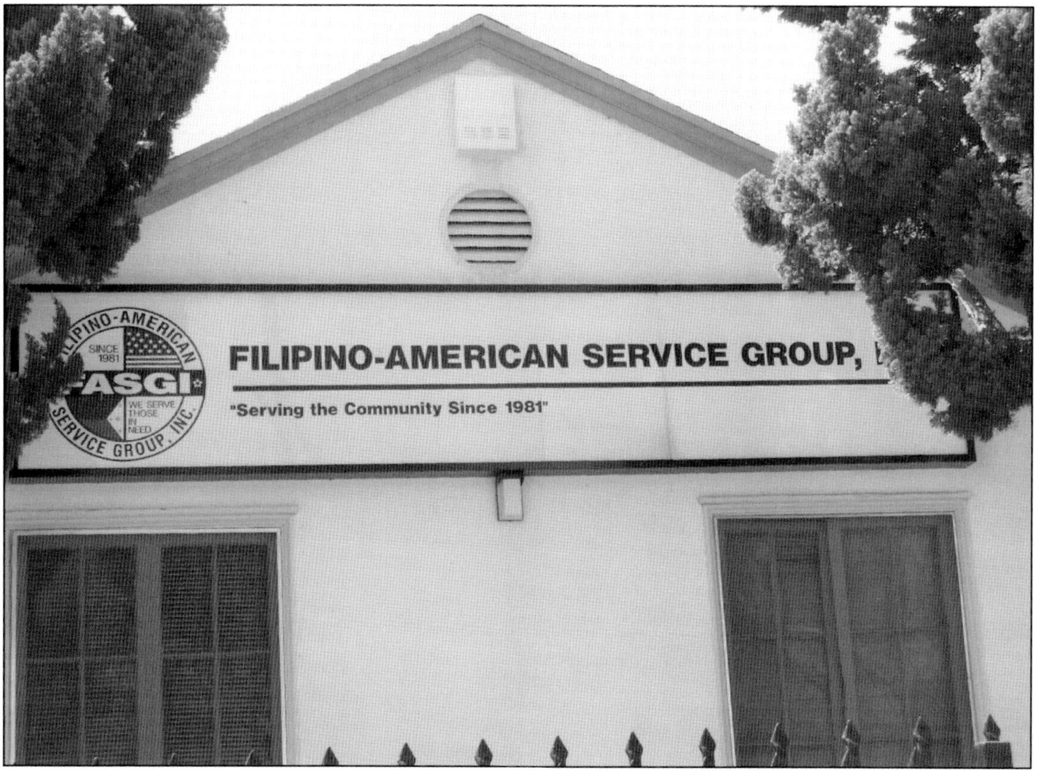

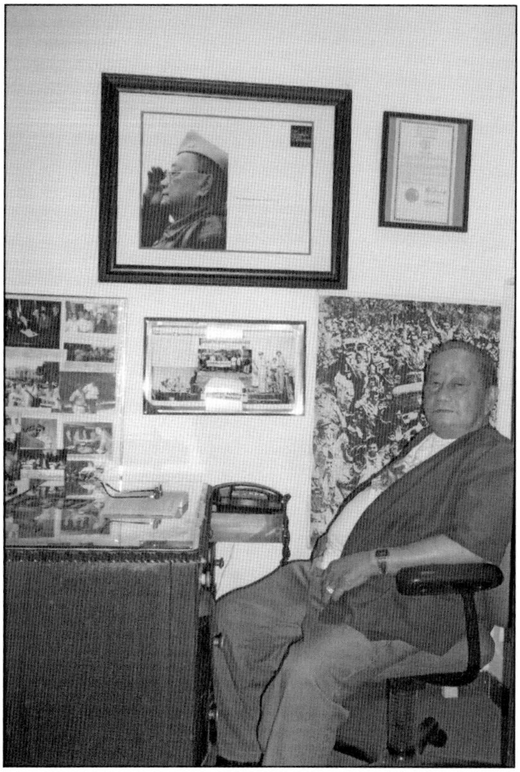

The Filipino-American Service Group, Inc., (FASGI) is one of the community's invaluable nonprofit organizations. Founded in 1981, it offers a wide range of services, including, but not limited to, crisis intervention, mental health counseling and referral, life skills training, and promotion of independent living. One of its contributions is its active social action in health advocacy and civic affairs, such as the equity campaign for Filipino World War II veterans. (Courtesy of the author.)

Faustino "Peping" Baclig is surrounded by photographs and awards for his involvement in, and his long quest for, equal rights for Filipino veterans' benefits as promised to them in 1942. This Filipino American World War II veteran is a survivor of the infamous Bataan Death March. He was instrumental in the creation of the Filipino World War II Veterans Memorial in Historic Filipinotown, and despite his age, his activism and dedication to FASGI is tireless. (Courtesy of the author.)

Five

A Sign of Distinction

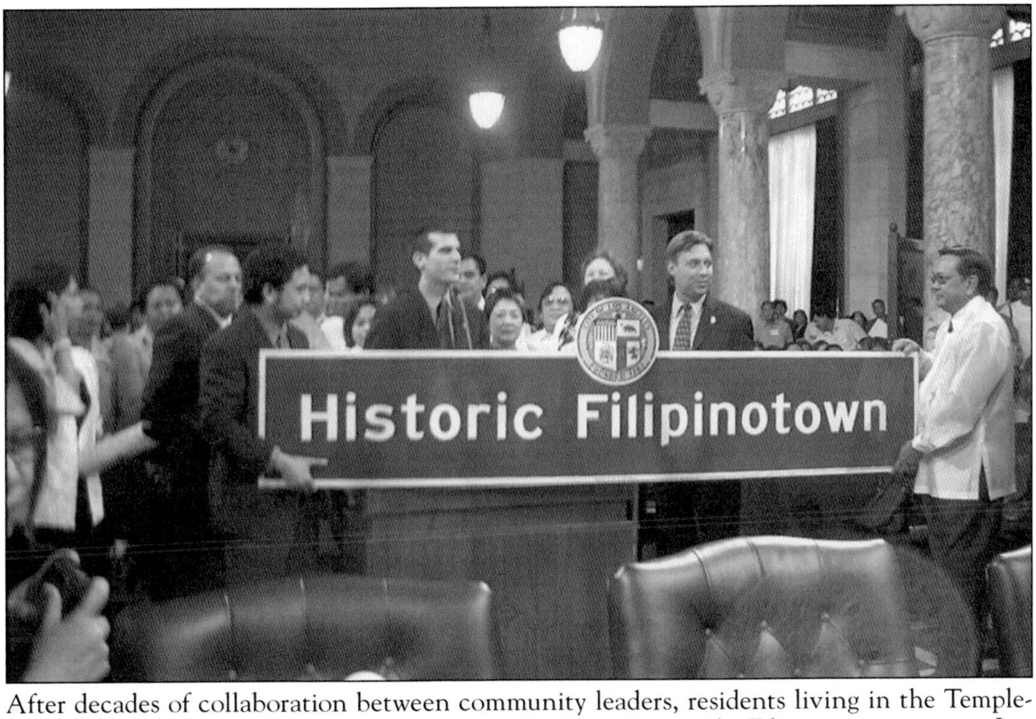

After decades of collaboration between community leaders, residents living in the Temple-Beverly corridor, business owners, and community organizations, the Filipino community in Los Angeles finally succeeded in obtaining an official designation of the Temple-Beverly corridor on August 2, 2002 as Historic Filipinotown. The designation acknowledged the Filipinos' tireless efforts to preserve and share the long history of their presence and experiences in Los Angeles. (Courtesy of Ernie Pena.)

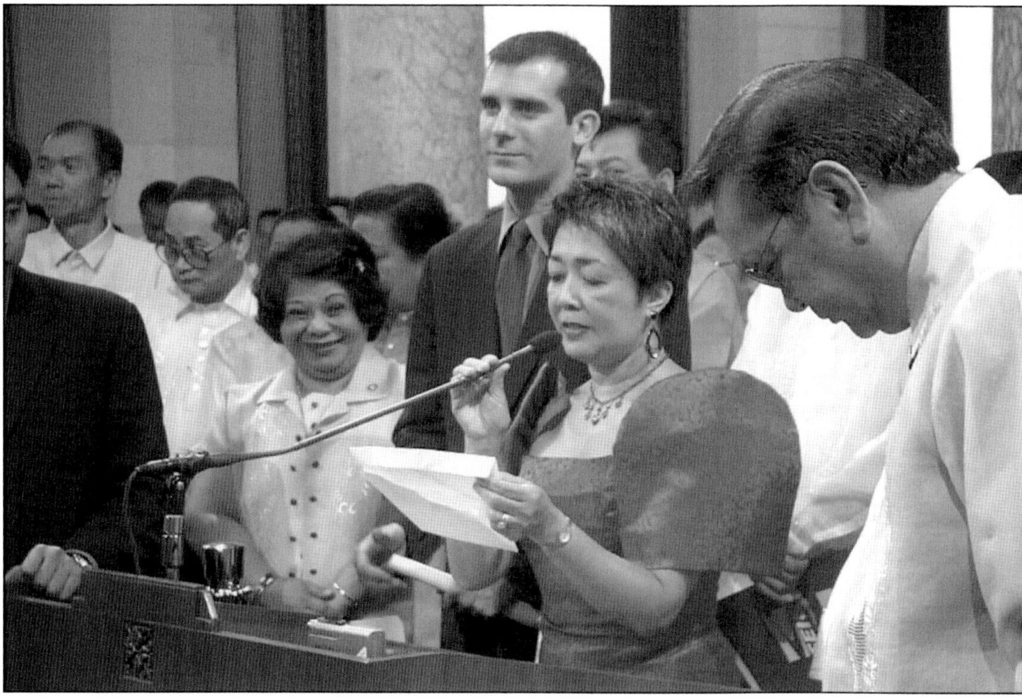

Above, Joselyn Geaga-Rosenthal (second from right), one of the Filipino community's notable leaders and activists, speaks at the ceremony during the official designation of Historic Filipinotown in 2002. Below, Filipino World War II veterans of the Los Angeles Filipino community attend the ceremony. (Both, courtesy of Elson Trinidad.)

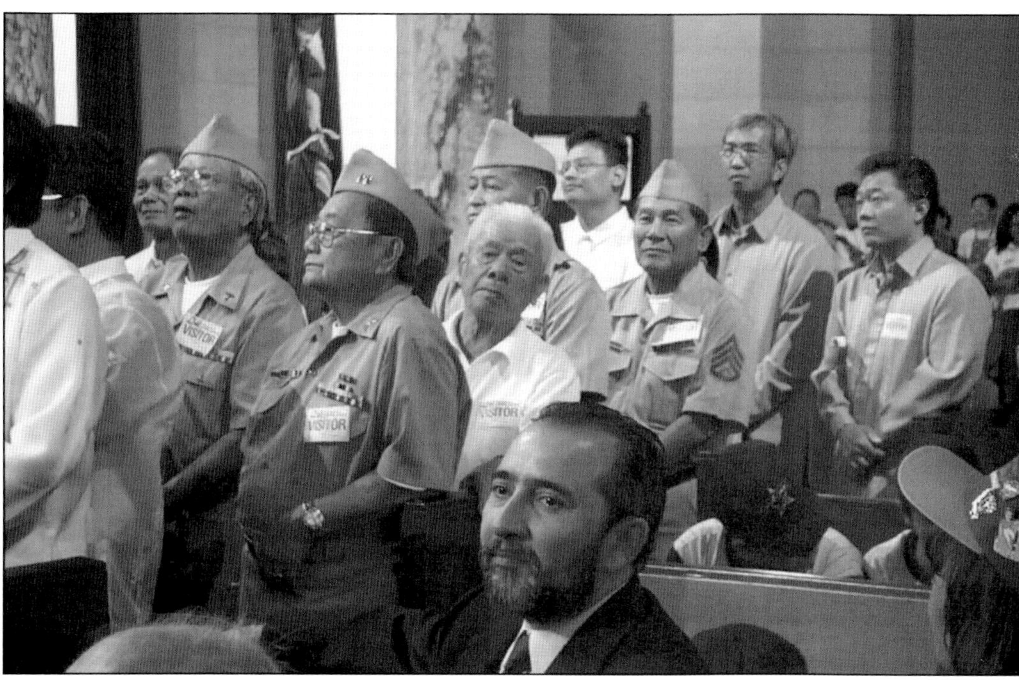

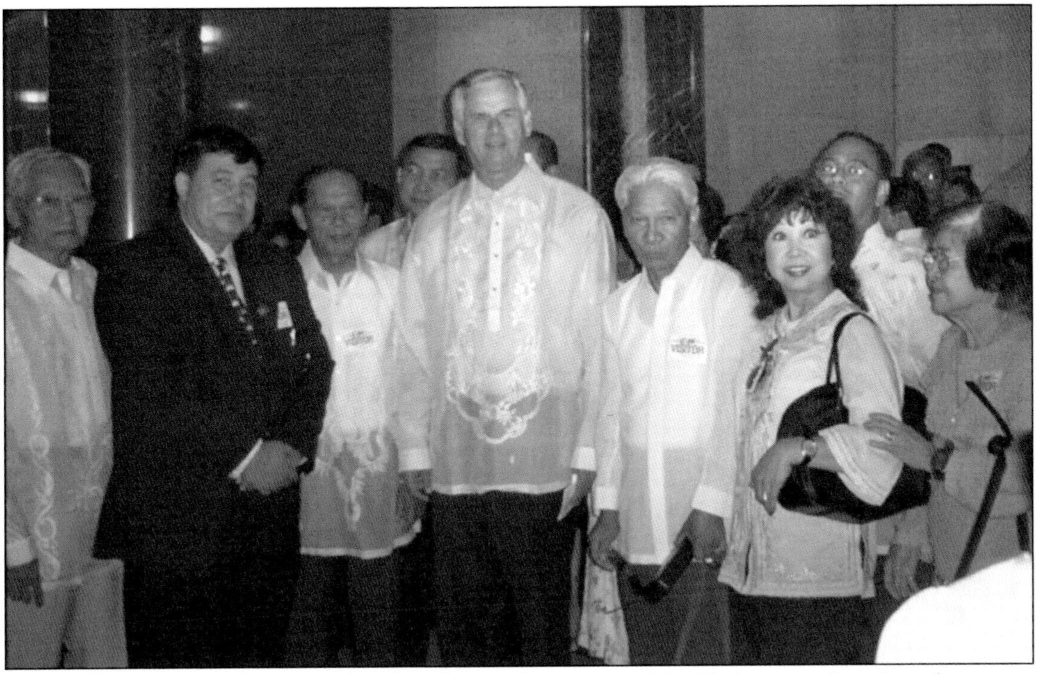

Wearing a *barong tagalog*, an embroidered formal garment of the Philippines, Los Angeles mayor James K. Kahn, (center) poses for this photograph with community leaders and members at the official designation of Historic Filipinotown ceremony held at city hall on August 2, 2002. (Courtesy of Elson Trinidad.)

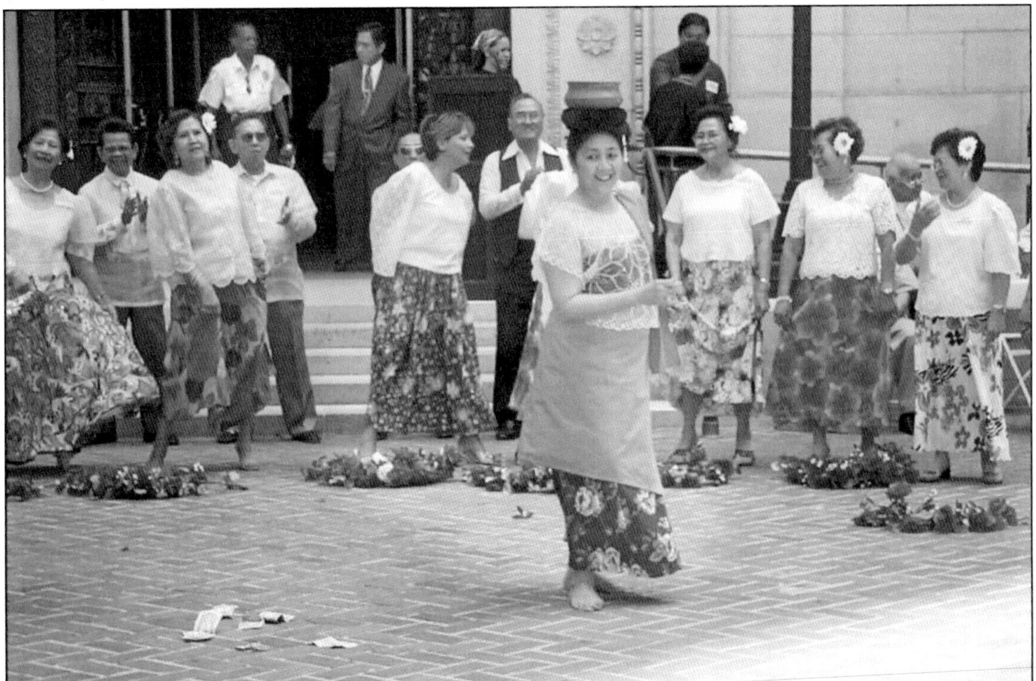

A traditional Filipino dance was featured as entertainment in celebration of the designation of Historic Filipinotown at city hall on August 2, 2002. (Courtesy of Elson Trinidad.)

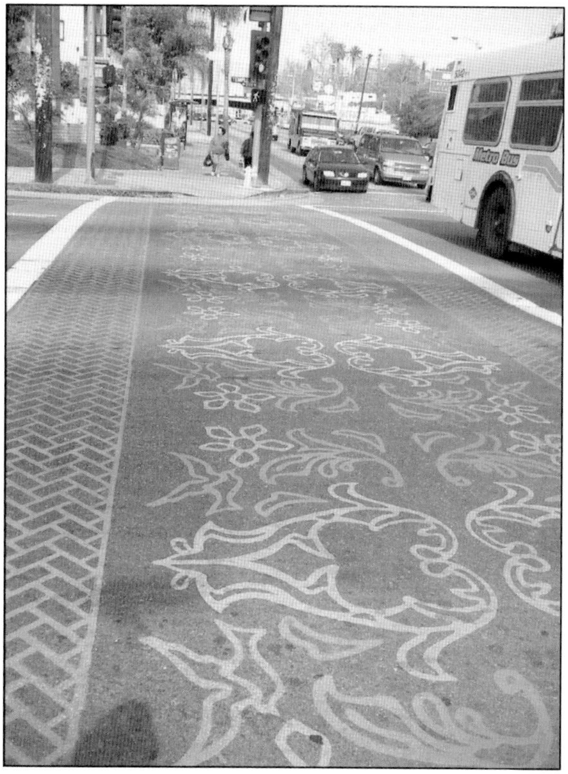

Pictured is the crosswalk at Temple and Alvardo Streets, which was designed by artist Erwin Federizo. His design incorporated traditional Filipino basket-weave patterns. The crosswalks were installed by the city's Bureau of Street Services at Temple Street and Glendale Boulevard and at Temple and Alvarado Streets as part of the Historic Filipinotown beautification project. (Courtesy of Debbie Sahagun.)

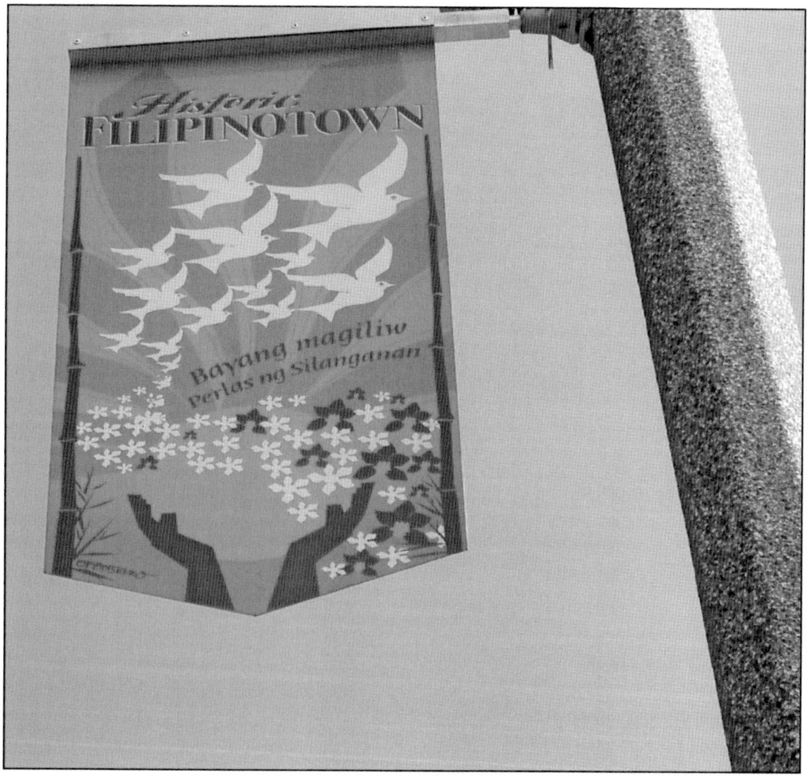

A Historic Filipinotown street banner boasts the words *Bayang magiliw Perlas ng Silanganan*, or "Beloved country, Pearl of the Orient." Banners are hung from streetlamps along major streets in Historic Filipinotown. (Courtesy of Debbie Sahagun.)

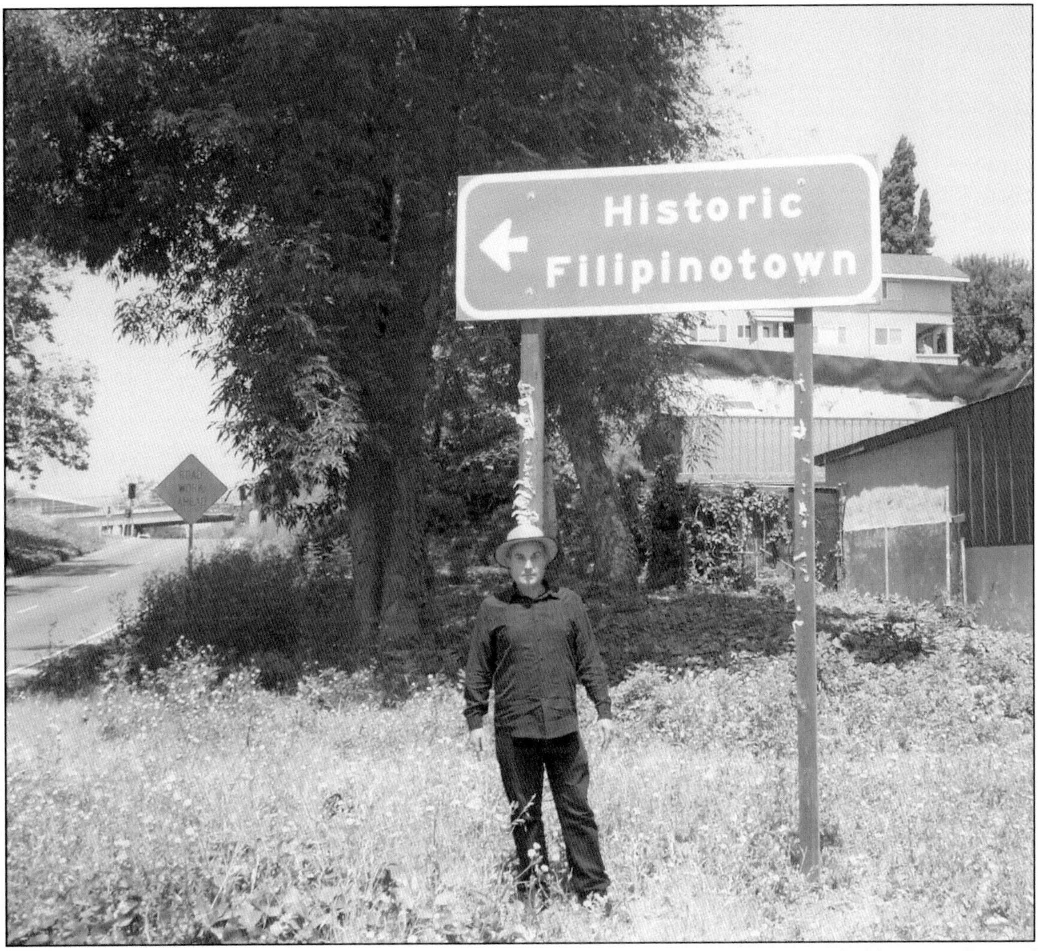

Pictured under the Historic Filipinotown freeway sign in 2008 is David Rockello, president of the Historic Filipinotown Improvement Association, vice president and chief information officer of the Historic Filipinotown Neighborhood Council (HiFiNC), and the elected vice president of the Greater Echo Park Elysian Neighborhood Council. Rockello's tireless dedication to the furtherance of Historic Filipinotown has been noteworthy. As the designer of the HiFiNC logo, he has displayed community activism and dedication to cultural community growth, among many other contributions that make him a fixture in and around Historic Filipinotown. Visible from U.S. 101 Freeway's Alvarado Street exit, this sign was unveiled by HiFiNC at the fourth anniversary festival celebration of the designation of Historic Filipinotown. The festival was sponsored by Pilipino American Network and Advocacy; Temple Westlake Neighborhood Development Corporation; Media Breakfast Club; Philippine Town, Inc.; Remy's on Temple; People's Core; Filipino American Service Group, Inc.; City of Angels Medical Center; Pilipino Workers' Center; Justice for Filipino American Veterans; the office of council president Eric Garcetti; the City of Los Angeles; and many other organizations and individuals. (Courtesy of Steven De La Vega.)

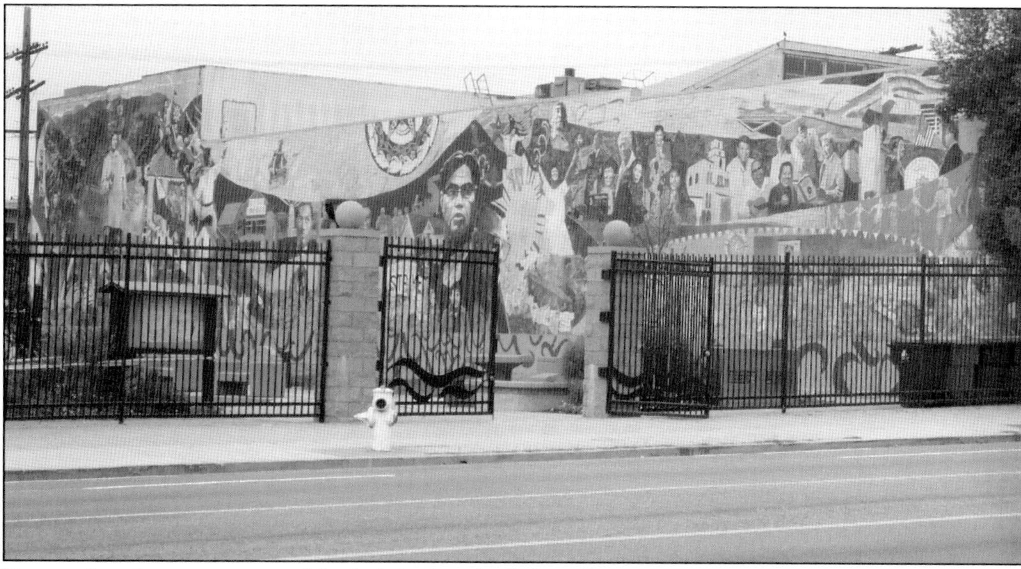

Pictured is the entrance to Unidad Park, which has the *Gintong Kasaysayan, Gintong Pamana* mural. Opened in 2007, the park was designed by Historic Filipinotown leaders and conceptualized by artist Eliseo Art Silva. The park's pathway was designed in the shape similar to the yo-yo. In the 1920s, Pedro Flores, a Filipino immigrant, was credited for manufacturing the first yo-yos in the United States, which introduced the yo-yo craze in America. Below, the park also features design enhancements along a community garden and throughout the park that were adapted from the rice terraces found in the Philippine Cordilleras, a United Nations Educational, Science, and Cultural Organization (UNESCO) World Heritage Site. The circular space in the center represents the *dap-ay*, a communal gathering place that is the social, educational, and tribal center of the Igorot people (Bontoc, Kankana-ey), an indegenous tribal community in Northern Luzon, Philippines. (Both, courtesy of Steven De La Vega.)

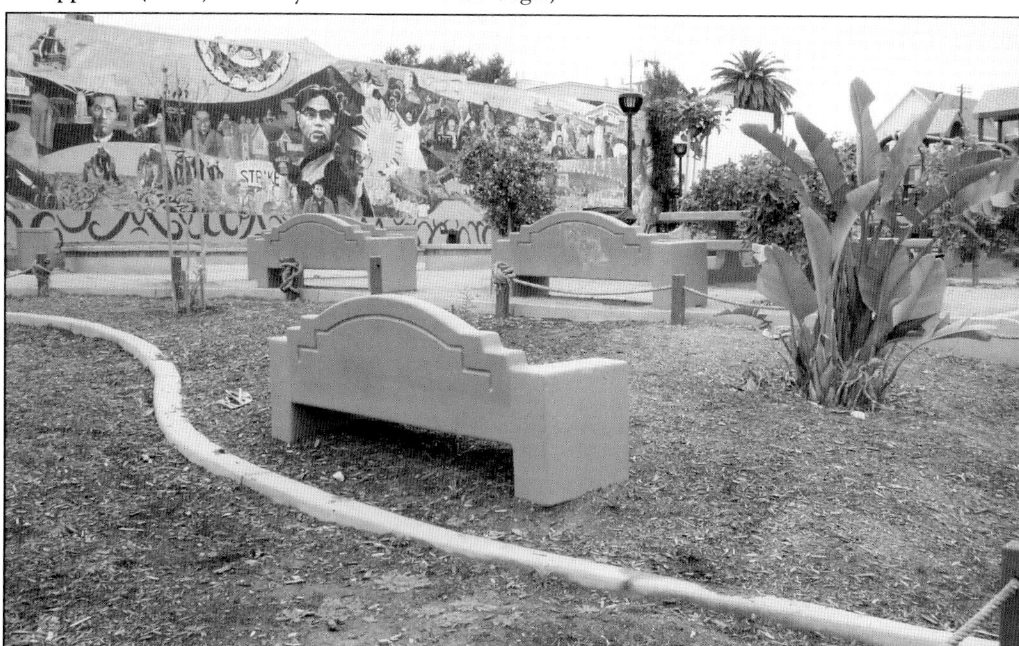

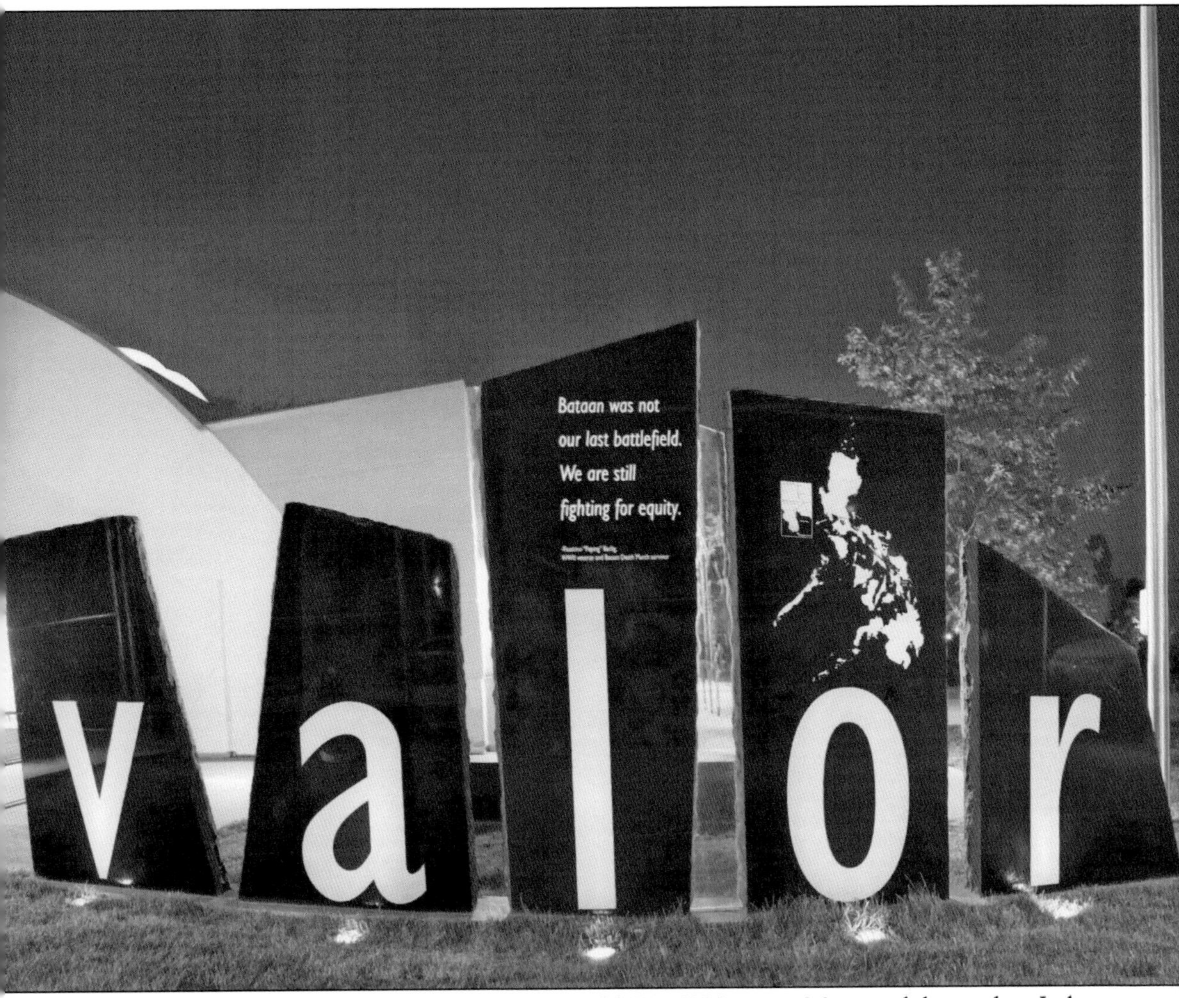

Designed by artist Cheri Gaulke, the Filipino World War II Veterans Memorial, located on Lake Street in Historic Filipinotown, was created to commemorate Filipino World War II veterans and their struggle for justice. Inscriptions on the first four stone stelae address the war years. At the center of the memorial is a sliver of dichroic glass in the crevice between two stones, representing an eternal flame. The fifth stela, standing slightly apart, tells of the struggle to regain the benefits that were promised to the veterans but were not given. The negative shape between the fourth and fifth stele forms a "V" for veteran, valor, and victory. Filipino veterans are the only national group that were denied full U.S. veteran status, while soldiers of more than 66 other allied countries who were also inducted into the service of the U.S. Armed Forces during World War II were granted full U.S. veteran status. The memorial was formally dedicated on Veteran's Day on November 11, 2006. (Photograph by Kevin O'Malley, courtesy of Cheri Gaulke.)

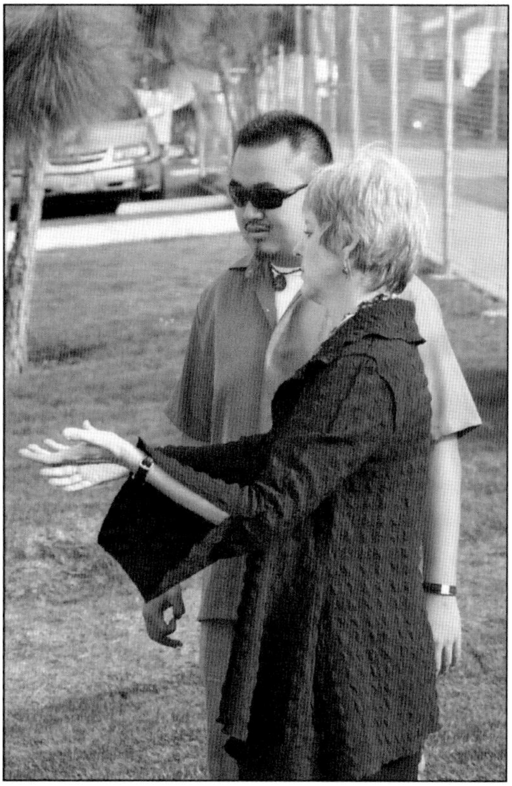

Joseph Bernardo (left), field deputy for Eric Garcetti's city council District 13 office and project manager of the memorial, was instrumental in introducing artist Cheri Gaulke (right) to the Filipino American Service Group where she met some of the World War II Filipino veterans, who shared stories of their horrific war experiences. (Photograph by Kevin O'Malley, courtesy of Cheri Gaulke.)

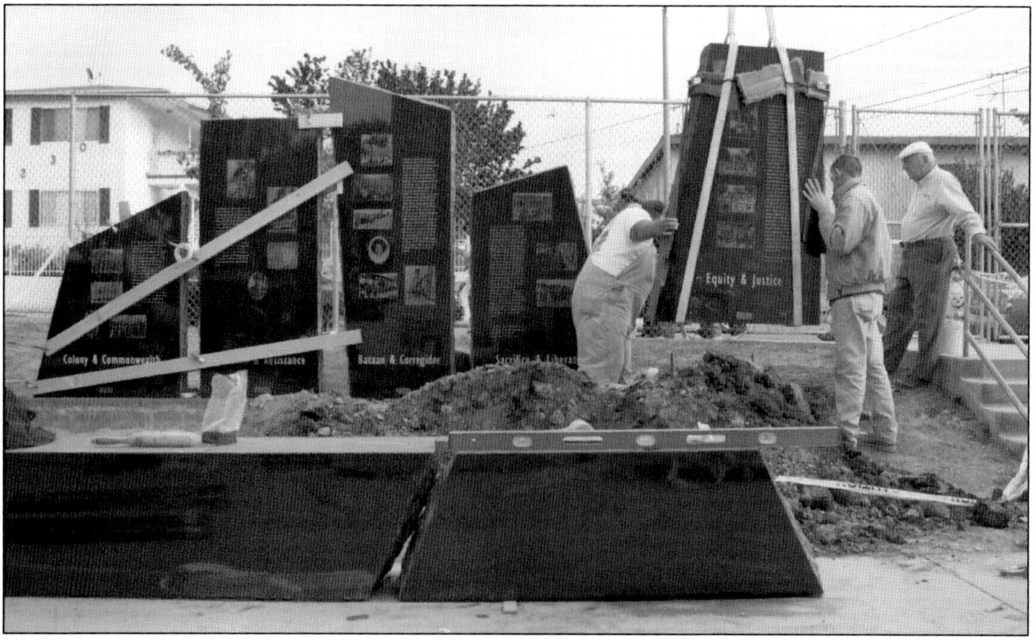

This photograph was taken during the memorial's construction. Workers guide a crane lowering a stone stela to its place in the memorial. Artist Cheri Gaulke divided the memorial into five chapters that are inscribed on the stone stelae. (Photograph by Kevin O'Malley, courtesy of Cheri Gaulke.)

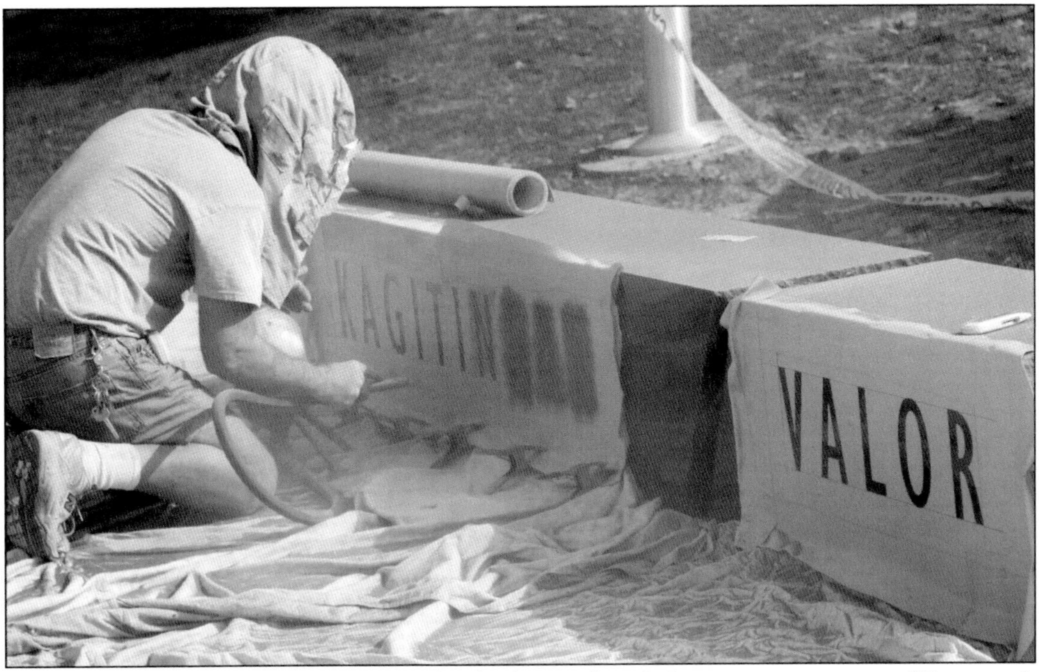

A worker bead blasts the word *Kagitingan* ("Valor") into a bench during its construction. (Photograph by Kevin O'Malley, courtesy of Cheri Gaulke.)

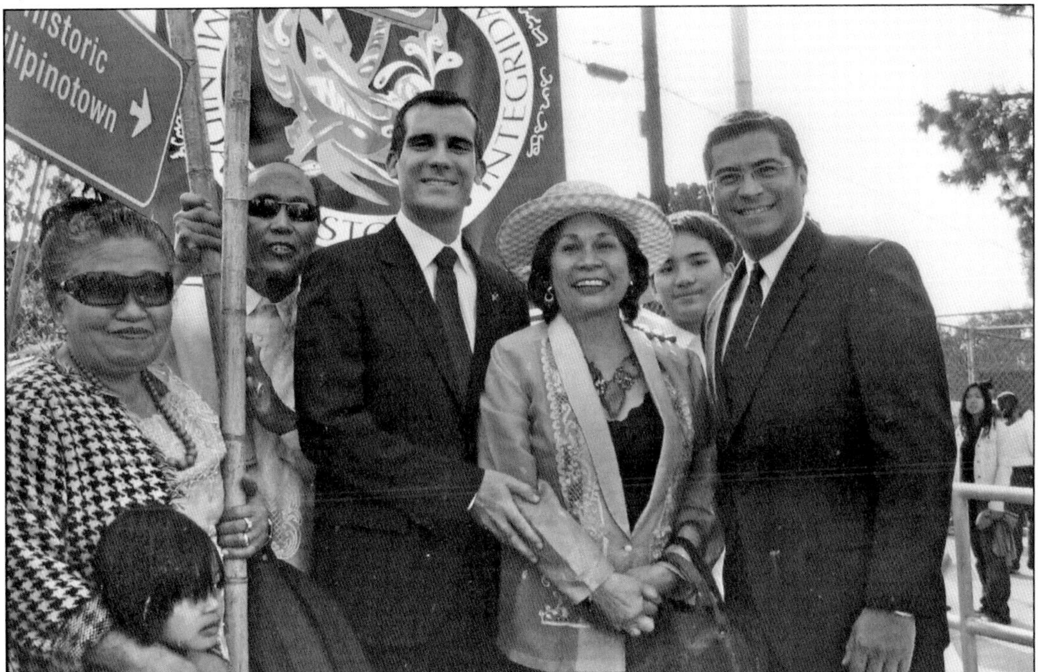

Filipino community leader Cecile Ramos (second from right), president of the Historic Filipinotown Neighborhood Council; community residents; Los Angeles city official Eric Garcetti (third from left); and U.S. Congress member Xavier Becerra (far right) attended the November 11, 2006, unveiling and dedication of the memorial. (Photograph by Kevin O'Malley, courtesy of Cheri Gaulke.)

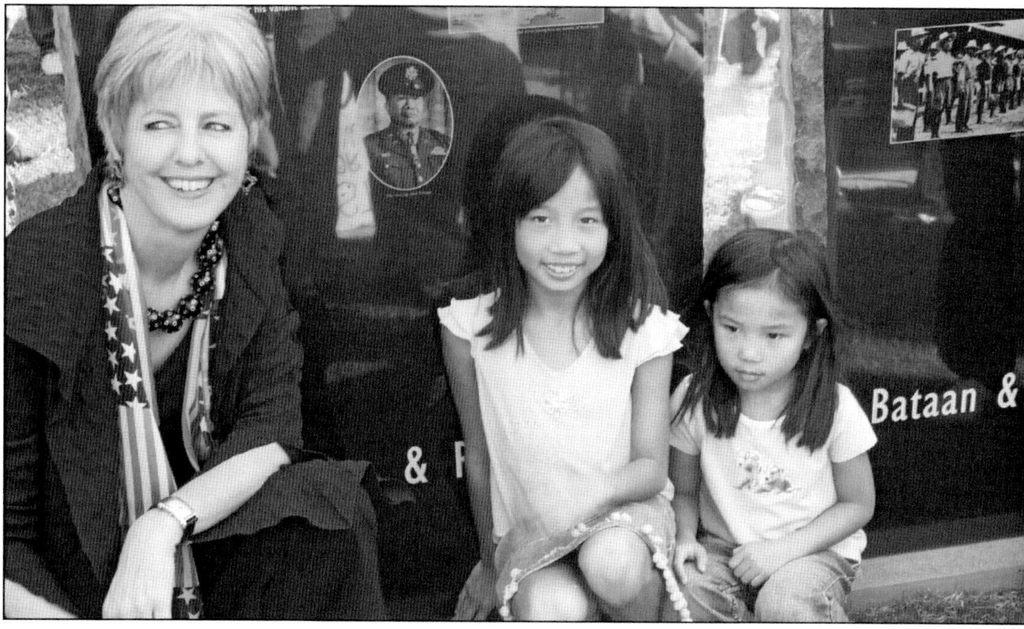

Artist Cheri Gaulke (left) is pictured with Sharla Calugas Chan (center) and Kayden Calugas Chan, who are visiting their great-grandfather's tribute at the memorial. Sgt. Jose Calugas Sr. received the Congressional Medal of Honor for his valiant actions in Bataan. He helped hold back the Japanese for five months, allowing the Americans to recover from the Pearl Harbor attack. (Photograph by Kevin O'Malley, courtesy of Cheri Gaulke.)

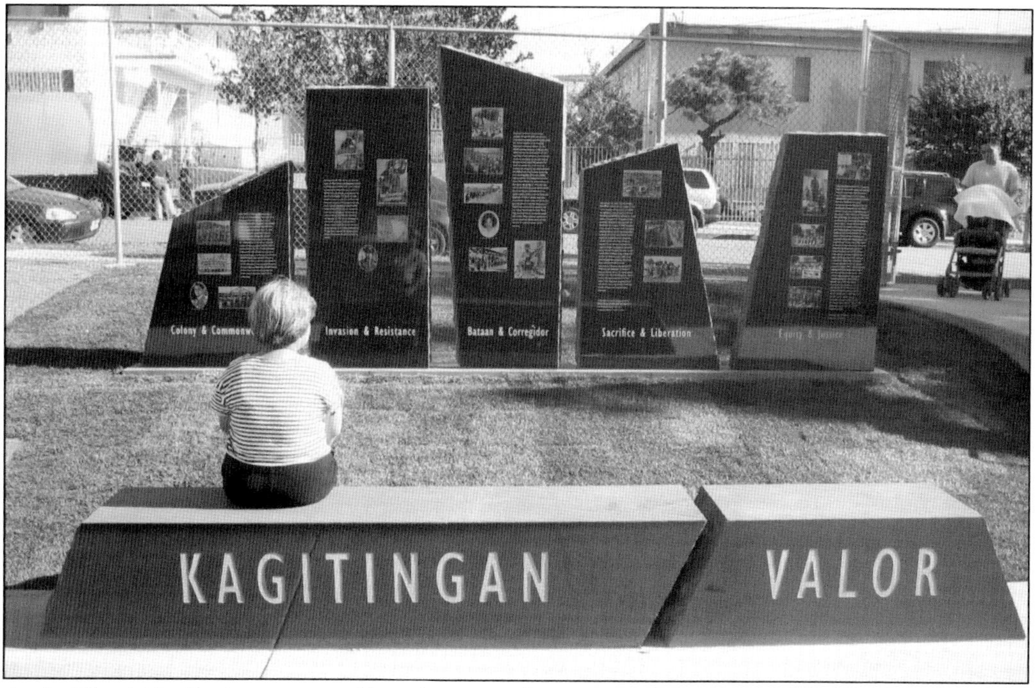

Artist Cheri Gaulke incorporated benches into the memorial to provide elderly veterans a place to sit, reflect, and tell their stories to visitors at the memorial. (Photograph by Kevin O'Malley, courtesy of Cheri Gaulke.)

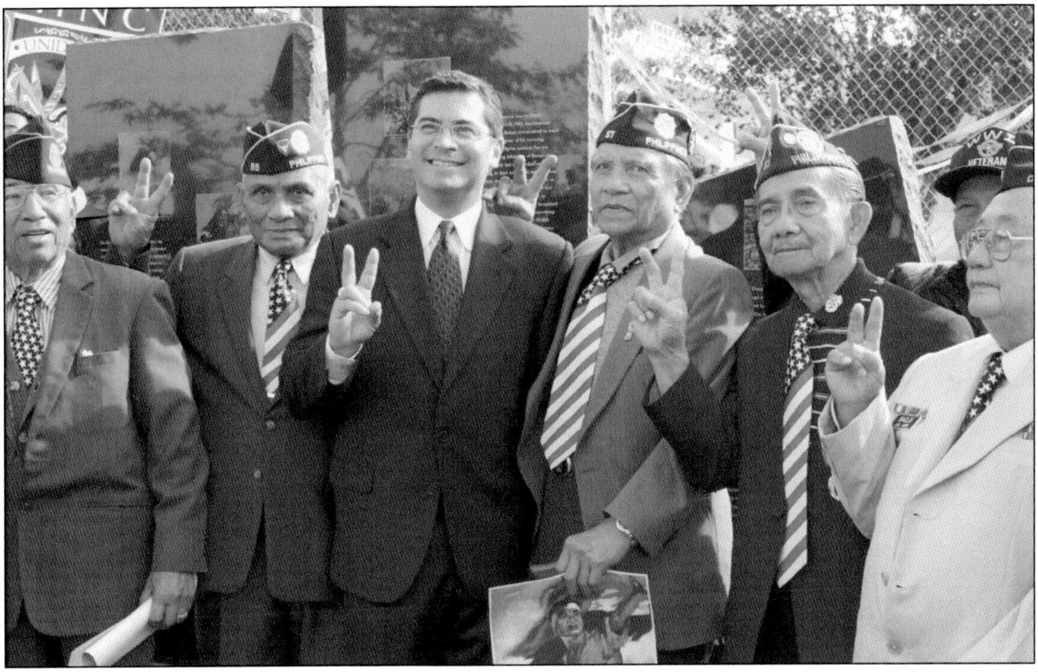

U.S. Congress member Xavier Becerra (third from left) is seen with Filipino veterans at the veterans' memorial unveiling ceremony. (Photograph by Kevin O'Malley, courtesy of Cheri Gaulke.)

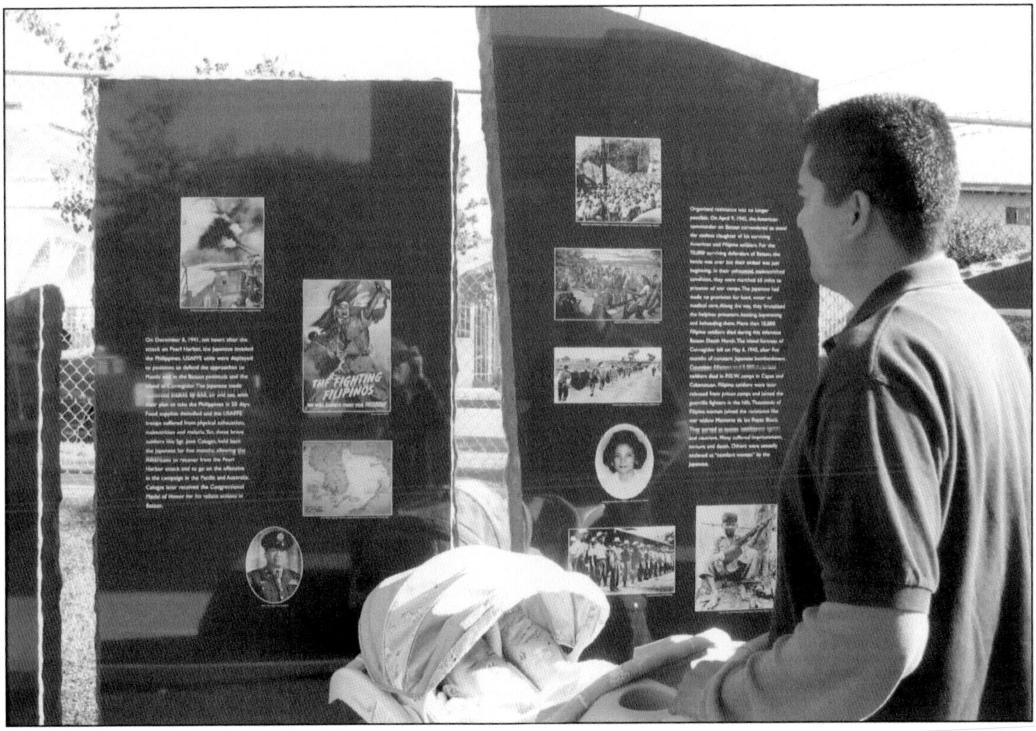

A crowd of more than 700 people attended the unveiling of the veterans' memorial dedicated to the Filipinos who served the United States during World War II. Pictured is a young father with his child at the unveiling. (Photograph by Kevin O'Malley, courtesy of Cheri Gaulke.)

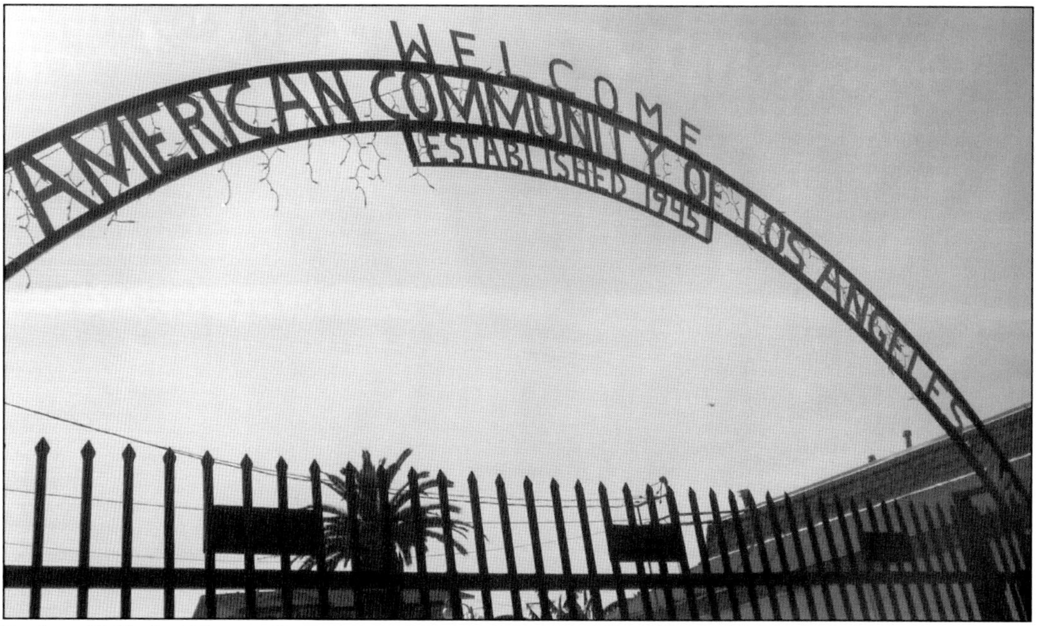

Built in 1965, the Filipino Community Center of Los Angeles is located on Temple Street in Historic Filipinotown. Registered with the State of California as the Filipino American Community of Los Angeles (FACLA) on April 26, 1945, it is one of the earliest Filipino American organizations in America. Ben Manibog and Remedios Geaga are two of the most notable past presidents of the center. (Courtesy of Debbie Sahagun.)

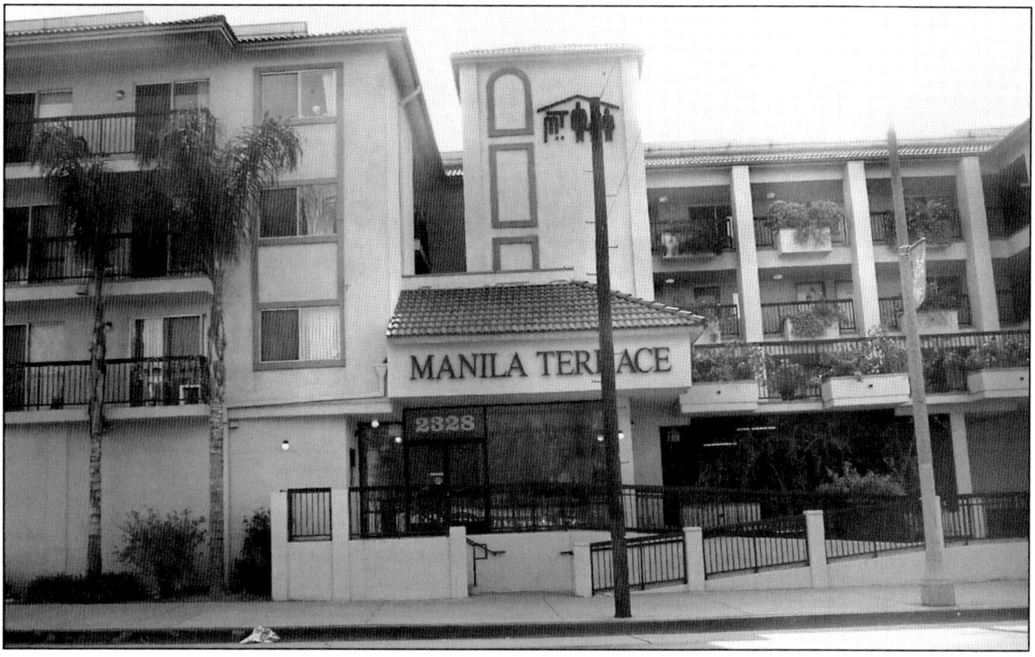

Manila Terrace was opened in 1996. It offers 30 units of affordable housing, and its residents are mostly Filipino and Latino families. Before Manila Terrace was opened, Mindanao Terrace, Mountain View Terrace, and the Villa Ramos apartments offered affordable housing to the Filipino and Latino community as early as 1987. (Courtesy of Debbie Sahagun.)

Bahay Kubo Natin is a popular Filipino restaurant that has a large patio with a replica of a *bahay kubo* (house hut), with woven nipa leaves and bamboo used as decorations. (Courtesy of Debbie Sahagun.)

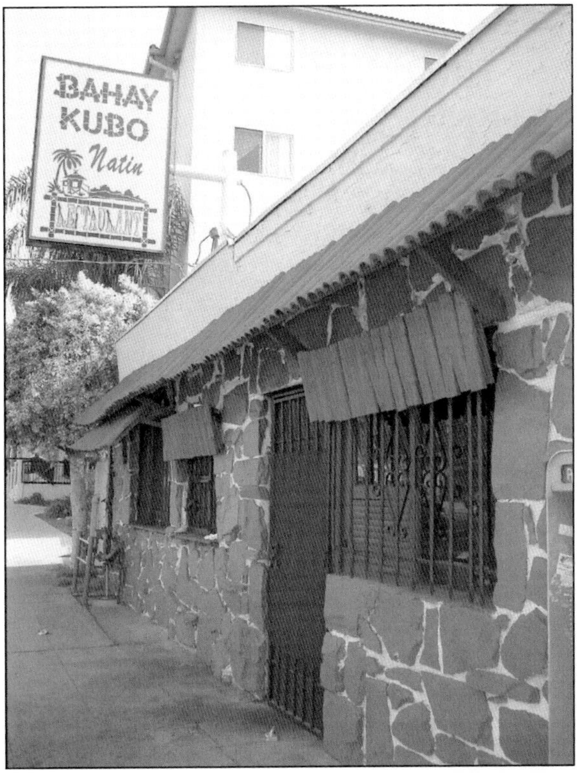

Little Ongpin Chinese and Filipino restaurant is popular because of its many ethnic dishes. It is located in the former location of a then-popular Filipino restaurant, the Morong Café, which was owned and operated by *Manongs*. The word *Manong* is a term of respect used when addressing an elder male. Other restaurants no longer in existence that were operated by *Manongs* include the Travelers Café and the Pasay Café. (Courtesy of Debbie Sahagun.)

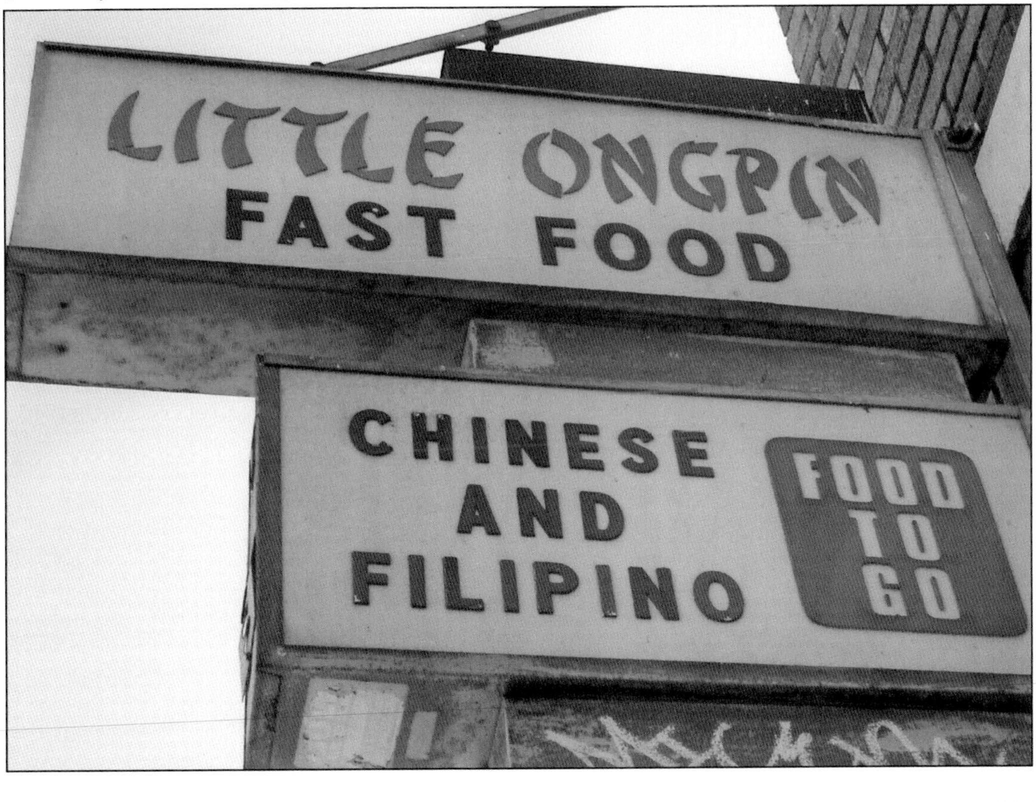

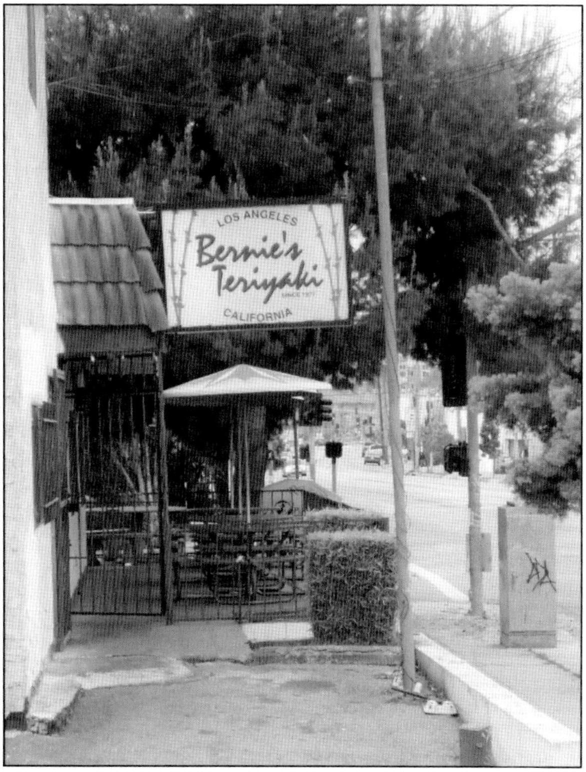

Founded in 1977, Bernie's Teriyaki is the oldest Filipino-owned restaurant in Historic Filipinotown. It is well known for its barbeque meats. (Courtesy of Debbie Sahagun.)

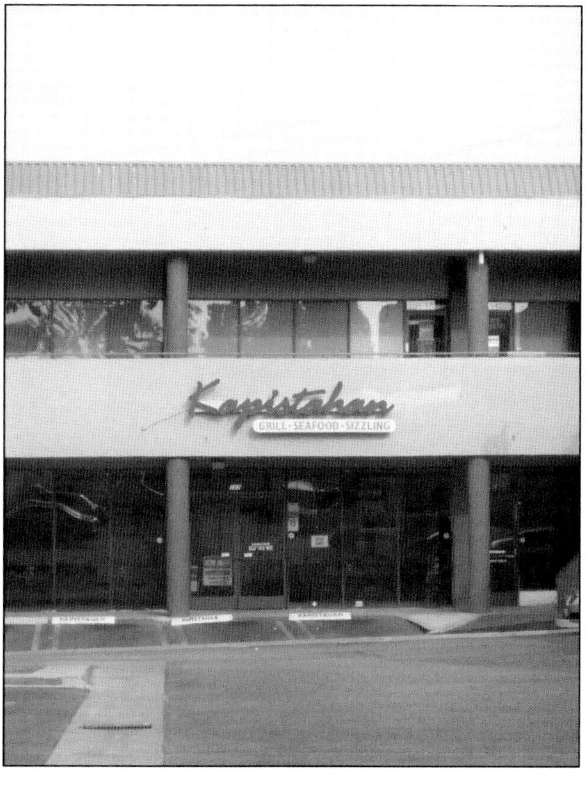

The Kapistahan Filipino restaurant was a new addition to Historic Filipinotown in 2008. Its extensive menu offers many freshly prepared ethnic foods. It is located in the Luzon Plaza next to SM Beauty and Cut, a beauty salon operated by Filipinas. A few blocks east of Kapistahan on West Temple Street is the Tribal Café, the former location of the Filipino Travelers Café. The Tribal Café is a unique community café decorated in tribal-themed colors and designs. It hosts open-mike nights, poetry readings, and music. Its menu offers gourmet coffee, teas, and sandwiches. (Courtesy of the author.)

Formerly located in an old firehouse in 1948 and rebuilt in 1968, St. Columban Catholic Church in 2008 still maintains a large number of Filipino parishioners. It was the first Filipino-owned and operated Catholic church in the United States. The church tower houses an old Spanish bell that was recovered from a shrine in Antipolo, Philippines. (Courtesy of Steven De La Vega.)

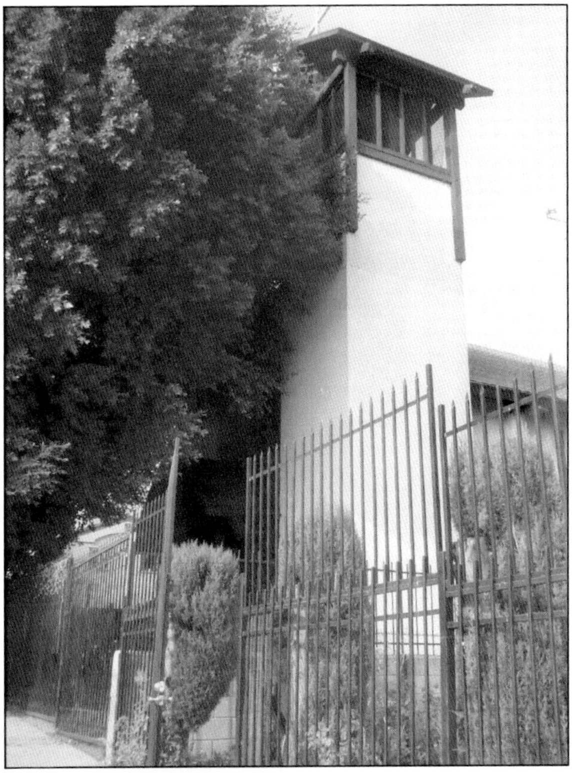

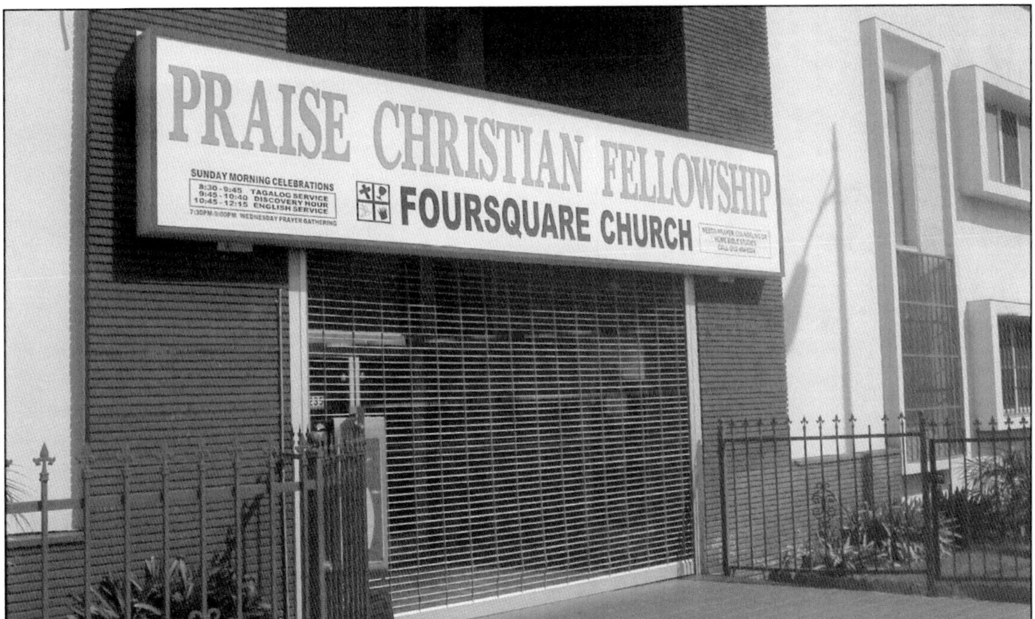

The pastors of Praise Christian Fellowship Church and the majority of its congregation members are Filipino. As part of the Foursquare Church that was established in the Philippines with churches in other countries all over the world, the church in Los Angeles conducts its service in Tagalog every Sunday morning. (Courtesy of Debbie Sahagun.)

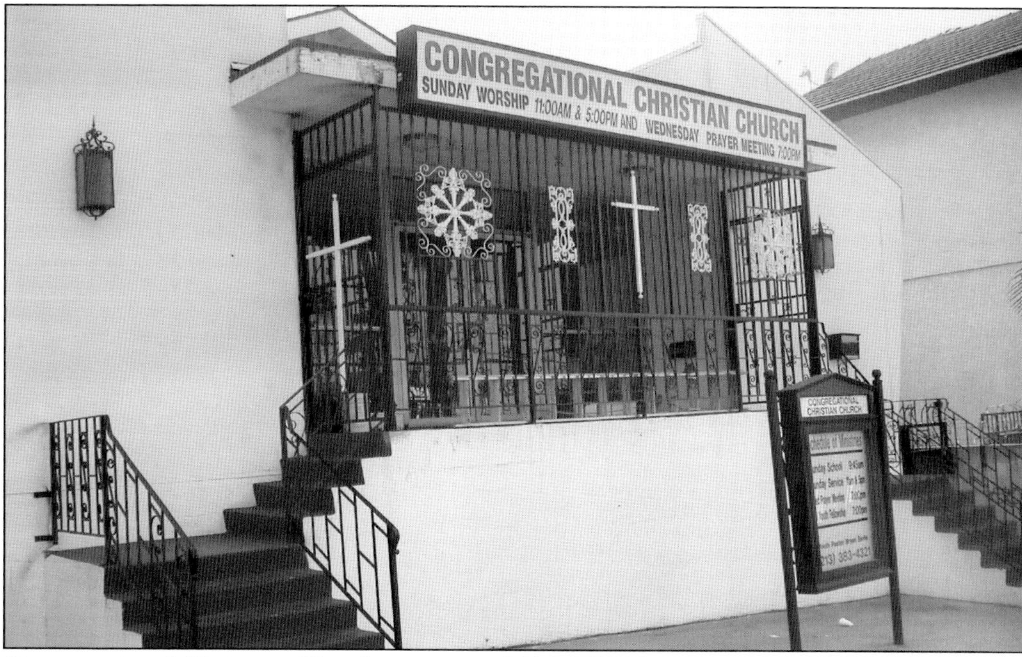

Congregational Christian Church is seen in 2008. The church was established in 1888, and because its members were predominately Filipino, Filipino pastors were solicited to lead the church. Another church in Historic Filipinotown, United Church of God Ministries, has a predominately Filipino membership and has services offered in Tagalog. (Courtesy of Debbie Sahagun.)

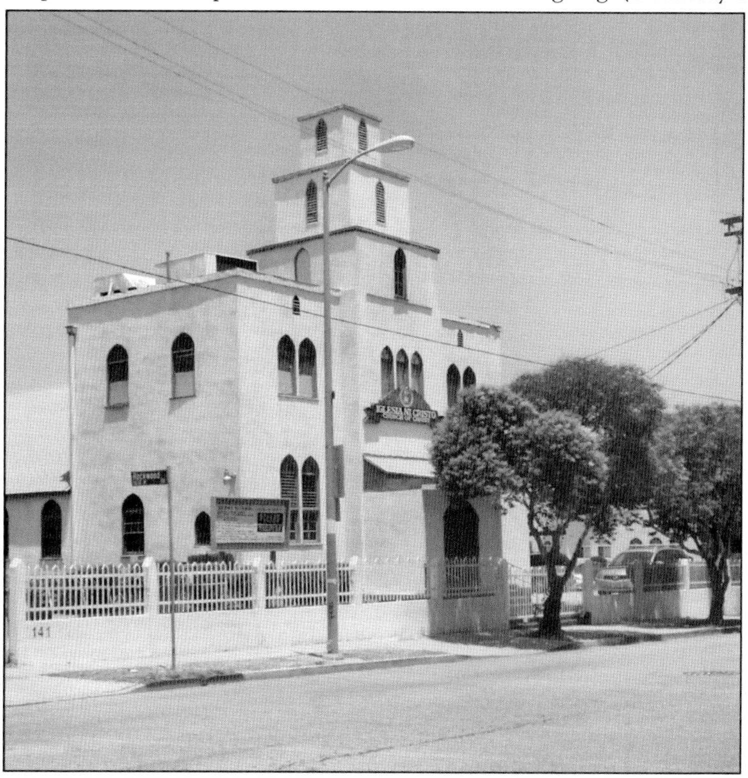

Founded in the Philippines in 1914, Iglesia ni Cristo is one of the oldest churches in Historic Filipinotown. Its chapel here in the United States, as well as its chapel in the Philippines, was constructed with narrow points on top of the buildings that are said to be representative of landmarks of major cities and provincial capitals in the Philippines. (Courtesy of Debbie Sahagun.)

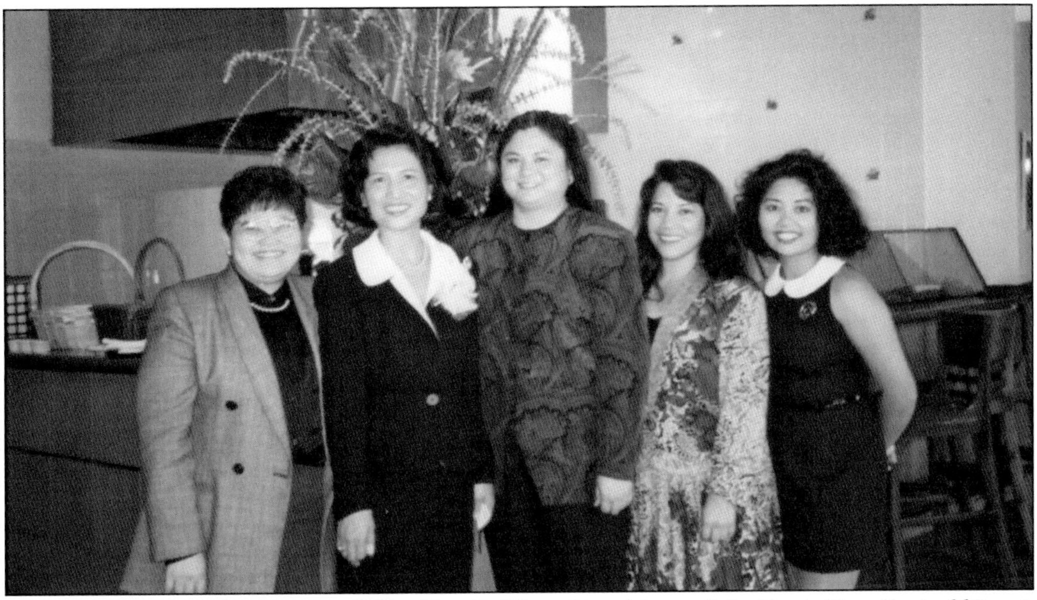

A 1996 West Coast book tour of *Why Should White Guys Have all the Fun?: How Reginald Lewis Created a Billion-Dollar Business Empire* was sponsored by the Pilipino American Reading Room and Library, Filipino American Heritage Institute, and UCLA Asian American Studies Center. The book was written by Reginald F. Lewis and Blair S. Walker. Pictured from left to right are Prosy Abarquez-Delacruz, Loida Nicolas-Lewis, Meg Malpaya Thornton, Liza Javier, and Maria Ventura. (Courtesy of Prosy Abarquez-Delacruz.)

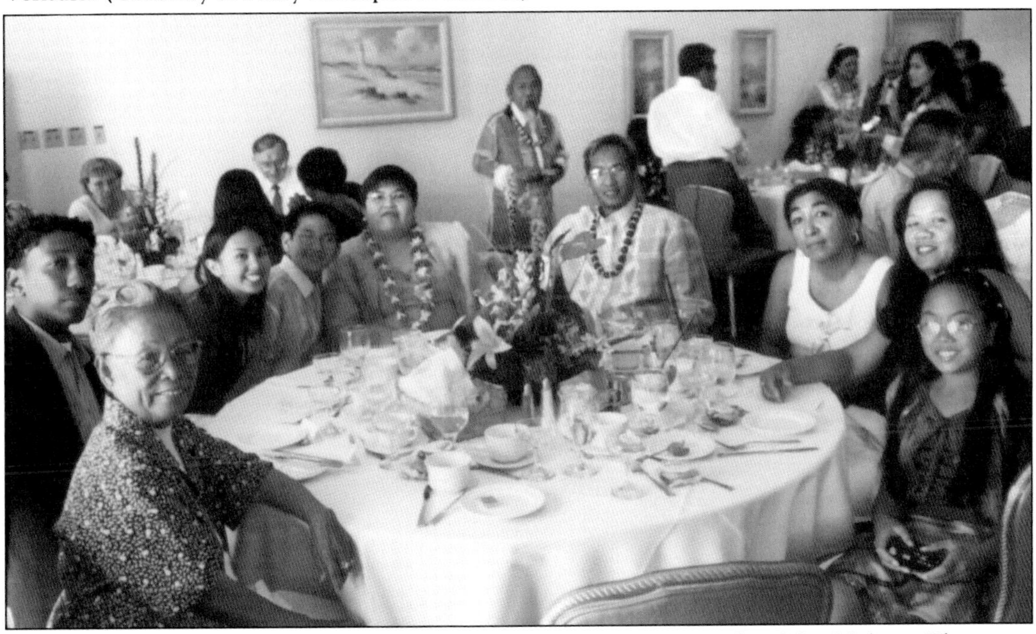

Community leaders and activists attend the wedding of SIPA past president Meg Malpaya Thornton. Pictured from left to right are Emily Soriano, Eduardo Soriano-Hewitt, Corina de la Cruz, Carlo de la Cruz, Prosy Abarquez-Delacruz, Enrique de la Cruz, Ester Soriano-Hewitt, Rose Ibanez, Michaela Ibanez, Roy Morales (standing), and (the bride and groom in far background) Meg Malpaya Thornton and Gil Ayuyao. All others are unidentified. (Courtesy of Prosy Abarquez-Delacruz.)

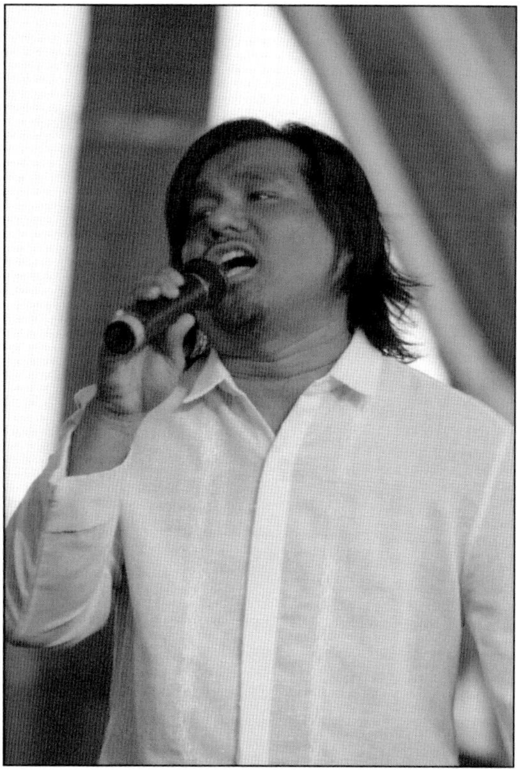

Elson Trinidad performs at the 2006 Lotus Festival in Echo Park. A community activist and freelance writer, Trinidad is also a member of the Soul Barkada band. (Courtesy of Elson Trinidad.)

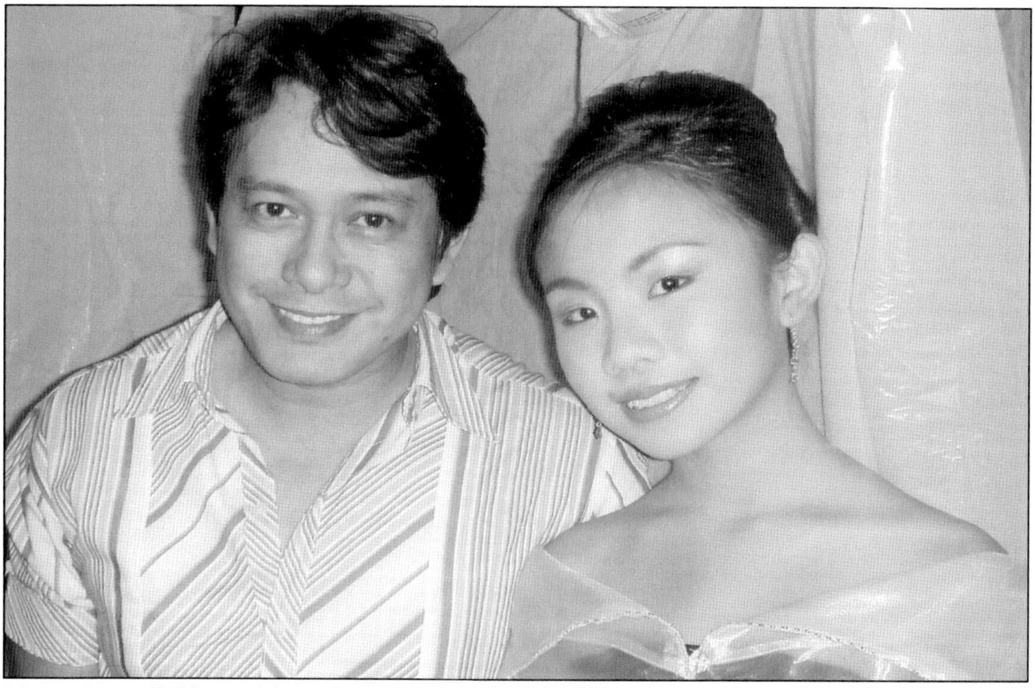

Marco Sison (left), a celebrated singer from the Philippines, is pictured with Claire Rodriguez. Rodriguez was awarded "Best in Talent" at the Historic Filipinotown Youth Ambassador Presentation Night in November 2007. (Courtesy of Imelda Rodriguez.)

The sixth annual Historic Filipinotown Festival was held on August 2, 2008. Pictured is Alvaro Vanegas (left) from Proyectos Saluda, an organization that promotes Hispanic cultures. His organization worked with Historic Filipinotown Neighborhood Council in cross-cultural sharing in festival activities. Also pictured is Benita Ibanez, master of ceremonies for the festival's events. (Courtesy of Sthanlee B. Mirador.)

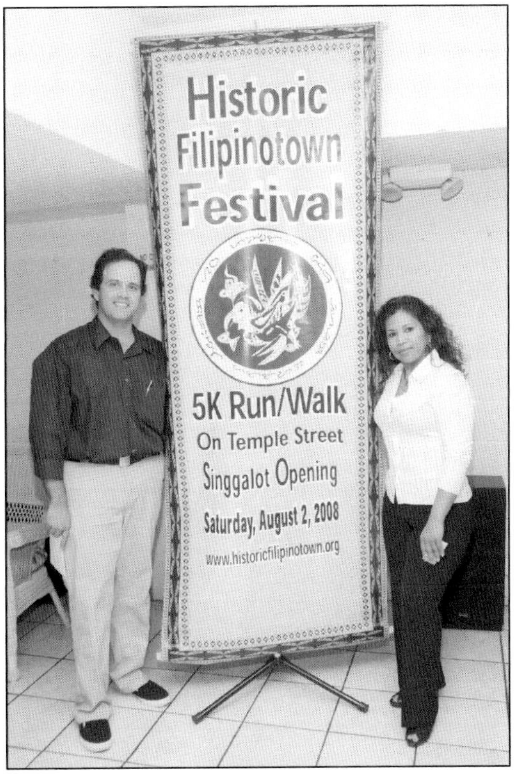

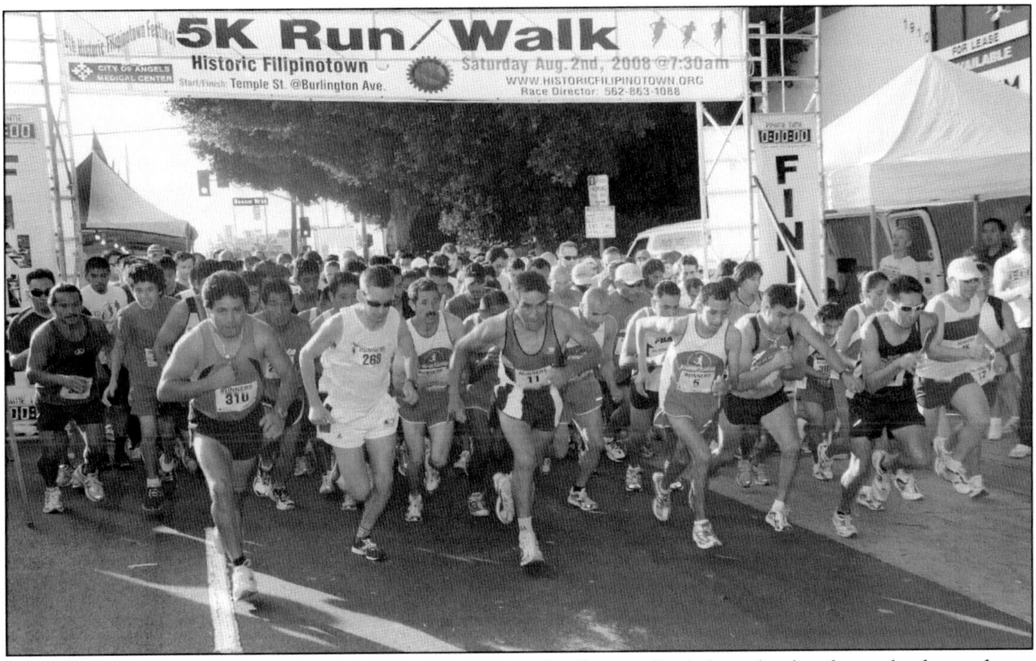

One of the festival's main attractions is the 5K run/walk, in which hundreds of people throughout Los Angeles come as participants and spectators. The spirit of Los Angeles's diverse ethnic community coming together to participate in this activity is in keeping with the spirit in which the festival was intended. (Courtesy of Sthanlee B. Mirador.)

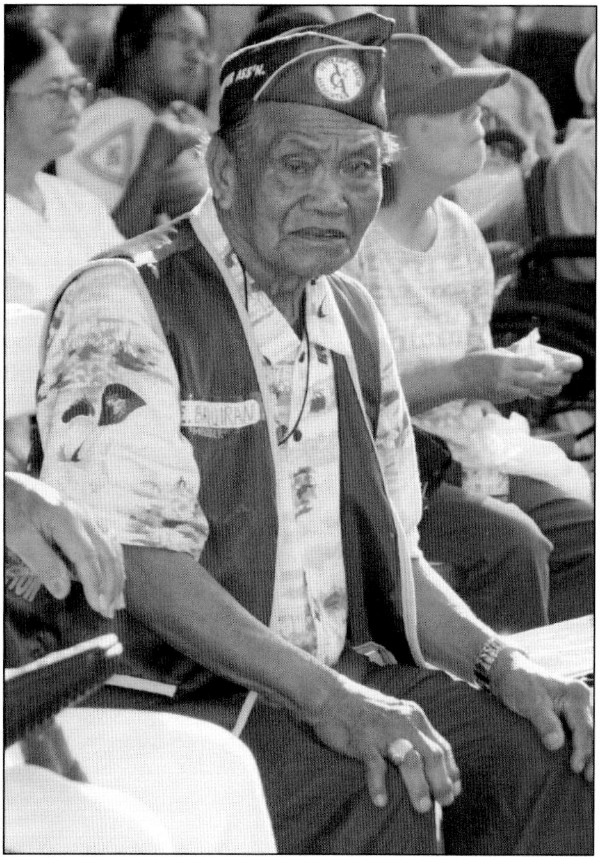

Pictured at left is Filipino World War II veteran E. Baquirin at the sixth annual Historic Filipinotown Festival. He is also shown below with fellow World War II veterans. Despite their age, some danced to the music of the Latin Rhythm Kings, who were featured as guest performers. (Both, courtesy of Peter Gonzaga.)

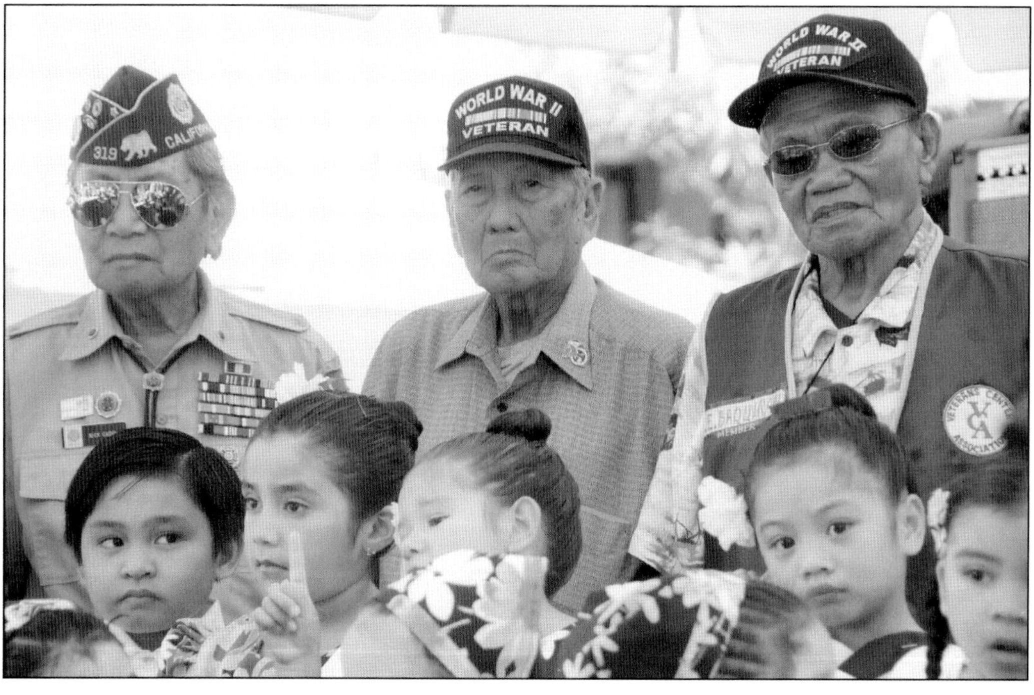

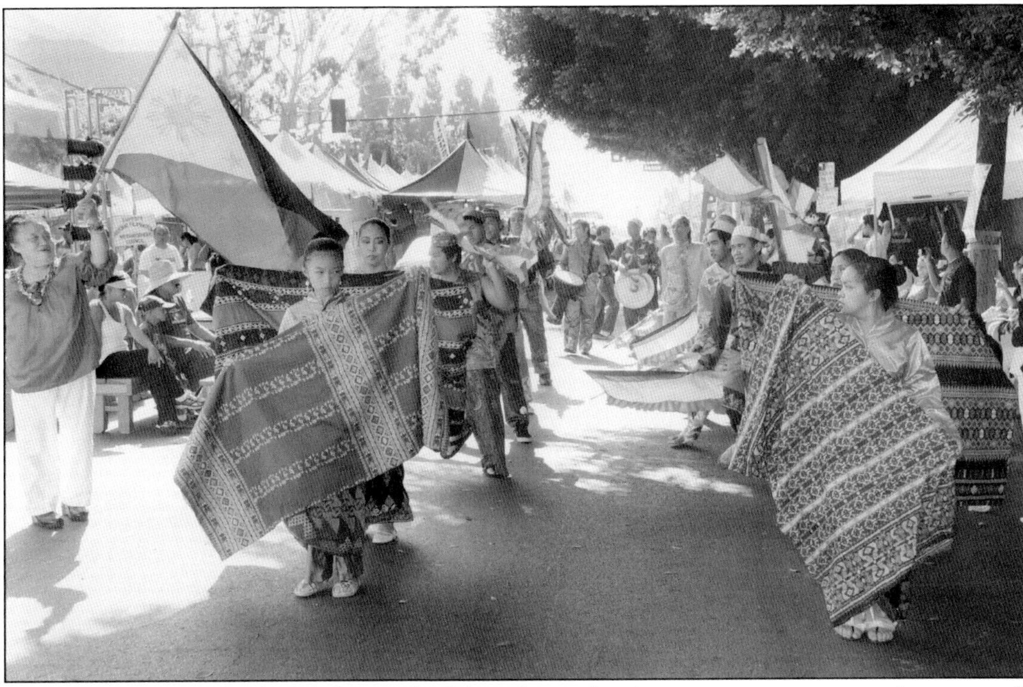

Philippine dancers displayed their colorful traditional-style costumes in a street dance parade during the festival. (Courtesy of Sthanlee B. Mirador.)

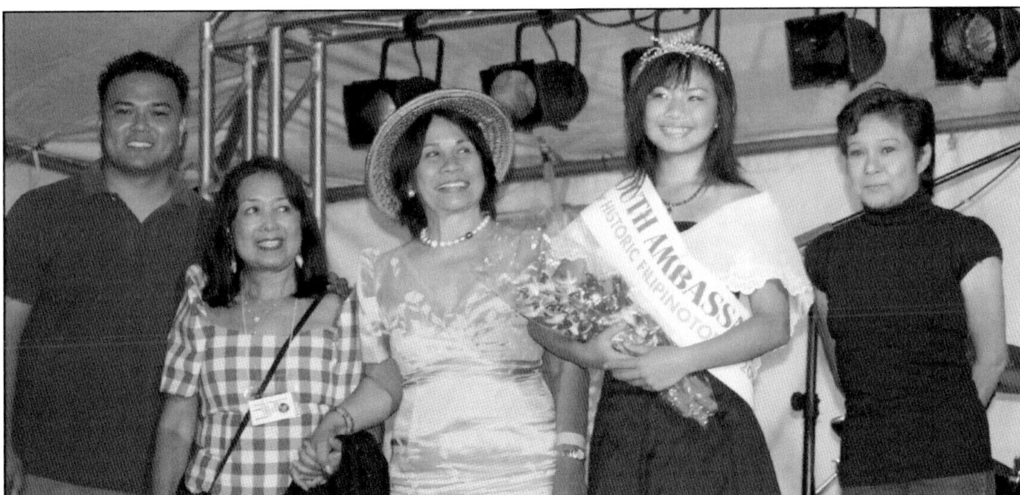

Claire Rodriguez was the winner of the title of Historic Filipinotown's first Youth Ambassador. Candidates were judged by academic excellence, talent, interview, extracurricular activities, and community service. Pictured from left to right are Ryan Carpio, Joselyn Geaga-Rosenthal, Cecile Ramos, Claire Rodriguez, and Philippine actress/singer Nora Aunor. (Courtesy of Imelda Rodriguez.)

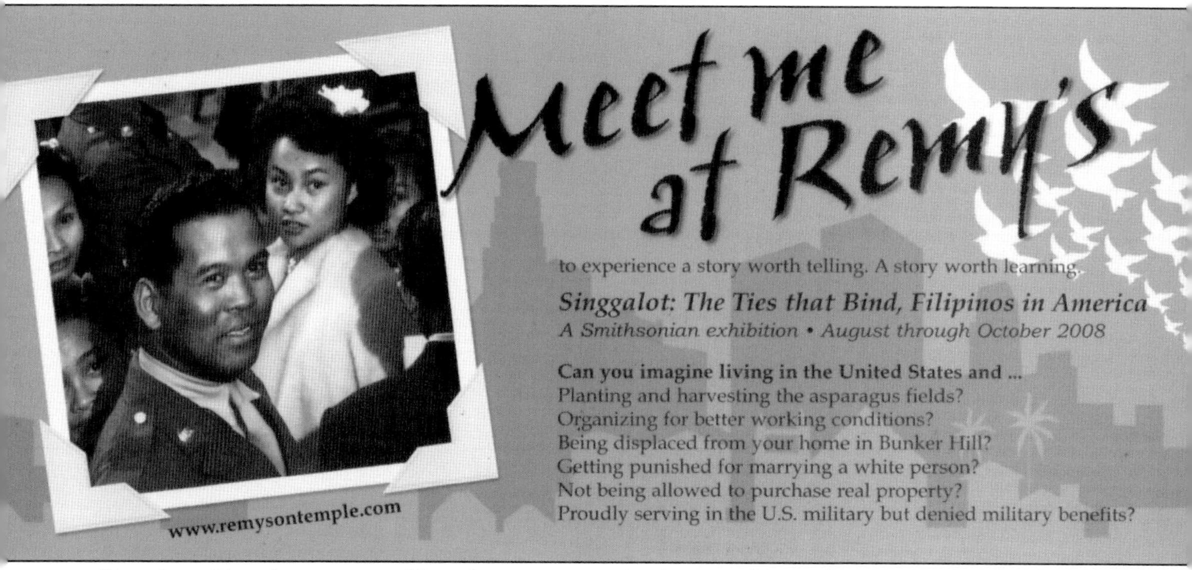

Remy's on Temple is an art gallery that was named in honor of Remedios V. Geaga, who dedicated most of her life to community involvement and political empowerment. The gallery opened in June 2004 and is a legacy of Geaga's commitment to building community partnerships and promoting creative expression. It is the first Filipino-owned gallery in Historic Filipinotown. Remy's was host to Singgalot: The Ties that Bind, a Smithsonian traveling exhibit, from August 1, 2008, to October 26, 2008. (Courtesy of Remy's on Temple.)

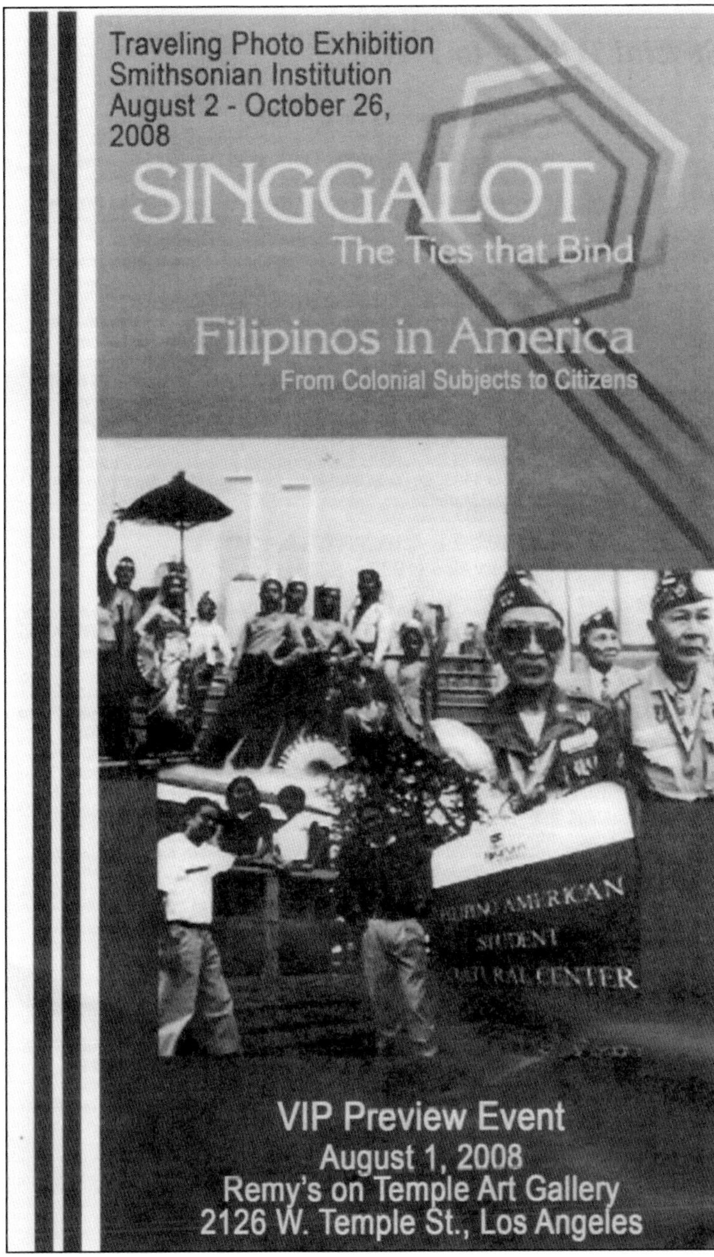

Singgalot: The Ties that Bind was an exhibition developed by the Smithsonian Asian Pacific American Program and was organized for travel by the Smithsonian Institution Traveling Exhibition Service. Consisting of 30 panels, the exhibit depicts the struggles, challenges, and successes of Filipino immigrants during the past 100 years. The exhibit highlights the contributions Filipino Americans have made in America from their labor in the Hawaii sugarcane fields, West Coast agribusiness, and the California and Alaskan seafood canneries, as well as achievements in U.S. military service, public service, literature, arts, sports, and health care. The exhibit not only preserves Filipino history, but it is an invaluable learning tool for everyone, especially for new generations of Filipino Americans, to understand through scholarly discussion Filipino Americans' history and legacy. (Courtesy of Carol Kimbrough.)

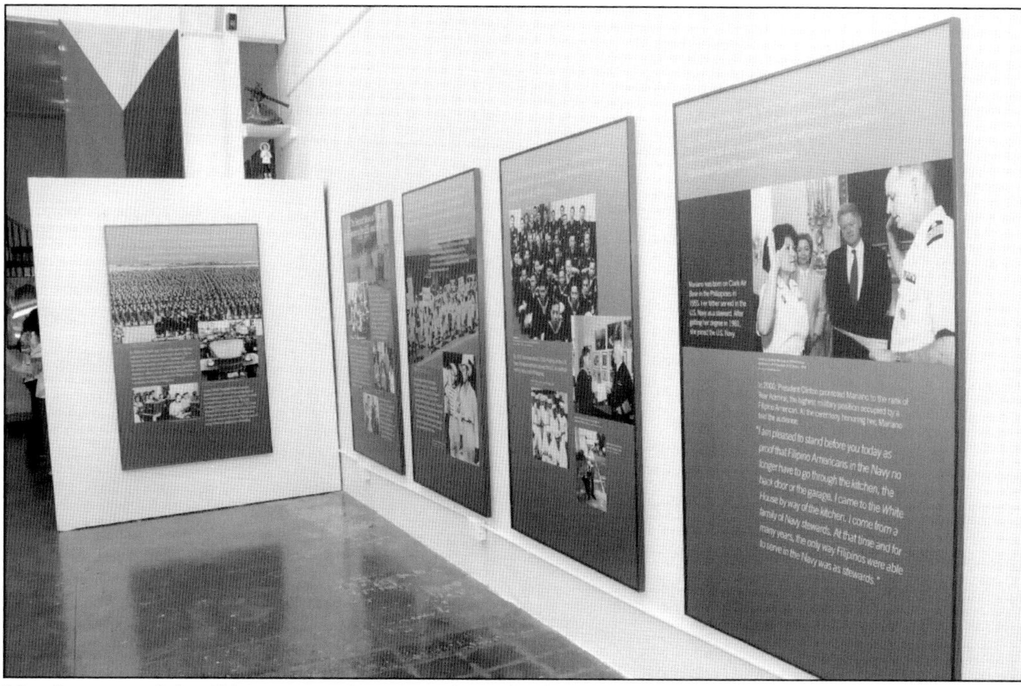

The history of the Filipinos in America dates back to 1565, and the Singgalot exhibit's aim is to tell the history of Filipinos in America through photographs depicted on panels. The exhibit opens up discussions on how Filipinos were viewed by Americans in the early 1900s: Who were the Filipino American pioneers?; What were some of the challenges faced by Filipino immigrants?; What are the differences and similarities among Filipino immigrants who arrived decades apart?; How is the Filipino immigrant similar to or different from other immigrants? (Both, courtesy of Sthanlee B. Mirador.)

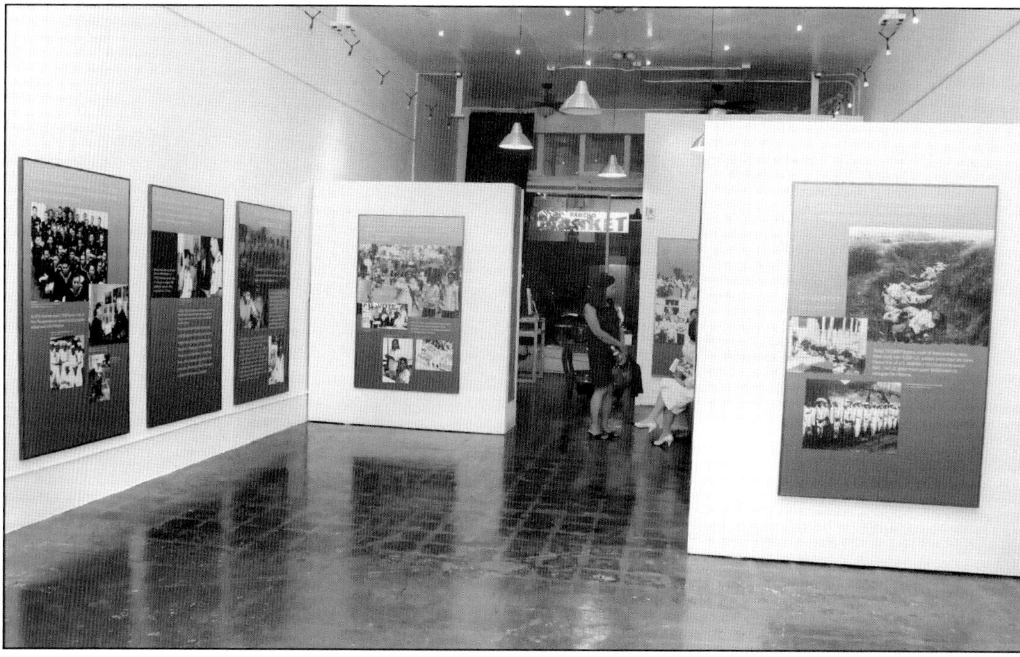

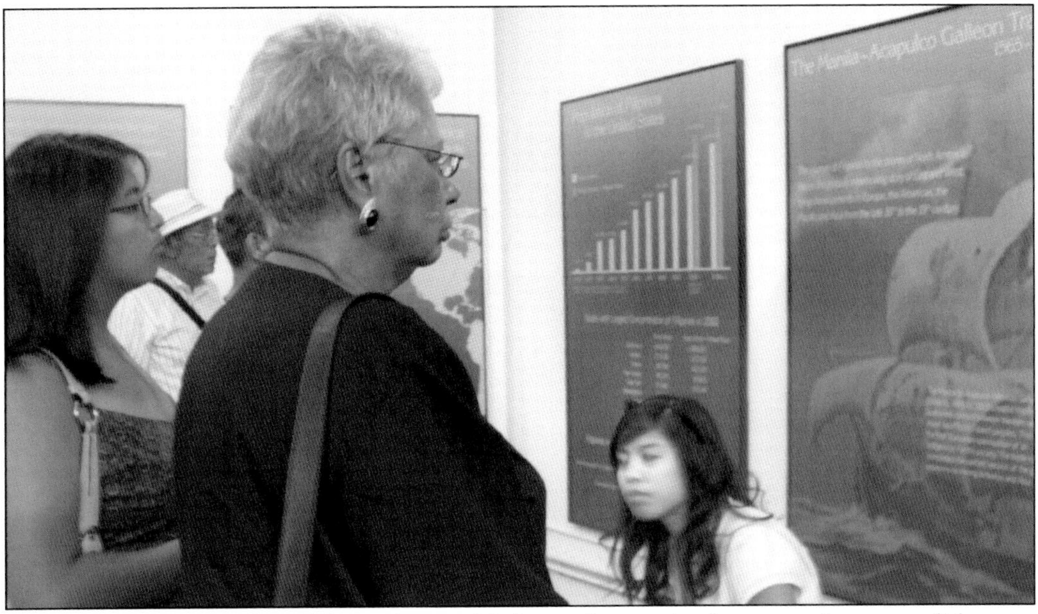

Visitors tour the Singgalot exhibit with mixed feelings of awe and sadness over the accomplishments as well as the injustices depicted in photographs covering the Filipino experience in America during the past 100 years. Viewing the exhibit with Shirley Dionzon (center) is Gabriela Delacruz (left) and Michaela Jane Delacruz (seated), a Singgalot volunteer. Dionzon reads with interest the stories on each panel, including the era of her father-in-law when he immigrated to the United States in the 1920s. (Courtesy of Christine Oshima.)

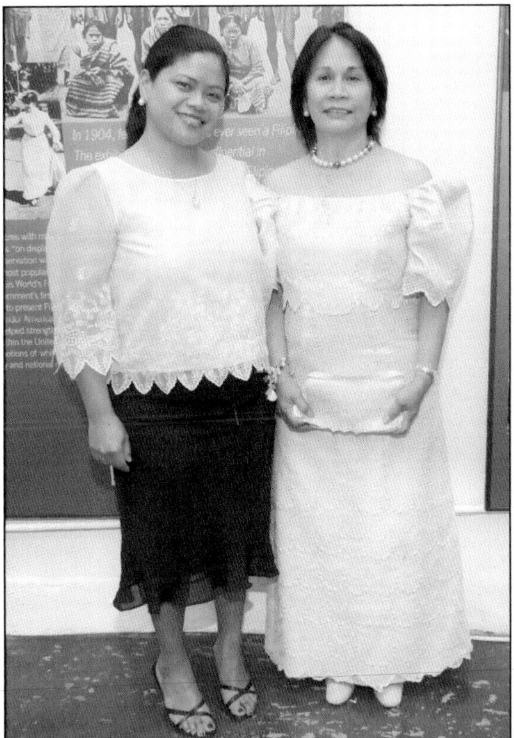

Historic Filipinotown Neighborhood Council president Cecile Ramos (right), and her daughter, Marisal Ramos, attend the private viewing of Singgalot held at Remy's on Temple on August 1, 2008. (Courtesy of Sthanlee B. Mirador.)

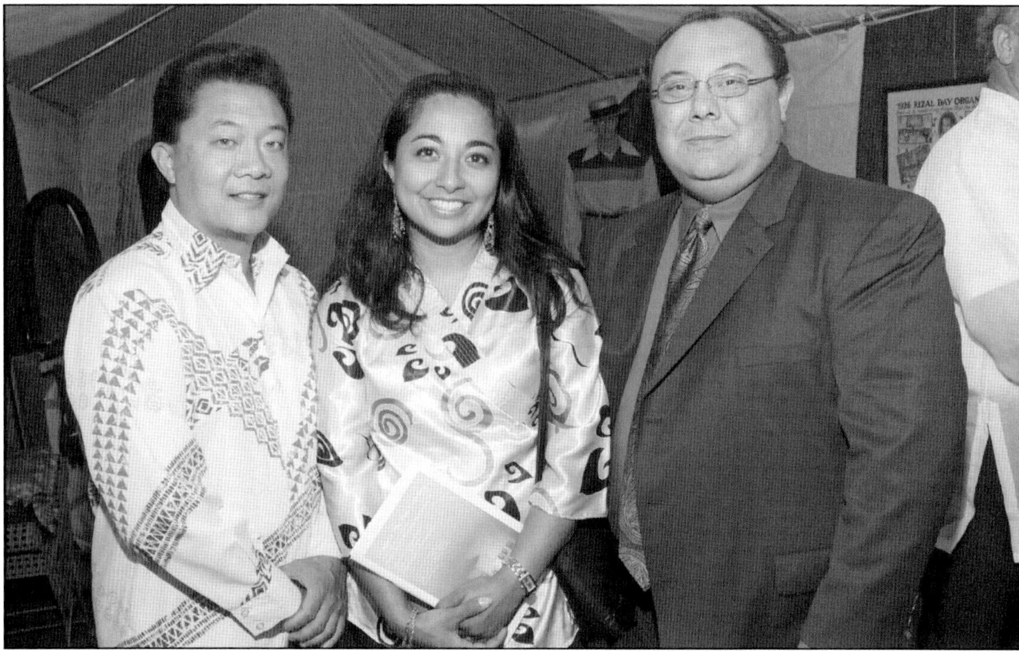

Guest speakers at the private viewing of Singgalot on August 1, 2008, are, from left to right, Joel Jacinto, executive director of Search to Involve Pilipino Americans (SIPA); Farzana Nayani, program manager of SIPA; and Joe Mazares, director of the Education Opportunity Program (EOP) at the University of California–Santa Barbara. (Photograph by Sthanlee B. Mirador.)

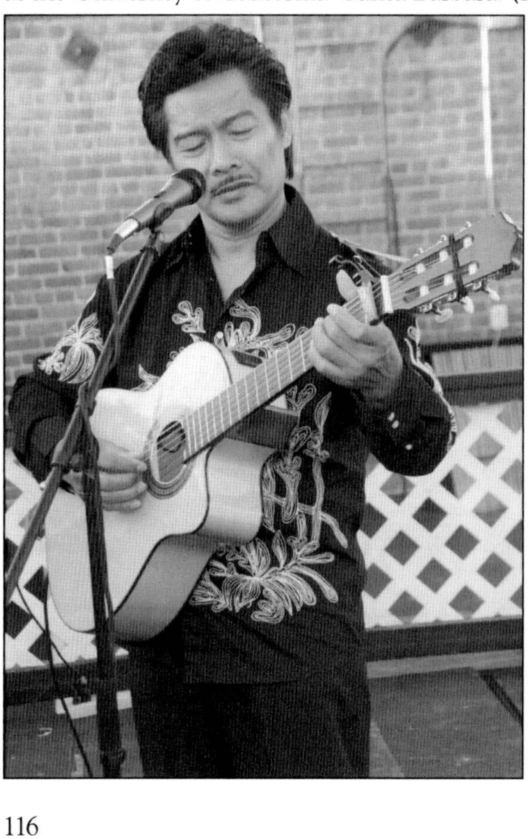

Mon David, one of the country's most respected Filipino singers, entertained guests with songs at the private and public viewing of Singgalot on August 1 and August 2, 2008. (Photograph by Sthanlee B. Mirador.)

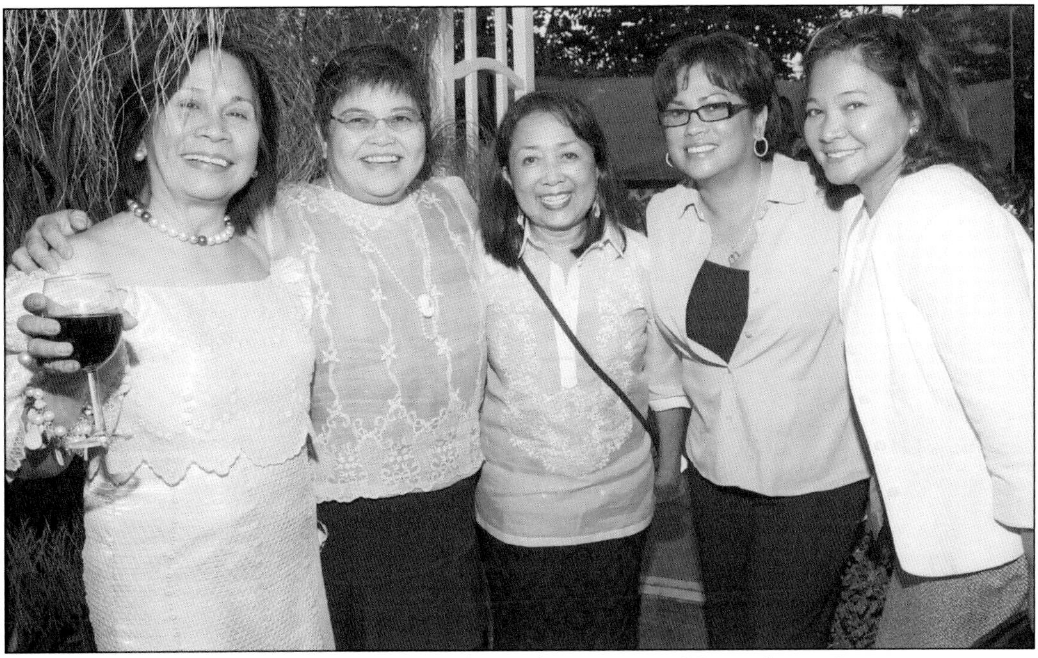

Singgalot exhibit committee members celebrate the opening of Singgalot at the private viewing held on August 1, 2008. Pictured from left to right are Cecile Ramos, Prosy Abarquez-Delacruz, Joselyn Geaga-Rosenthal, Carina Forsythe, and Thelma Sugay, events and marketing specialist. (Courtesy of Christine Oshima.)

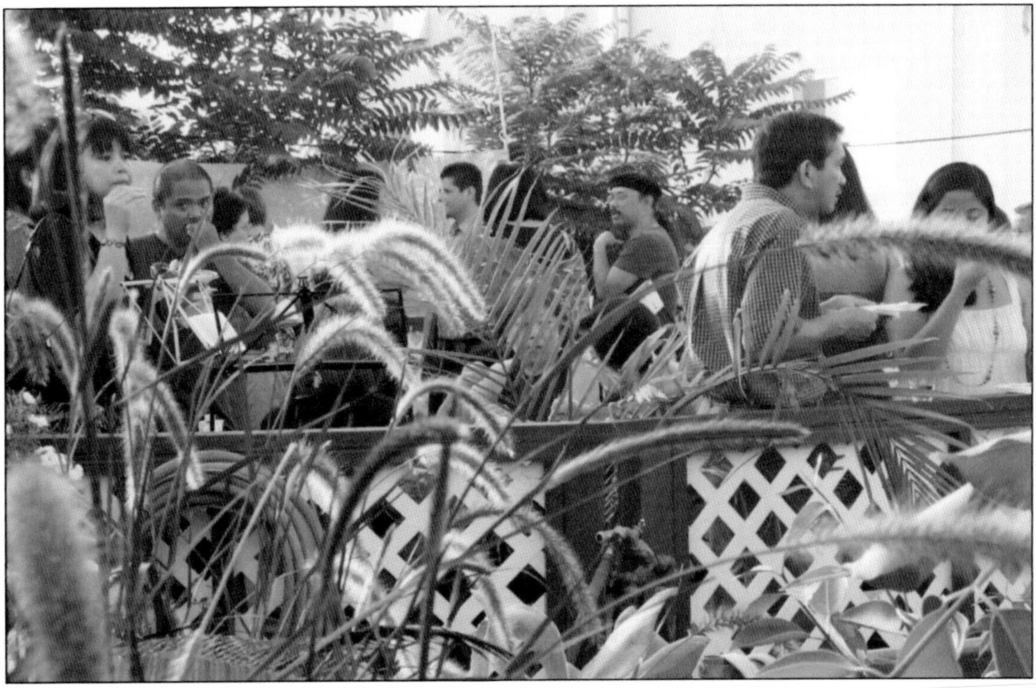

Guests attending the public opening of the Singgalot exhibit enjoy refreshments around the sculptured Asian-theme garden located outside in the back of the gallery. (Courtesy of Christine Oshima.)

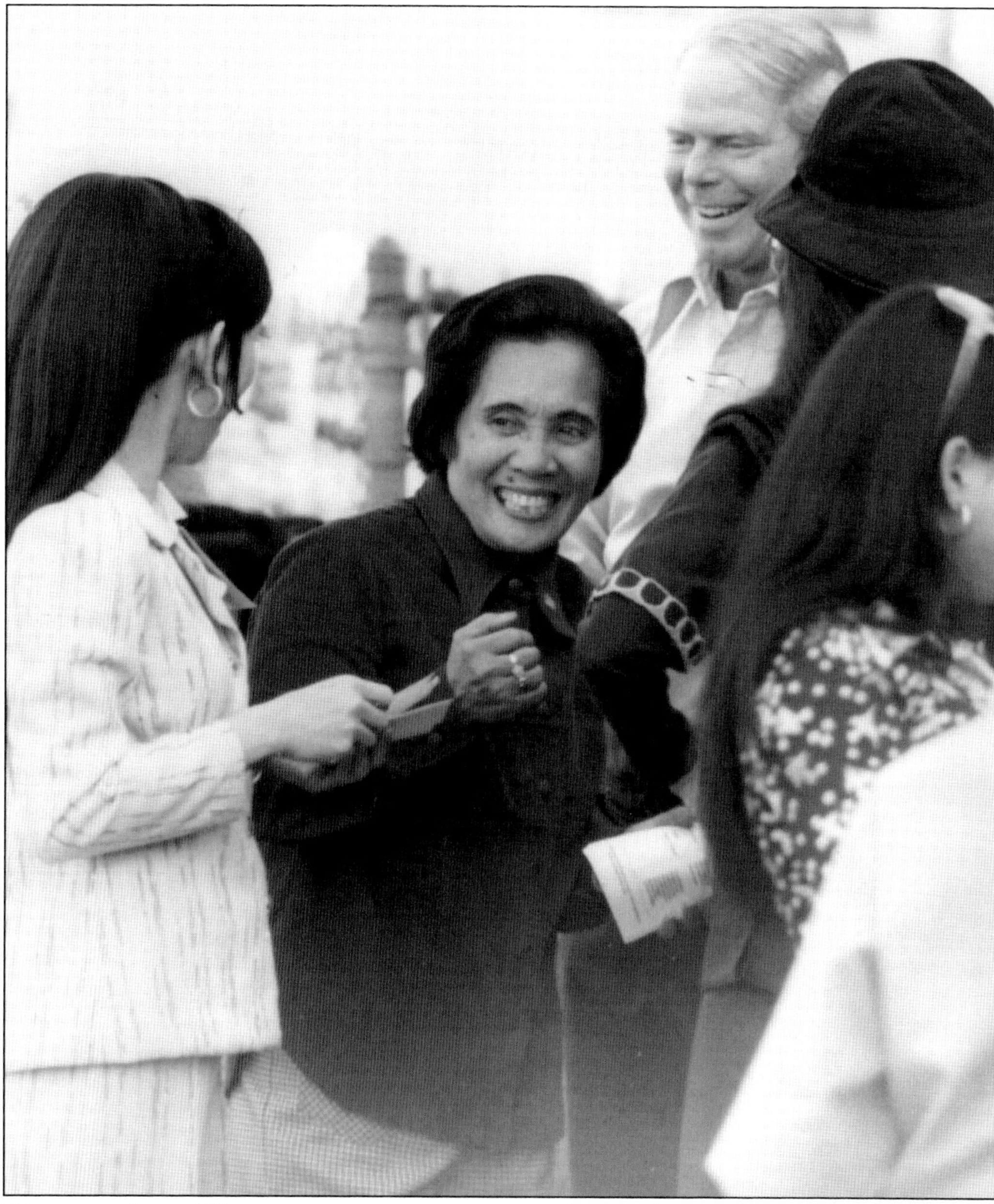

Three prominent Filipino community activists were honored at the Singgalot exhibit public opening on August 2, 2008. Honored were Remedios Geaga (center), Roy Morales, and Ester Soriano. Remedios Geaga (1916–1997) was a strong advocate for political empowerment and was a four-time president of the Filipino American Community of Los Angeles (FACLA); president of the Sampaguita Women's Circle; cofounder of the Bayanihan Seniors Association; and cofounder of the Filipino American Service Group, Inc. (FASGI). (Courtesy of Carol Kimbrough.)

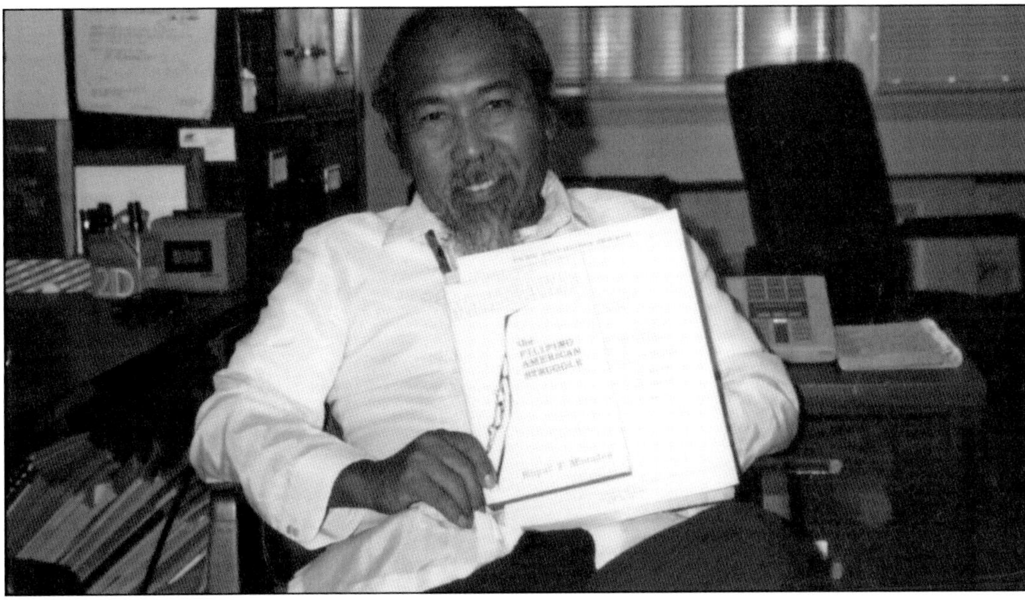

Honoree Roy Morales (1932–2001) is seen here in 2000. Roy was cofounder of Search to Involve Pilipino Americans (SIPA), the Pilipino American Reading Room and Library; the Pacific Asian Alcohol Program; and the Asian American Community Mental Health Center of Los Angeles. He also originated the tour of Little Manila in Los Angeles for his Pilipino American Experience classes, which he taught at several local campuses for more than 15 years. (Courtesy of Carol Kimbrough.)

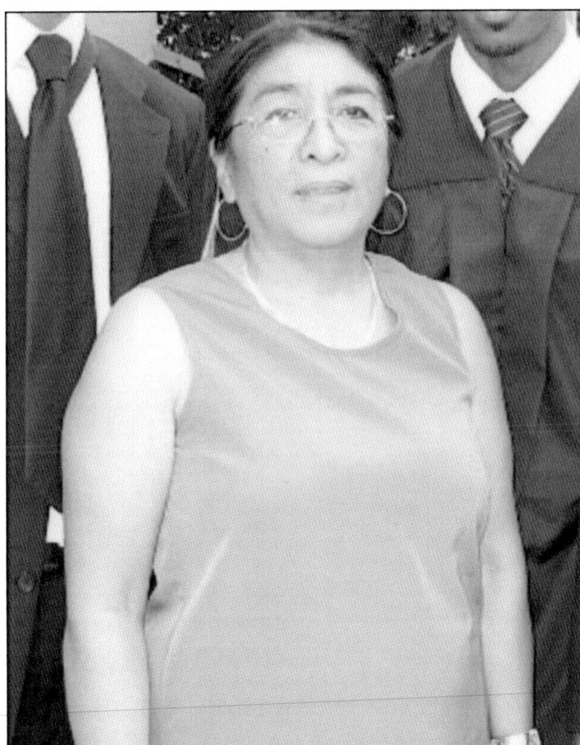

Honoree Ester Soriano-Hewitt (1946–2008) was a community activist and helped found several nonprofit social service and political groups, including the Search to Involve Pilipino Americans with Roy Morales; the Asian American Drug Abuse Program; the Pacific Asian Consortium in Employment; and the National Committee for the Restoration of Civil Liberties in the Philippines. (Courtesy of Carol Kimbrough.)

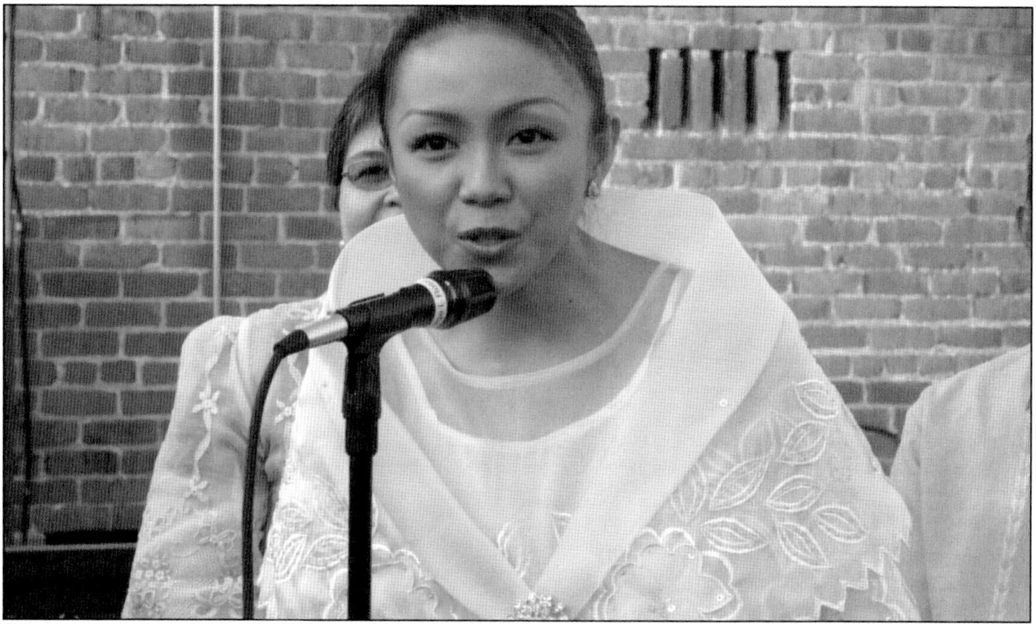

Jannelle So, host of Los Angeles television's Channel 18 *Kababayan LA* show, also hosted the public opening of Singgalot in Los Angeles. Her dedication to the Filipino community's efforts to further cultural awareness has been unflagging. So volunteers her time and services at many community events. (Photograph by Christine Oshima.)

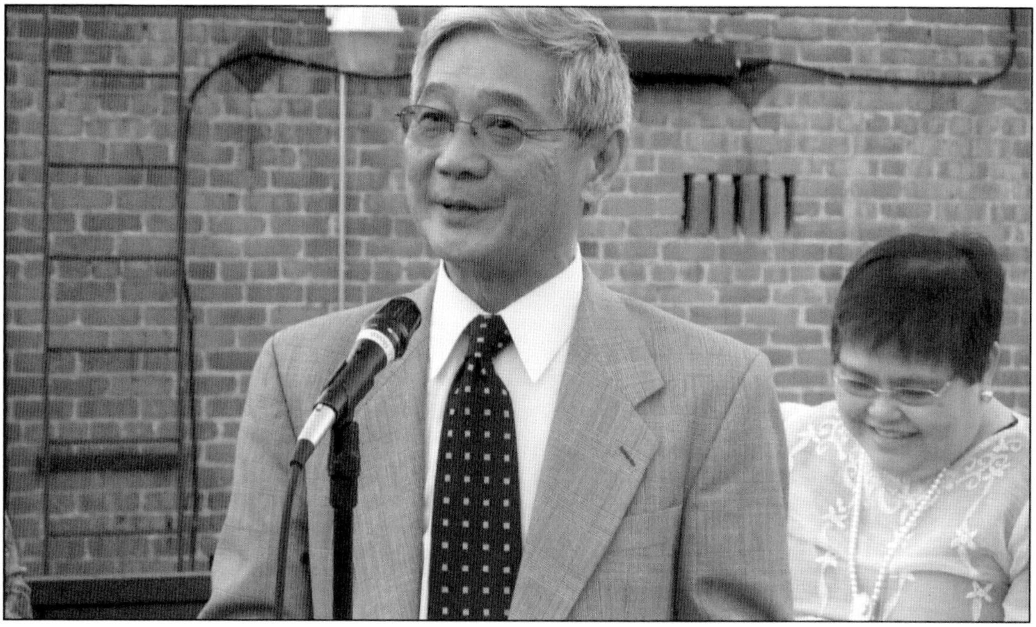

Pictured is Asian American author, scholar, activist, and historian Dr. Franklin Odo, a keynote speaker of Singgalot's August 2, 2008, public opening at Remy's on Temple art gallery in Historic Filipinotown. He has served as the director of the Asian Pacific American Program at the Smithsonian Institute since the founding of the program in 1997. Behind him is Prosy Abarquez-Delacruz, the convener of the Singgalot committee that hosted and planned for the exhibit to be held at Remy's on Temple. (Photograph by Christine Oshima.)

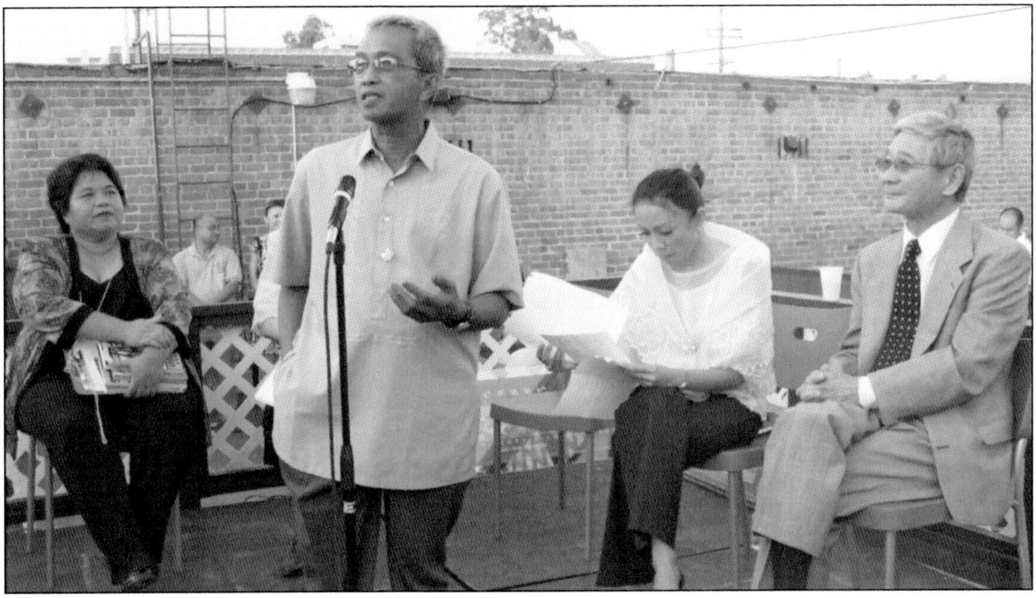

Enrique de la Cruz, Ph.D., another key speaker at the Singgalot public opening, described how Filipinos are part of nation-building as they build their communities in America. Coauthor of *The Forbidden Book*, Dr. de la Cruz is a professor of Asian American studies at California State University–Northridge and is the former assistant director of the UCLA Asian American Studies Center. Seated are Carol Ojeda Kimbrough (left), cochair of the Singgalot committee; Jannelle So (center); and Dr. Franklin Odo (right). (Photograph by Christine Oshima.)

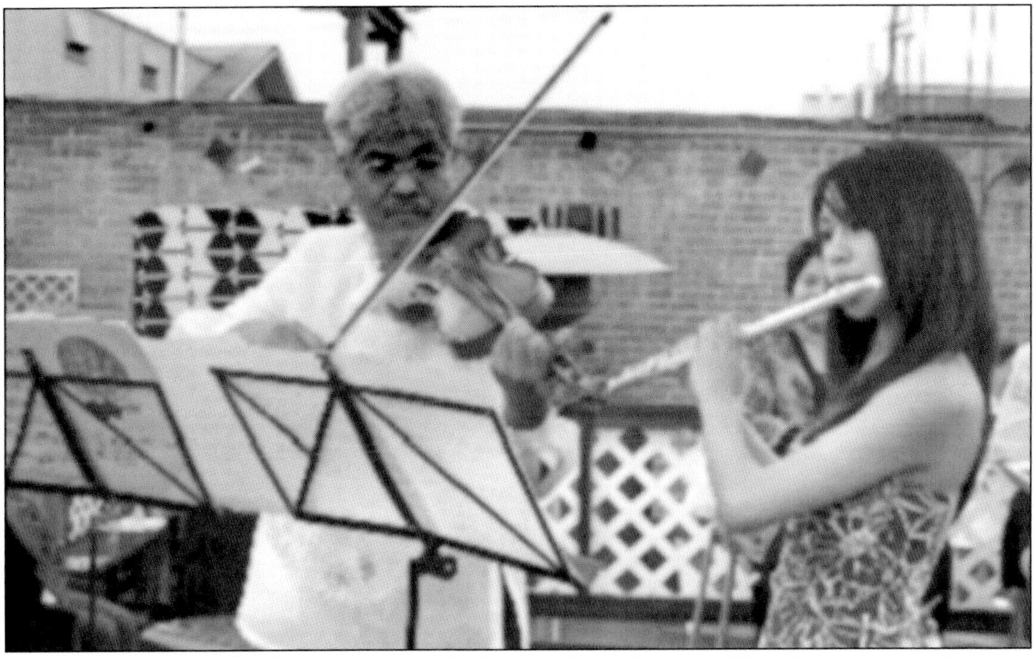

Pictured are Nonoy Alsaybar, who holds a Ph.D. in anthropology at UCLA (left), with his daughter Jenica Alsaybar. Nonoy is a master violinist, and Jenica is a flutist. Together they performed a musical duet that they composed for the public opening of Singgalot in Historic Filipinotown. (Courtesy of Christine Oshima.)

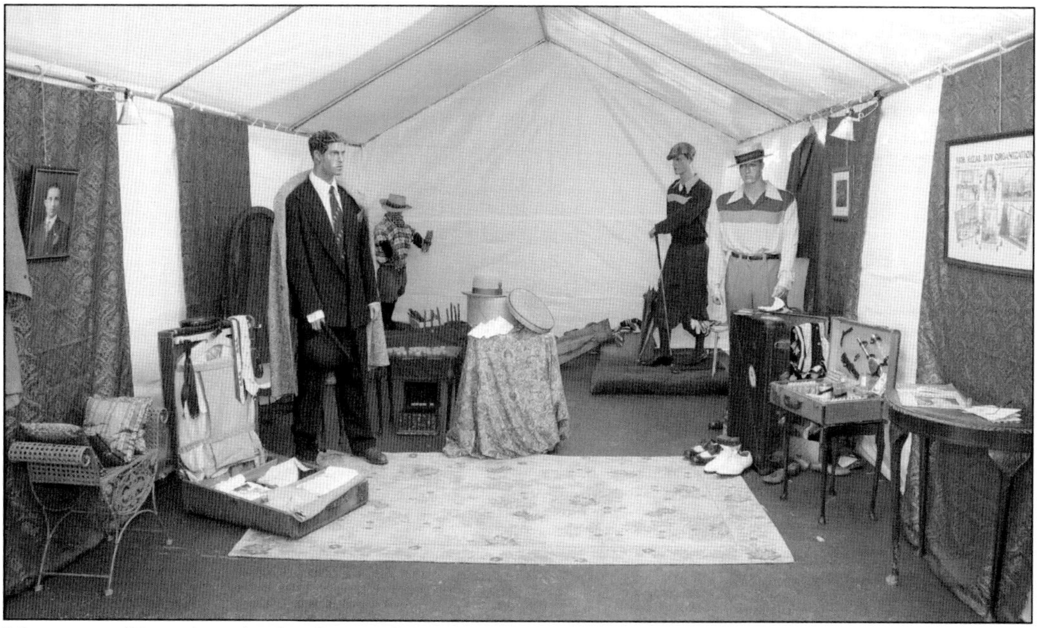

Manongs of Los Angeles by Carina Monica Montoya was featured at the opening of Singgalot at Remy's on Temple on August 1, 2008. The theme was "transformation of self," using original McIntosh-brand clothes and items dating back to the 1920s. The exhibit was supplemented with music from the era and a slide show of vintage photographs of Manongs in Los Angeles between the years 1920 and 1950. (Courtesy of Sthanlee B. Mirador.)

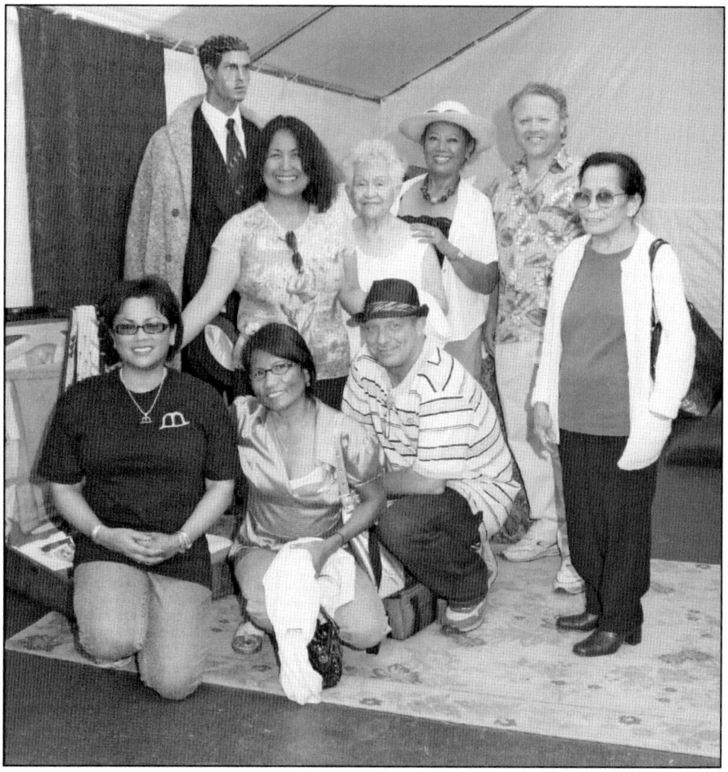

Board members of the Filipino Federation of America, Inc., from Stockton, California, attended the Manongs of Los Angeles exhibit. Many of the vintage clothes and items in the exhibit belonged to Hilario C. Moncado, founder of the federation. Pictured from left to right are (first row) Carina M. Montoya, Ellen Loomis, and Don Loomis; (second row) Alma Pader, Angie Orlanes, Elvisa Ordonio, Todd Pader, and Pasita Sugano. (Courtesy of Peter Gonzaga.)

John Mina, president of the Filipino American Library, attended the Manongs of Los Angeles exhibit dressed in Manong style. (Courtesy of Sthanlee B. Mirador.)

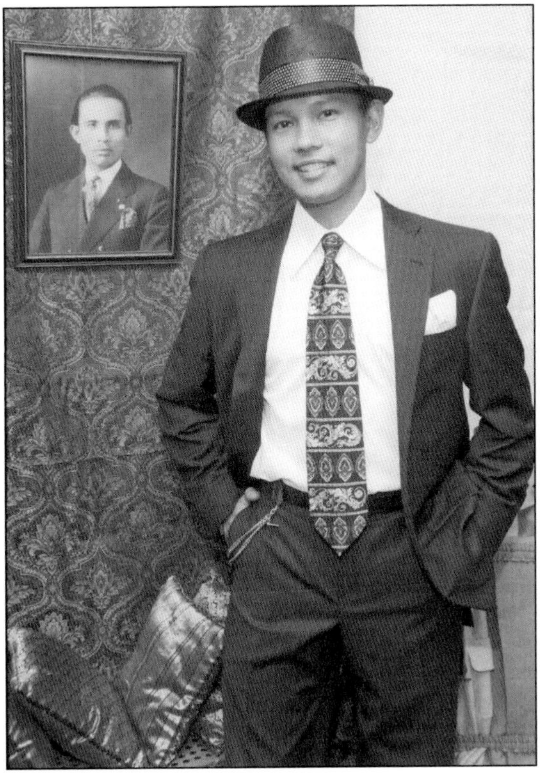

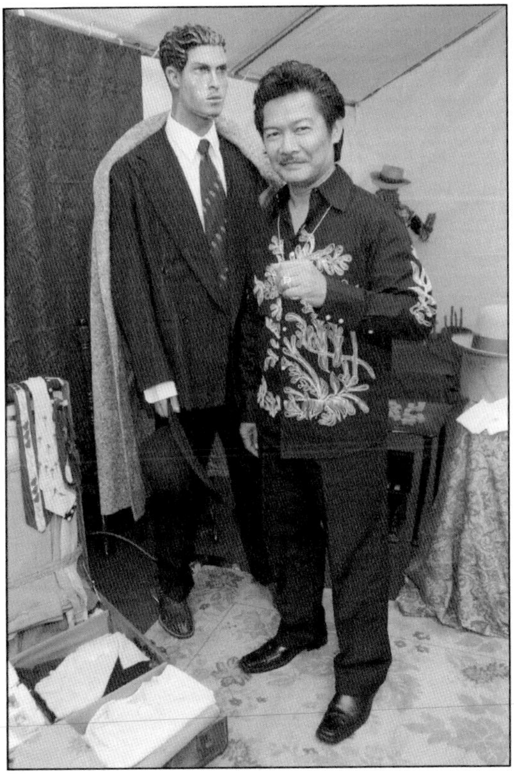

Singer/musician Mon David posed with one of the mannequins featured in the Manongs of Los Angeles exhibit. (Courtesy of Sthanlee B. Mirador.)

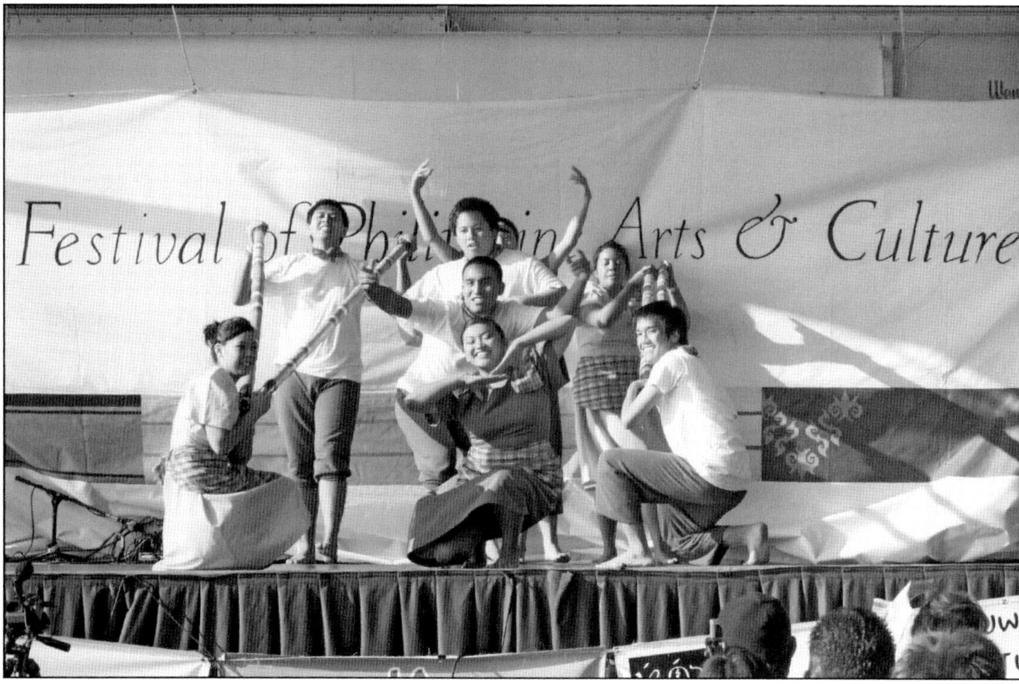

Tinikling dancers, above, perform at the 17th Annual Festival of Philippine Arts and Culture, held in September 2008 at Point Fermin Park on the cliffs above the ocean in San Pedro. Below, people gather around the main stage to watch the shows and listen to live music. (Both, courtesy of Sthanlee B. Mirador.)

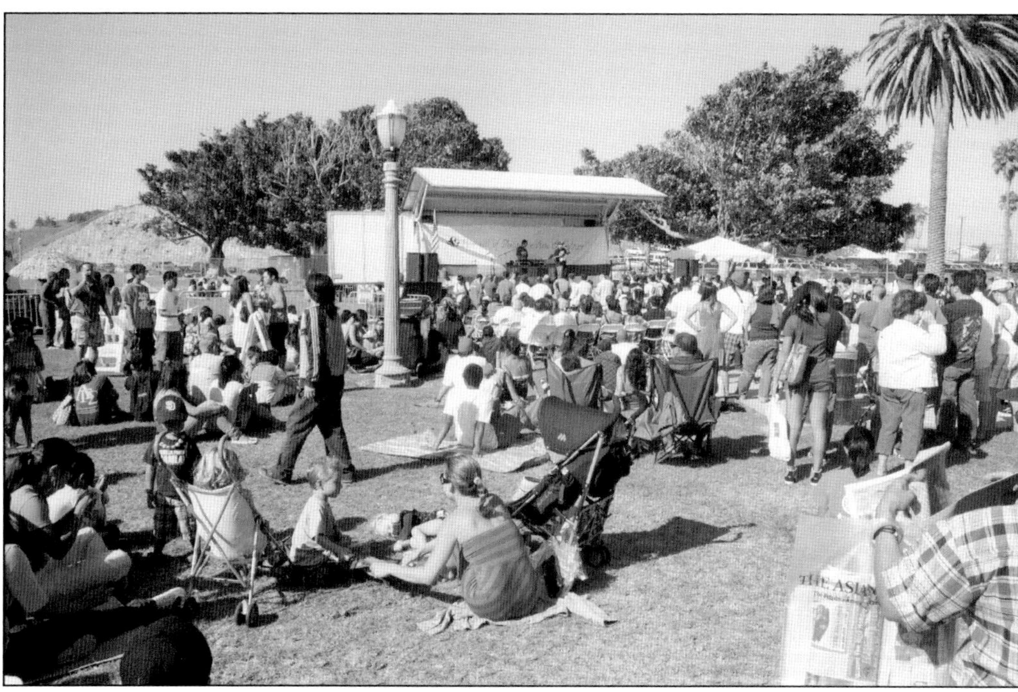

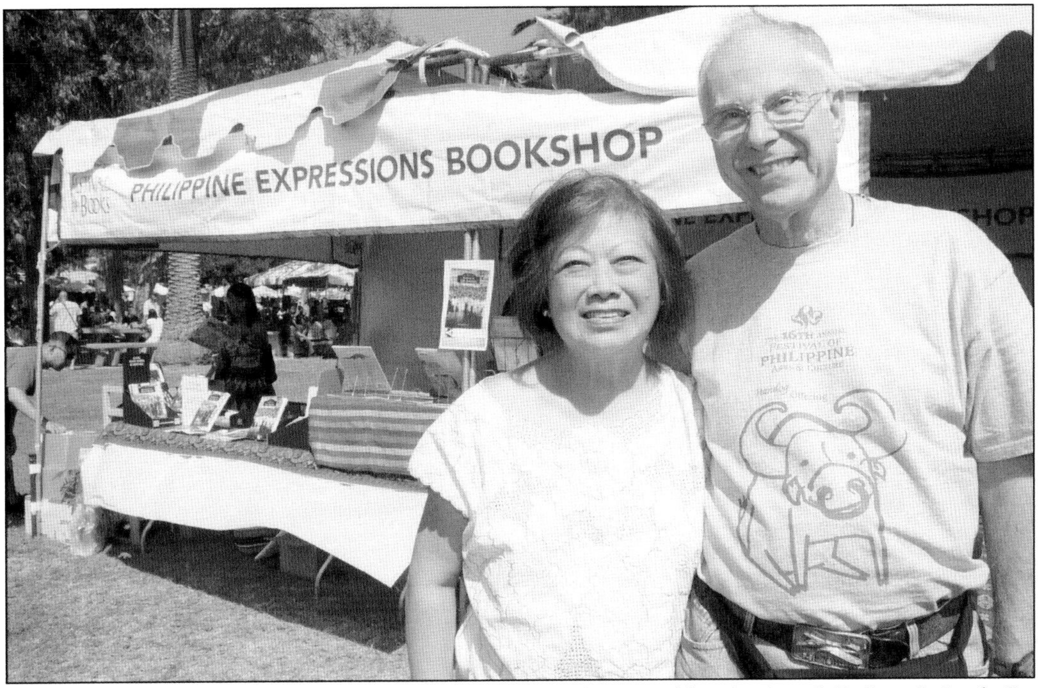

Linda Nietes, owner of Philippine Expressions Bookshop, and her husband, Robert J. Little Jr., pose for this photograph in front of their booth at the annual Festival of Philippine Arts and Culture. (Courtesy of Sthanlee B. Mirador.)

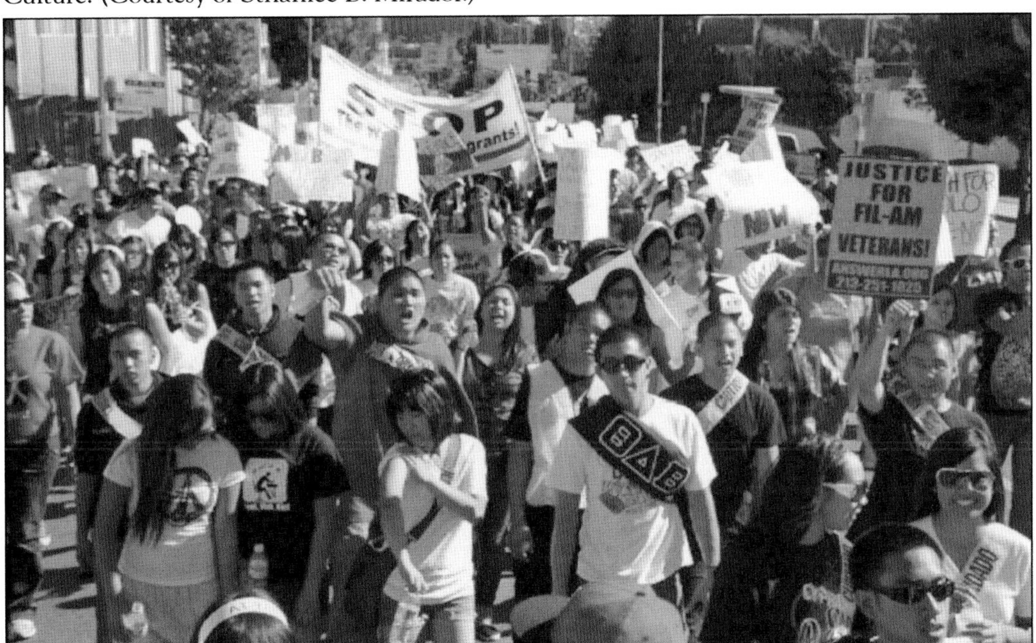

The World War II Filipino American veterans continue to fight for the right to benefits promised to them in 1943 but were rescinded by the U.S. Congress in 1946. Pictured is a march and rally in November 2008 in Historic Filipinotown, which was attended by Filipino American veterans, students, community leaders, area residents, and individuals. (Courtesy of Dion Bagaporo.)

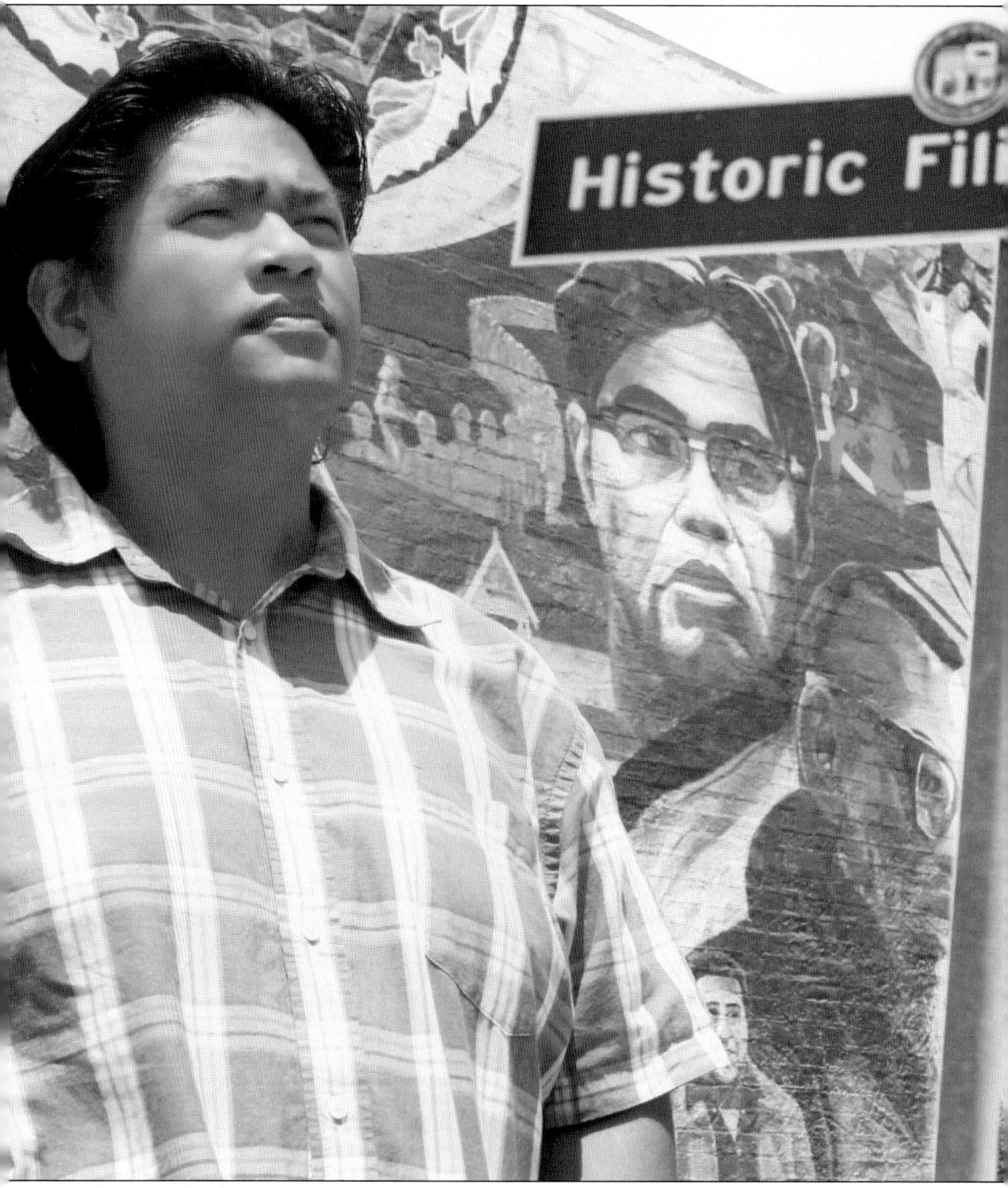

The growth of Historic Filipinotown today is credited to the tireless efforts of community organizations, leaders, and individuals who all share in the common goal of giving back to the community. Having founded the first major celebrity photo agency that concentrates on Asian and Latino representation through photograph coverage, professional red carpet photographers Peter Gonzaga (left) and Sthanlee B. Mirador volunteer their time and talents in photograph

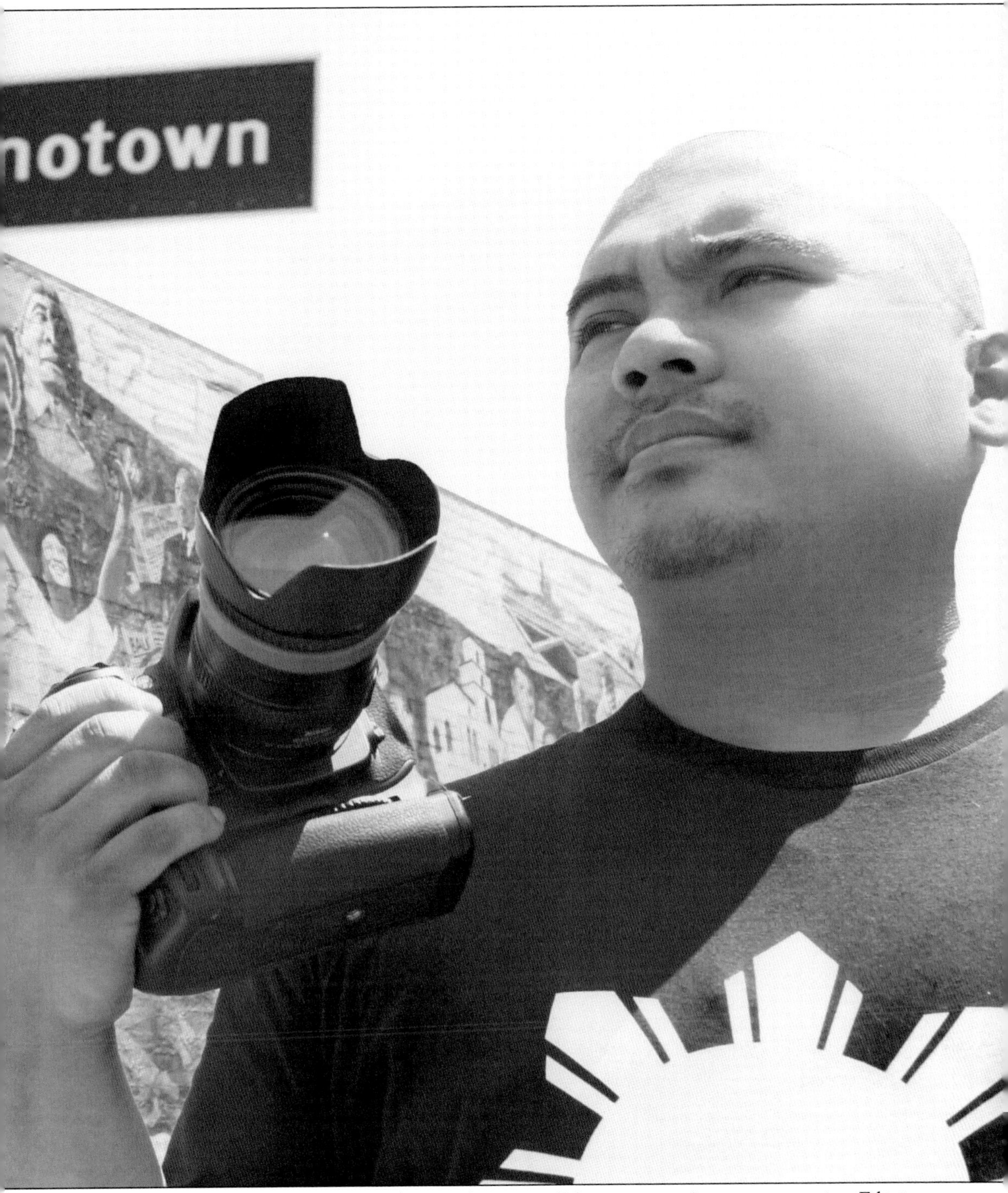

coverage of events and festivals in and around Historic Filipinotown. As new generation Filipino Americans, both Gonzaga and Mirador share in the collective efforts to preserve Filipino history and are keeping in the spirit in which the original Filipino community of Los Angeles was founded. (Photograph by Sthanlee B. Mirador, Peter Gonzaga, and Alexander Sanchez.)

ACROSS AMERICA, PEOPLE ARE DISCOVERING SOMETHING WONDERFUL. *THEIR HERITAGE.*

Arcadia Publishing is the leading local history publisher in the United States. With more than 4,000 titles in print and hundreds of new titles released every year, Arcadia has extensive specialized experience chronicling the history of communities and celebrating America's hidden stories, bringing to life the people, places, and events from the past. To discover the history of other communities across the nation, please visit:

www.arcadiapublishing.com

Customized search tools allow you to find regional history books about the town where you grew up, the cities where your friends and family live, the town where your parents met, or even that retirement spot you've been dreaming about.

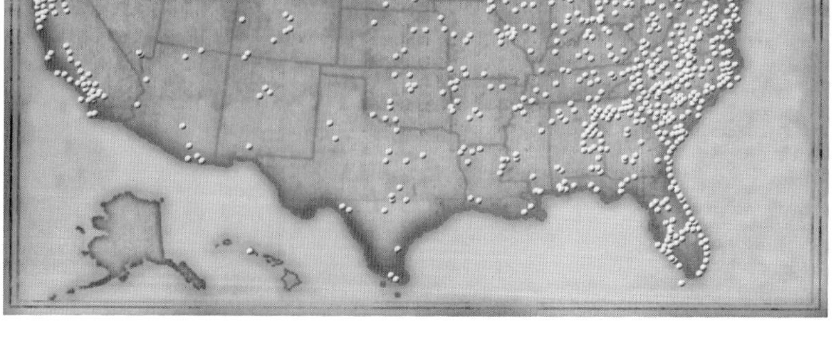